P9-DFN-234

GUIDE TO TRANSFORMATIONAL GRAMMAR

Guide to

Transformational Grammar

HISTORY, THEORY, PRACTICE

John T. Grinder
University of California, Santa Cruz

Suzette Haden Elgin
California State University at San Diego

HOLT, RINEHART AND WINSTON, INC.
New York   Chicago   San Francisco   Atlanta
Dallas   Montreal   Toronto   London   Sydney

Copyright © 1973 by Holt, Rinehart and Winston, Inc.
All Rights Reserved
Library of Congress Catalog Card Number: 72–79088
ISBN: 0–3–080126–5
Printed in the United States of America
3 4 5 6   038   9 8 7 6 5 4 3 2 1

HOLT, RINEHART & WINSTON

6 ²²

28 FEB. '74

Preface

In the past few years there has been such an upsurge of interest in the field of generative transformational grammar that every few months has seen the publication of a new introductory text. Now here we are, offering you the same thing—yet another introduction to what already may look like an overintroduced subject. We feel that this calls for an explanation that will make clear the reason we feel another such text is needed.

The majority of the available texts in this field are of two types. First there is the specialized text, bristling with theory and formulas and symbols and squiggles, and aimed primarily at the graduate classes of universities, where the students often already have undergraduate degrees in linguistics. These books are "introductory" only if you are already quite knowledgeable about the subject.

The second type of text is the "introduction to language" text. It will contain information on such things as the history of language families, the acquisition of speech by children, the fact there is no such thing as a primitive language, some materials on the history of linguistics, and so on. In addition, there will be sections on transformational grammar. Such a text is suitable for introducing basic concepts about language to students whose primary interest may or may not be linguistics. But for a course dealing exclusively with transformational grammar, it is hopelessly inadequate.

Our text is intended for the average class in introductory transformational grammar at the undergraduate level, intended for students who have little or no background in linguistics, and taught by instructors whose own background is not necessarily that of a transformational grammar specialist.

The text we have written does not assume that the student has a background in any kind of linguistics at all, although it would serve as an excellent text to follow a course in traditional linguistics using one of the standard traditional texts. It does not assume that the instructor has any extensive experience with transformational linguistics. The text introduces each of the basic concepts in transformational grammar, with thorough

49651

explanations, in the order that they will be needed by the student. All terms are carefully defined. At the end of each chapter are exercises that not only are intended to give the student an opportunity to practice what he has learned but are in addition teaching exercises, developing further the concepts introduced by the chapter. We have provided answers for these exercises, with careful explanations of those answers.

We have included in this book extensive material describing the recent developments in the field that are so rapidly altering the theory. We have included, wherever pertinent, material from publications not generally available. The bibliography is as complete as we could make it and is intended to refer the student and teacher to supplementary material in every aspect of transformational grammar dealt with in the text, with especially valuable sources indicated as such.

Certainly we do not make any claim that this book constitutes the perfect text. It undoubtedly contains errors and inadequacies. But we are confident that teachers and students with only a minimal background in transformational linguistics, or with no background at all, can take this text and work with it.

In our preparation for the writing of this book we have profited greatly from our association with professors and colleagues, both in formal class situations and in conversation. There is not space to thank each one individually, and we will therefore simply acknowledge our indebtedness to all of them. For the above-mentioned errors and inadequacies, of course, we alone are responsible.

San Diego, California   *J. T. G.*
November 1972   *S. H. E.*

To the Teacher

This text is intended for one quarter's work for advanced students, or for one semester's work at the early college level. We suggest that the most useful way of dividing the text would be as outlined below.

ONE QUARTER

WEEK 1 $\begin{cases}$ Why Linguistics Is Worth Doing (Chapter 1)
 The Task of the Linguist (Chapter 2) $\end{cases}$

WEEK 2   The Historical Antecedents of Transformational (Generative) Grammar (Chapter 3)

WEEK 3   The Beginning of Generative Grammar—Noam Chomsky's *Syntactic Structures* (Chapter 4)

WEEK 4 $\begin{cases}$ Early Transformational Syntax (Chapter 5)
 Families of Transformations (Chapter 6) $\end{cases}$

WEEK 5   Early Semantics (Chapter 7)

WEEK 6 $\begin{cases}$ The First Complete Model—Chomsky's *Aspects of the Theory of Syntax* (Chapter 8)
 The Cycle (Chapter 9) $\end{cases}$

WEEK 7   Generative Semantics versus the Extended Standard Theory (Chapter 10)

WEEK 8   The Application of Transformational Grammar to Literary Analysis (Chapter 11)

WEEK 9   Generative Phonology (Chapter 12)

WEEK 10   Universal Grammar (Chapter 13)

ONE SEMESTER

If it is desired to extend the course over a longer period of time, we suggest that the text be supplemented by assigned readings from works referred to in the text and bibliography.

We should point out that although the time given to various portions of the text is, of course, at the instructor's discretion, the *order* is not: that is, students will not be able to read and understand Chapter 6 before they have completed Chapter 5. The necessary terminology and theory is introduced step by step in the text, and we recommend that the order of chapters be maintained as presented in order to obtain the best results.

Because of the highly theoretical nature of the material, we suggest that the students not be assigned readings from the bibliography until *after* they have completed the chapter for which those readings are relevant.

The exercises provided with the chapters are intended to be such that the student will discover for himself the principles involved, in the course of doing the exercises. The exercises are therefore an integral part of the text rather than simply a supplement; we believe that the use of other exercises than those indicated would not be likely to give good results and is not recommended.

The authors of this text would be very grateful to have any suggestions, criticisms, or comments of any kind from teachers using this text or considering its use.

To the Student

A preface is presumably a place where the writers get to say a few words concerning what you are about to read. We wanted the book to be a pleasure as well as a learning experience; whether we have succeeded is something you will have to decide for yourself. Here are a few remarks that may help you in your evaluation and use of this text.

First of all, the book suffers from the same handicap as do most texts. That is, it presents a misleading picture of the discipline it describes. When a body of theory has been set in final-looking black print, and bound between covers, there is a tendency to accept it as something finished, complete, and changeless. This text encourages that tendency. It presents, as far as we can tell, the impression that transformational grammar is a well-defined, coherent set of analytic principles that, when applied to a natural language, yields an elegant set of formulas (the transformations) enumerating the set of well-formed sentences of that language with their structural descriptions. That is, of course, the *ideal;* the reality is that there are a group of people, linguists, who are struggling to bring this ideal about. By the time this text—or any text—reaches you, the changes in the field it purports to teach will be extensive. Many of the conventions and principles used in transformational analysis are relatively arbitrary, in the sense that they could be replaced by some other set of principles and conventions. The important thing, it seems to us, is not the particular formulation or notation chosen, but rather the abstract properties that any adequate formulation has. This is true because these properties form a component of the human mind. Therefore, at the same time that we are presenting one conceptualization of the phenomena of natural languages, we wish to strongly encourage you to investigate and develop alternative conceptualizations of your own.

In Chapter 1 we describe a number of introspective experiences that are valid for us when dealing with linguistic material having certain properties—for example, the property of ambiguity. We suspect that these experiences will be valid for, and available to, everyone. We hope that when people become acquainted with this approach to the study of language systems, they will understand that the enjoyment they derive from such study is simply an enjoyment derived from exploration, in this case from the exploration of inner space. When dealing with linguistic material, it is necessary to tune in constantly to a portion of the internal landscape. In constructing a grammar, you are attempting to describe something that is literally within your own head. We hope that there will be a sense of discovery about yourself and that you will find that you are better acquainted with your own mind as a result of this study.

It may be useful for us to suggest something about the mechanics of using this book. For us, the real core of the book is contained in the following sequence of chapters: 1, 2, 4, 5, 9, 11, 13. If you feel obliged to skip or slight any portion of the text, don't choose one of these chapters to do it to. If you become discouraged at what appears to be the heaviness and difficulty of some of the material, we suggest that you reread Chapter 1 and then read Chapter 13. These two chapters will tell you why the whole book is worth your while. Finally, we have indicated with a double dagger (‡) those bibliographic references that we feel are valuable and that tend to point in a particularly interesting and intelligible way toward new methods of approaching the analysis of human language systems.

It is important to remember that the example sentences used throughout this text represent only the dialect of the writers. They do not represent that mythical entity known as *The Correct Way to Speak the English Language*. It may well be that your own judgments about the data presented will differ from ours, and in certain cases that is what we would expect to happen. Any native speaker using this text will have to decide on the basis of his or her own intuitions what is the form of the grammar that he or she has internalized. It is precisely by being sensitive to those features of language that vary across dialects that one begins to distinguish between properties of language systems that are universal and those that are specific to some particular language or dialect. In the context of this book, such a distinction corresponds to *innate* versus *learned properties* of language systems. We wish, therefore, to point out the obvious: namely, that to accept a formulation for a particular grammatical phenomenon for no other reason than that it is elegant, or has been proposed and motivated by someone of "great stature" in the field of linguistics, or someone in your own group or class, is to do both this subject matter and yourself a violence.

Your intuitions are a part of you—they are natural. Be sensitive to them, respect them.

This leaves us only a brief note to indicate what motivated us to write this book. First of all, it was fun to do, of course. Second, we are convinced that it is not possible to escape or transcend more than temporarily any system unless one thoroughly understands the structure of that system. It is ignorance of this fact that is displayed by the museum visitor who looks at an abstract painting by Picasso and claims that his or her three-year-old brother could do as well blindfolded. Revolution, whether in the arts, the sciences, the political or economic sphere, or anywhere else, cannot take place in any meaningful way unless more is happening than just the exchanging of one set of surface phenomena—colors, stylistic conventions, names, faces, terminologies—for another. It appears to us that progress is dependent upon the ability to see clearly the structure of whatever system is under investigation; in the case of this book, that system is the structure of human language, and thus a portion of the structure of the human mind.

We had intended to call this book *The Demystification of Transformational Grammar*. Whatever it is called, however, it remains an attempt to do just that, to demystify, as a step toward a general program of demystification of knowledge that is badly needed, now and always. All of us are so close to our own natural language system that we fail to see the distortions it induces; we hope that this book will help in making these distortions more apparent. It is only by understanding the effect of the language system that it is possible to liberate yourself from the distortions that are thereby induced.

And, finally, we recommend to your attention the following quotation:

". . . The suggestion is that the function of the brain and nervous system and sense organs is the main *eliminative* and not productive. Each person is at each moment capable of remembering all that has ever happened to him and of perceiving everything that is happening everywhere in the universe. The function of the brain and nervous system is to protect us from being overwhelmed and confused by this mass of largely useless and irrelevant knowledge, by shutting out most of what we should otherwise perceive or remember at any moment, and leaving only that very small and special selection which is likely to be practically useful." According to such a theory, each one of us is potentially Mind at Large. . . . To make biological survival possible, Mind at Large has to be funneled through the reducing valve of the brain and nervous system. What comes out the other end is a measly trickle of the kind of consciousness which will help us to stay alive on the surface of this particular planet. To formulate and express the contents of this reduced awareness, man has invented and endlessly elaborated those symbol-systems and implicit philosophies which we call languages. Every individual is at once the beneficiary and the victim of the linguistic tradition into which he has been born—the beneficiary inasmuch as language gives access to the accumulated record of other people's experience, the victim in so far as it confirms him in the belief that reduced awareness is the only awareness and as it bedevils his sense of reality, so that he is all too apt to take his concepts for data, his words for actual things.—ALDOUS HUXLEY, *The Doors of Perception* (New York: Harper & Row, 1954), pp. 22–23.

Contents

GUIDE TO TRANSFORMATIONAL GRAMMAR

Chapter 1

Why Linguistics Is Worth Doing

The sole purpose of this chapter is to get you interested in the rest of the book. The purpose of the book itself is to turn you on to one of the systems that you carry around in your head—your language system. If our experiences are in any sense typical, we are certain that the mere mention of the word "grammar" will produce in you an immediate feeling of severe nausea, and we begin this book with that certainty firmly in mind. The source of the nausea is not difficult to discover. It is most probably rooted in your past experience with grammar classes.

For some reason that is not clear to us, the world seems to be full of grammar teachers who excel (and in fact, in many advanced cases, rejoice) in the issuing and enforcement of arbitrary rules. It seems that, in general, the "teaching" of grammar calls forth in a person all the arbitrary repressiveness that that person possesses. There appear to be two major causes of this strange situation. In the first place, the position "teacher" has about it an aura of authoritarianism that appears to be built in; in the second place, so little is known about the structure of language that the language itself appears to be arbitrary. The interaction of these two factors results in statements like the following:

Thou shalt not split infinitives.
Whom, not who.

It also results in responses to student questions like the following:

$$\text{Because that's the way it's} \left\{ \begin{array}{l} \text{done} \\ \text{written} \\ \text{said} \\ \text{pronounced} \end{array} \right\} \text{in} \left\{ \begin{array}{l} \text{this} \\ \text{my} \end{array} \right\} \text{class.}$$

This version of the "because I say so" school of explanations (and other statements like it) belongs jointly to the fields of study known as psychiatry and prescriptive grammar, and is by no means restricted to the latter field. However, perhaps because grammar is so centered about the concept of "rule(s)," the percentage of acute cases of the "because I said so" syndrome seems to be higher among grammar teachers than could be predicted on the basis of probability theory alone.

We feel that transformational grammar is neither prescriptive nor particularly pathological. On the contrary, we personally consider linguistics, or the study of grammatical systems, to contain some of the most attractive questions yet asked by man about himself. It is, in fact, a "head" science. This book is perhaps best regarded as our attempt to tell you what it is about this activity that fascinates us so.

We have tried to write this book in such a way as to make it teacher-proof. This is not because we have anything personally against teachers as such; in fact, some of our best friends are teachers. It is because one of the major causes of the repressive environment, which is called to mind when someone says "grammar," is the teacher $\left\{ \begin{array}{l} \text{herself} \\ \text{himself} \\ \text{itself} \end{array} \right\}$, and we have deliberately attempted to bypass this problem by appealing directly to the student. It is possible that our attempt will fail, given the intricate intertwining of the systems of education, social life, economy, and so on. We hope not.

Evidently people have always wondered about and asked questions about "the world around them." The more systematic the questioning, the more scientific the endeavor has been assumed to be. Natural language forms, or serves as, the vehicle for these extended lines of questioning. The overwhelming proportion of both the questions and the tentative answers to these questions is forced into the mold of natural language.

People in some areas of the activity called science have been dissatisfied with their understanding of the syntax, or rules of combination, of natural language. In addition, they have not considered adequate their understanding of the types and amounts of ambiguity present in natural languages. They have then selected a rather highly restricted portion of what had formerly been expressed in the natural language, formalized the syntax, and thus reduced or minimally identified the ambiguities present in the resultant system. These impoverished systems are usually referred to as artificial languages. Portions of mathematics, in particular mathematical logic (or, if Russell and Whitehead are to be believed, portions of logic, in particular mathematics), form the most advanced of these formal languages.

We would maintain that the study of natural language systems has profited greatly from this activity. Indeed, the model of natural language presented in this book serves as the focal point of active research today, largely because its initiator, Noam Chomsky, proceeded on that basis. Chomsky, making use of various results and suggestions from the research conducted on artificial languages, was able to articulate in a brilliant, explicit, and unequivocal manner the inadequacy of the previous models employed by linguists in their attempts to describe natural language systems. He also presented in clear terms a system that allowed the formal statement of the systematic body of intuitions hinted at by traditional grammarians and shared by the native speakers of the languages concerned.

We would like to point out that the object referred to as "the world around us" is not in fact a simple inventory of what exists around us. While we do not subscribe to solipsism—that philosophy which explicitly denies the possibility of distinguishing between what exists in the mental life of the individual (what he perceives to be "out there") and what is "in fact" out there—we are convinced that language systems systematically distort the model of what's "out there" that we create in our heads.[1] It seems to us that there are two ways in which language systems accomplish this distortion.

T1. What is to be described apparently has to be described within a particular natural language system that consists of a series of rules, categories, and other elements whose effect is to force one to express experiences in a form sometimes unintentionally ambiguous, and to use words that presuppose or imply more or less than was actually intended by the speaker.

It is not unusual for people desperately trying to make themselves understood to comment that "There just isn't any way to say what I want to say," or "That's not really what I wanted to say." Such remarks clearly point to the speaker's awareness that there is a serious discrepancy between what he or she wishes to convey and what it is possible to express using the instrument of natural language; that is, between what is being experienced and what can be said.

Consider a rather simple case of ambiguity, as shown in the following sentence.[2]

E1. All of the people weren't represented.

There appear to be three major dialects, or three different ways, of interpreting this sentence. One group of native speakers of American

---

[1] Clearly, then, the object referred to as the *real world out there* is, in fact, inside our heads.

[2] These facts were first described by G. Lakoff (1970a).

English will state flatly that it is unambiguous and that it describes roughly the same situation as in sentence E2:

E2. None of the people were represented.

Another group of native speakers will leap up to protest in horrified tones that E1 could never mean what E2 means, but rather that it presents the same situation that E3 describes:

E3. Some of the people weren't represented.

The first group of native speakers will in turn be astonished to discover the existence of a group of people who presumably speak the same language they do and with whom they have associated—perhaps even lived for an extended period of time—and who have an understanding of E1 that is totally distinct from their own. The third group will probably smile and ask what all the furor is about, since it is "obvious to any speaker of English" that E1 is ambiguous and describes the same general situation as *either* E2 or E3.

One of the characteristics of this first type of distortion is the awareness the native speaker has of the discrepancy between what is intended and what is expressed.

Then there is the second type of distortion, which is even more insidious and even more difficult to illustrate.[3]

T2. It has been claimed that these same sets of rules, this same set of categories, that structure your native language themselves structure perception as well. Specifically, these categories, or rather the distinctions presupposed by them, operate on the information being carried in the nervous system at the preconscious level, performing a transformation on this material, grouping, summarizing, deleting, and in effect introducing distortions, prior to the nervous system's presenting the resultant impoverished picture of the "world out there" to the conscious mind.

It is obvious, for example, that such a process is implied by remarks such as "That must be a _____," where the blank may be filled by any well-formed description in English. This remark is to be contrasted with

---

[3] This second type of distortion is apparently the basis for the famous Whorfian hypothesis, named after Benjamin Whorf, its author. Whorf's description (1956) of the tense system of the Hopi Indians is an excellent example of the phenomenon. This is not to suggest that the Hopi language distorts the *real world* that English accurately describes; rather it is obvious that the distortion introduced by Hopi is different from the distortion introduced by English.

the utterance "That is a _____," where the blank may be filled by any well-formed description in English.

The second expression is a rather straightforward description of a phenomenon. The first, however, would seem to be the linguistic reflex of the speaker's awareness that there is a perceptually ambiguous situation confronting him, and that "_____" is his best approximation, the linguistic entity that designates the "real world" entity that most closely approximates the situation at hand.

This expression is not, of course, the distortion we want to illustrate, since the remark of the speaker indicates some measure of awareness of the actual discrepancy. The process to which we refer is the principle that lies beneath the experiments of psychological "set" when the set is induced linguistically. Figure 1.1 is an illustration of a bug crawling up the *inside*

Fig. 1.1.

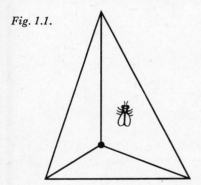

of a three-dimensional transparent pyramid. Look at Figure 1.1. But Figure 1.1 can also be seen as an illustration of a bug crawling up the *outside* of a three-dimensional *opaque* pyramid. The illustration is, of course, a perceptually ambiguous figure. Whether one sees it as showing a bug on the inside or the outside of the geometric object is determined in part by the set induced by the linguistic objects that immediately precede the presentation of the figure itself. In other words, the resolution of ambiguities in some sense modalities may be determined by the set induced by the language system in such a way that the individual involved is never aware that the ambiguity exists.[4] Thus, it may be that the so-called straightforward description of "_____" is not nearly so straightforward as it first appeared to be.

[4] There is some experimental evidence to show that while the speaker is unaware of certain linguistic ambiguities by introspection, these ambiguities have behavioral repercussions. See Bever (1970) for a discussion of the experiments. Interestingly enough, the general finding seems to be that ambiguities predicted by the linguistic analysis, but which the speaker has no awareness of, are present only until the clause or sentential unit in which they occur is completed.

The situation described above for Figure 1.1 has a counterpart, linguistic rather than visual, in many natural languages. Consider, for example, the distinctions that are presupposed for some of the Amerindian languages, and which appear to restrict speakers of these languages on very much the same basis.

The examples below are from Navajo, a member of the Athabaskan family of Amerindian languages. The underlined word is in each case the verb of the sentence.

E4. Ásaa' kǫ́ǫ́ si'á.
    (There's a pail here.)
E5. Bichidí kǫ́ǫ́ sizį́.
    (His car is here.)
E6. Tó kǫ́ǫ́ siyį́.
    (There's some water here.)
E7. Łį́į́' ła' kǫ́ǫ́ sitį́.
    (There's a horse here.)
E8. Gish kǫ́ǫ́ sitá.
    (There's a cane here.)

In all examples E4 to E8, the shape that the word will finally have as spoken by the native speaker depends upon a classification of objects into sets, which are described in various ways as "round," "long and stick-like," "in or not in a container," and so on. And it is not always possible to see upon what basis the objects have been sorted out into these categories. For example, the sequence 'bee nahlzhoohí' (meaning *broom*) is in the set classified as *long and stick-like,* and the word béésh (meaning *knife*) is not. It is obvious that there are cases in which the linguistic category may appear to contradict the perceptual evidence available to the native speaker.

As a final example, consider the following situation. If a native speaker of Hsilgne desires to describe the length of a pole- or sticklike object, he has the following choices: If the object does not possess great length, he may refer to it as a 'trohs' object. If the object does possess considerable length, he is forced to choose one of two descriptive terms:

a 'llat' object   if the object is situated such that it is perpendicular with respect to the surface of the earth.

a 'gnol' object   if the object is situated such that it is parallel with respect to the surface of the earth.

Notice that the same speaker will be forced to describe the *same object* by *different words* as a function of the object's attitude with respect to the surface of the earth, but only in the case where the object possesses considerable length.[5] The linguistic distinction is not present when the object is not of considerable length; that is, when the object is neither 'llat' or 'gnol'.

The exotic language being described here is not usually considered very "exotic" by Americans. It is, of course, English, or 'Hsilgne', spelled backward. The words of Hsilgne presented above have the following equivalents in English:

trohs = *short*
llat = *tall*
gnol = *long*

The distinction described, however, is perfectly accurate. Using a flagpole as an example, we point out that whether the flagpole is lying on its side on the ground or standing upright, as good flagpoles are expected to do in our culture, we may describe it as 'trohs' in Hsilgne or more commonly as *short* in English if it has no great length. Not so, however, if the flagpole has considerable length. In this latter case, if the flagpole is upright or perpendicular to the surface of the earth (even if upside down), E9(a) but not E9(b) is a possible description.

E9. (a)   That is a tall flagpole.
     (b)   That is a long flagpole.

The converse is true if we wish to describe the same object as it lies on the ground. The problem arises when the native speaker of American English wishes to describe only the length dimension of the flagpole. He will succeed if the flagpole is short; he will fail to describe only its length if he describes it as being *tall* or *long* because these words include information about the flagpole's orientation with respect to the visual horizon.

This last example from Hsilgne, or English, illustrates one of the initial difficulties often encountered by people when they are first exposed to linguistics, namely, the question of what the content of linguistics could be. It seems to come as a surprise to most people that there are grammatical or linguistic phenomena that are poorly if at all understood. This attitude itself has a linguistic reflex, which is reflected in the ambiguity of the meaning of the word *know*. The expression *so and so knows English* means that so and so knows how to speak and understands English, not that so and so consciously knows the structure of English. Every native speaker of English can be said to know the structure of English: His fluency pre-

[5] By the phrase *has some length,* we intend to point out that the object described as having some length is three-dimensional, with one of the dimensions exceeding the other two by some considerable although undetermined amount. Notice that the term *length* itself shows phonological similarity to *long,* but does not carry the same information about the attitude of the object being described.

supposes this knowledge. This knowledge is, however, in general not available to consciousness. The word *grammar* is used by linguists to refer to two objects; one, the internal representation of the set of rules, categories, and so on, in the native speaker's nervous system; and two, the external representation of this same set of rules, categories, and so on—that is, the description or object that the linguist is trying to construct. The point is that if the speaker can be said to know the structure of English already, and further has a complete, explicit grammar inside of his head already, it would appear that there is nothing left to be done. The individual usually expresses rather pleasant surprise when phenomena such as the *long-short* distinction are pointed out to him, marveling at the existence of such an "exotic" phenomenon in his own language. It is this psychological closeness to one's native language (or, indeed, any language in which one is fluent) that prevents the individual from recognizing or noticing the intricacies and richness of that system.

If our earlier discussion is in any sense accurate, then the activity called *linguistics* will be the single most important activity in liberating one's head from the structure imposed by one's native language. In the attempt to construct an explicit set of formal statements that reflect the structure of the language being analyzed, one becomes aware of the categories and distinctions inextricably interwoven in the fabric of the language system itself. This awareness or bringing to consciousness of the systematic distortion induced by one's language system gives one the opportunity to escape from the unconscious or preperceptual distortion mentioned above. We devote the remainder of this introductory chapter to the presentation of several phenomena in hopes of arousing interest in linguistic phenomena in general and of pointing out some phenomena in the reader's native language that his psychological closeness to the language prevents him from seeing.

Ambiguity

The first phenomenon is an example of what the linguist calls ambiguity.[6]

E10. Eleanor took Theodore's coat off.

A sentence is said to be ambiguous if native speakers agree that there is more than one meaning or more than one distinct situation described by it (a more formal characterization will be presented later). One of the

---

[6] This particular ambiguity was first described by Postal (1970c). The transformation or operation that produces the ambiguity is called *Apparel Pronoun Elision* by Postal.

most interesting features displayed by ambiguous sentences such as E10 is that many native speakers will deny that they are ambiguous and will persist in their denial until the "other" meaning is presented in detail. It is not an uncommon experience for the person who has been denying that the sentence could have another meaning suddenly to experience a "flash," "rush," or mental flip-flop, and the "other" meaning comes to occupy his or her attention to the exclusion of the first or previously "only" meaning. (The sentence E10 is still sitting there.)

The entire experience of discovering an ambiguity in a sequence where one would have previously sworn that none exists is a particularly instructive experience in a number of respects. It points out that while the intuitions that a native speaker has form the data base for the analysis of the language (discussion in Chapter 2), it may be necessary to work for such intuitions. This feature is often referred to as the Competence-Performance distinction. (The sentence E10 is *still* sitting there.) That is, it is clear that once the two meanings of sentences like E10 are explained, the native speaker will agree that both such meanings can be represented by the same sentence; in making this judgment, he is relying rather directly on his competence. The fact that he was unable to detect the ambiguity in the first place without assistance is said to be due to some performance problem. Perhaps, say, he was distracted by something around him or by some gesture on the part of the utterer of the sentence in question. For most speakers of American English, sentence E10 can be paraphrased by E11.

E11. Eleanor took Theodore's$_i$ coat off him$_i$.
 where identical subscripts or Noun-Pronoun pairs indicate that both forms refer to the same individual.

The other meaning of E10 has probably become apparent to most readers; it can be represented by the sequence E12, which for some speakers is not well formed.

E12. Eleanor$_i$ took Theodore's coat off her$_i$.

We now have an example of a case, E10, in which the same sequence describes two very different situations; one, E11, where Theodore has his coat on initially and it is removed by Eleanor; two, E12, where Eleanor is wearing Theodore's coat initially and she subsequently removes it. The ambiguity may be compounded by adding Noun Phrases with the possessive suffix (*'s*) immediately after the word *Theodore's* in sentence E10 as, for example, in E13:

E13. (a) Eleanor took Theodore's sister's coat off.
 (b) Eleanor took Theodore's sister's boyfriend's coat off.
 (c) Eleanor took Theodore's sister's boyfriend's mother's coat off.

Although admittedly difficult,[7] it is possible to understand E13(c) say, as a well-formed sequence that describes a situation in which any of the individuals—*Eleanor, Theodore, Theodore's sister, Theodore's sister's boyfriend,* or *Theodore's sister's boyfriend's mother*—were initially wearing some coat and had it removed by Eleanor.

Differential Patterns

The second phenomenon that we will consider is represented by the difference between the sentences E14(a) and (b):

E14. (a) Henry is eager to please.
      (b) Henry is easy to please.

These two sequences have the same superficial, or surface, structure. If one were asked, for example, to construct a formula using traditional terminology or labels that gives the syntactic structure of these two, the results would be identical, as in E15:

E15. Noun   Copula   Adjective   Infinitive

But this identity can be shown to be an identity at only the most superficial level of analysis. Consider the following differential patterns of syntactic behavior:

E16. (a)   Henry is eager to please someone.
      (*b)   Henry is easy to please someone.
      where the symbol * indicates sequences not acceptable as well formed in the judgment of native speakers.

E17. (*a)   It is eager to please Henry.
      (b)   It is easy to please Henry.

E18. (*a)   Henry is eager for someone to please.
      (b)   Henry is easy for someone to please.

E19. (*a)   The one who it is eager to please is Henry.
      (b)   The one who it is easy to please is Henry.

E20. (a)   Henry is eager and able to please.
      (*b)   Henry is easy and able to please.

[7] The fact that the intuitional judgments about sequences in E13 are difficult to make is usually attributed by linguists to performance factors. In general, this is not considered relevant for the linguistic analysis. This distinction between facts that are relevant for the construction of the grammar and facts concerning performance, usually felt to be in the domain of psychology but not linguistics, is discussed further in Chapter 2.

E21. (*a)   Henry is eager and fun to please.
    (b)   Henry is easy and fun to please.

E22.   *Henry is eager and easy to please.

E23. (*a)   Henry is eager to talk to.
    (b)   Henry is easy to talk to.

This list of differential syntactic patterning could be extended even further; the point, however, is that while the surface forms of these two sequences, E14(a) and (b), are indistinguishable, they are indeed very different syntactic animals, as the differences in E16 through E23 demonstrate. The linguist will account for such differences by distinguishing two levels of analysis, often referred to as Surface Structure (E14), and Deep Structure, which for the sequence E14(a) is not unlike the sequence E16(a), and for the sequence E14(b) is not unlike a combination of the sequences E17(b) and E18(b). These two levels of analysis will then be related by formal devices, which must then account for the fact that from such diverse Deep Structures the same Surface Structure may result.[8]

Structure Sequence

The majority of American English speakers would agree that the sequences in E24 are well formed.

E24. (a)   Abraham told me where the drinking gourd was.
    (b)   Abraham asked me where the drinking gourd was.

However, for a black dialect of American English spoken in Harlem, E24(b) sounds very peculiar. A speaker of this dialect would express the meaning of the sequence E24(b) as E25.[9]

E25. Abraham asked me where was the drinking gourd.

Conversely, E25 sounds peculiar for the majority of American English speakers unaccustomed to this dialect. Is there some principled way for the linguist to predict whether the verbal form *was* will precede the subject Noun Phrase, *the drinking gourd,* as in E25 or follow as in E24? The fact that E26 is ill formed for both speakers of the dialect in Harlem and those

---

[8] See Chomsky (1966) for further discussion.
[9] See Labov (1968) for the first report of this dialect feature. It appears that the dialect variation concerning inversion in structures such as those under discussion in the text is not restricted to Harlem but is also a characteristic of other areas; for example, southern Missouri.

outside that dialect means that the presence of the word *where* is not the factor that determines whether the verbal form precedes or follows the phrase *the drinking gourd.*

E26. *Abraham told me where was the drinking gourd.

The following examples from the black dialect of Harlem will assist in determining what, in fact, the relevant factor is.

E27. (a)   Abraham wondered where was the drinking gourd.
     (b)   Abraham demanded to know where was the drinking gourd.
     (c)   Abraham asked the question where was the drinking gourd.

E28. (a)   Abraham knew where the drinking gourd was.
     (b)   Abraham remembered where the drinking gourd was.
     (c)   Abraham decided where the drinking gourd was.

If the sequences of E27 are changed so that the subject Noun Phrases *the drinking gourd* are preceded by the verbal forms *was,* then they are judged to be unacceptable by speakers of the Harlem dialect. The converse is true of the sequences of E28. The factor common to the sequences of E27 and E25, but not possessed by the E24(a) or E28, is that each of the former but none of the latter describes situations that are requests for information. In American English, for all dialects, a question or request for information, when not preceded by any other material, is always associated with the sequence *Verbal form + subject Noun Phrase.* The same linguistic principle is then occurring in the case of requests for information when the sentence that makes the request is preceded by other linguistic material (that is, when the sentence expressing the request for information is embedded within another sentence) in the black dialect but not for speakers outside of this dialect.

Contraction Sequence

Notice the difference between the two versions of E29:

E29. (a)   Marxists are convinced that Abbie is having too much fun.
     (b)   Marxists are convinced that Abbie's having too much fun.

Such a reduction of the copular verbal form *is* is traditionally referred to as contraction. If the reader spends some time rummaging through his conscious linguistic file composed of sentences that contain the verb *is,* he is likely to conclude that contraction may occur anywhere; that is, if there is a grammatical or acceptable sentence of English that has the sequence *Noun Phrase + is,* then there is another sequence of English, also perfectly grammatical or acceptable, of the form *Noun Phrase's.* Notice, however, that E30 shows that this is not a fully accurate general statement.[10]

E30. (a) Huey is laughing harder than Jane is.
 (*b) Huey is laughing harder than Jane's.

There are independent syntactic reasons for believing that the Deep Structrue of E30 is closer in form to the form of E31 than to the form of E30.

E31. Huey is laughing harder than Jane is laughing.

The sequences of E32 show this same exceptional behavior with respect to contraction.

E32. (a) Serious though Sam is, he sometimes makes sense.
 (*b) Serious though Sam's, he sometimes makes sense.

Once again, there are independent syntactic reasons for believing that the Deep Structure of E32 more closely approximates E33 than E32.

E33. Though Sam is serious, he sometimes makes sense.

Notice that both E31 and E33 themselves may undergo the contraction operation without any deviancy being introduced.

E34. (a) Huey is laughing harder than Jane's laughing = E31 + contraction.
 (b) Though Sam's serious, he sometimes makes sense = E33 + contraction.

If one were to state the difference between the acceptable and the unacceptable versions of the preceding examples, one would ultimately discover that in the well-formed cases there is an element that immediately succeeds the contraction and that is also found in the Deep Structure in the same position in E31 and E33. On the other hand, in the ill-formed cases with contraction, the element that succeeded the verbal form that undergoes contraction in Deep Structure is no longer there [E30(b) and E32(b)]. This is apparently the factor that determines whether contraction may occur. In other words, if the element that followed the copula in Deep Structure is removed (either deleted as in the case of E30 or moved as in

---

[10] First reported by King (1970).

the case of E32 to a new position in the sentence), then contraction will produce an unacceptable sequence. The identification of which of the sequences may undergo the process of contraction presupposes the distinction first mentioned in "Differential Patterns," the distinction between deep and surface forms of the same sequence.

We have attempted in this chapter to show you what types of problems interest the linguist. We have indicated to some extent what we feel are the general motivations for studying linguistics. If either these general motivations or the specific phenomena briefly described here are of interest to you, read on.

EXERCISES

1. Parallel to the example from the language Hsilgne given in the text, there appear to be interesting differences in the following sets of words:
    (a) barrel versus bucket
    (b) handkerchief versus kerchief versus bandanna versus scarf
    (c) apron versus pinafore
    (d) narrow versus slender
    Identify and discuss the differences in the use and meaning of these pairs.
2. Find similar examples of pairs like those in Exercise 1 from your own dialect. Then proceed as in Exercise 1.
3. In the text we were able to show that what is superficially an identical pair of constructions must come from different Deep Structures; namely,

Henry is *eager* to please.
Henry is *easy* to please.

By using a number of different syntactic contexts in which one of the pair but not the other was substitutable, we were able to show that these two were in fact different. The following sentences are of the same superficial structure; find a series of syntactic environments in which one, but not the other, is possible.

John and Sam are *similar*.
John and Sam are *happy*.

4. Find in your own language system some distinctions of the type *long-tall*. Attempt to find the exact conditions of their usage.

5. Break the class into small groups and present your sets of word pairs developed under Exercise 3 above. Be sensitive to dialect differences: it is

probable that the same set of factors (geography, social class, and so on) will be relevant in this exercise.

ANSWERS

1. A sample, from the dialect of one of the authors:
   - (a) *barrel*—must be wooden, either having no taper or tapering at both ends, and having no handle.
     bucket—metal or plastic, tapering from top to bottom, and having a handle.
   - (b) *handkerchief*—cloth, square, and carried rather than worn (except in the sense of *worn* in a pocket).
     kerchief—cloth, square or triangular, worn on the head.
     bandanna—cloth, square or triangular, brightly patterned, worn on the head.
     scarf—cloth, almost any shape, worn on the head or around the neck.
   - (c) *apron*—cloth, fastens around waist, may or may not have bib, worn by either child or adult, worn for work and nonwork activities.
     pinafore—cloth, must have bib, always worn by a child, usually worn for nonwork activities.
   - (d) *narrow*—applies to streets, rivers, doors, and the like, never to people; appears to refer to size in terms of distance to be traversed.
     slender—applies to people, columns, trees, and so on, never to streets; appears to refer to size in terms of sight.
2. Depends on individual student.
3. John and Sam are $\left\{ \begin{array}{l} \text{similar} \\ \text{happy} \end{array} \right\}$.

   John is $\left\{ \begin{array}{l} \text{happy} \\ \text{*similar} \end{array} \right\}$ and so is Sam.

   John is as $\left\{ \begin{array}{l} \text{happy} \\ \text{*similar} \end{array} \right\}$ as Sam is.

   John is $\left\{ \begin{array}{l} \text{similar} \\ \text{*happy} \end{array} \right\}$ to Sam.
4. *Fat* versus heavy. The word *heavy* refers to the weight of an entity with regard to the actual operation of *lifting* it, while *fat* refers to weight from the standpoint of appearance. You would say a woman was "heavy" only if lifting her was actually intended. Notice that when you talk of a "fat" book you are referring to the way it looks. (There are dialects of American English where this does not hold. In such dialects the remark "John is getting too heavy" is synonymous with "John is getting too fat.")

Chapter 2

The Task
of the Linguist

In this chapter we take up two major questions: First, what is it that a linguist does? Second, what are the data with which the linguist does what he does?

We begin by discussing two sets of objects that linguists consider to be the proper concern of linguistic investigations.

1. The collection of all well-formed utterances or sound sequences in some natural language; call this Set A.

2. The collection of all well-formed meanings, or semantic representations, in some natural language; call this Set B.

If you are a native speaker of some language, you are able to identify the two sets above for that language without any particular difficulty, although there will be times when such judgments will require more of your attention than others. Consider the following examples:

E1. (a)   Max lost his pants.
     (b)   Martha held her breath until the gas dissipated.
     (c)   Margaret winked her left eye at Harry.

E2. (*a)   Pants his lost Max.[1]
     (*b)   Martha held breath until the gas dissipated.
     (*c)   Teragram dekniw reh tfel eye ta yrrah.

[1] The use of the symbol * by linguists is subject to rather wild variations. The symbol itself, of course, is well defined only within a perfectly explicit and complete theory of grammar. Unfortunately, none exists. The symbol will be used here to identify orthographic representations of sequences that are judged to be excluded from the cross product of the two sets A and B.

The sound sequence represented by E2(a) is, of course, the same as E1(a) with the word order reversed. The sequence E2(b) is the same as E1(b) with the word *her* deleted. The sequence E2(c) is the same as E1(c) with the sound segments within each word (represented by the letters, since we have only written material) reversed.

Analogous examples for Set B of English would be as follows, with the sequences of E3, but not of E4, being considered members of the set:

E3.   (a)   John Mayer eats Wheaties.
      (b)   Hermione's daughter smokes.
      (c)   The Massachusetts legislature demanded that all troops be withdrawn from New England.

E4. (*a)   Wheaties eat John Mayer.
   (*b)   Richard followed himself into court.
   (*c)   Jack held Mary's breath.

It is, of course, possible that there might be some contexts in which some of the sequences of E4 could be meaningful, and we will take up this question in a later chapter. For the moment, however, we will assume that the sequences occurred in ordinary straightforward discourse and that they are therefore not acceptable as members of Set B.

Sets A and B, for any given language, constitute the answer to our second question. The data with which the linguist does what he does are the well-formed sound sequences and the well-formed semantic representations for the language with which he is working.

Now, given these data, we can answer the first question: What does a linguist do? The task of a linguist is considered to be the construction of an explicit statement that will specify which sound sequences are associated with which meanings. That is, the linguist's major concern is the pairing of members of Set A with their corresponding members in Set B. Such an explicit statement is usually referred to as a grammar.

The detailed construction of such a statement will be the subject of later chapters of this book. At this point, however, there are some general characteristics of the association that can profitably be noted.

Consider the (a) and (b) variants of E5 and E6.

E5.   (a)   Jerry sent an honorary Yippie card to George.
      (b)   Jerry sent George an honorary Yippie card.

E6.   (a)   The gentleman was unaware of the plight of the migrant workers.
      (b)   The gentleman was unaware of the migrant workers' plight.

The (a) and (b) versions of both E5 and E6 express the same thought, or semantic representation; that is, they are synonymous, or paraphrases of each other. The fact that a paraphrase relationship exists shows us that the grammar will not in all cases associate one and only one sound sequence (member of Set A) with each meaning (member of Set B). The grammar must account for this fact.

The converse situation, in which the grammar associates more than one meaning (member of Set B) with each sound sequence (member of Set A), is easily constructed. For example, consider the following sentence:

E7. Murdering peasants can be dangerous.

The sound sequence represented by E7 can be associated with the meanings represented by both E8(a) and (b).

E8. (a) Murdering peasants is sometimes dangerous.
     (b) Murdering peasants are sometimes dangerous.

A sound sequence like E7 is said to be ambiguous (that is, it corresponds to more than one semantic representation) and this fact must be accounted for by the grammar.

The phenomena of synonymy and ambiguity make it clear that the pairing of Set A and Set B is not going to be a simple matter of one-to-one mapping. In fact, it is not a simple matter at all, and yet any native speaker of a language can do it without either being a linguist or even knowing that there is such an entity as a linguist.

Another general characteristic that turns up when the problems of A/B pairing is examined is that there exist sound sequences that appear to be members of Set A but which have no counterpart in Set B. A famous example of such a sequence is Noam Chomsky's "Colorless green ideas sleep furiously."[2] The sequence seems to have no related well-formed meaning. The converse case, where there exists a well-formed meaning without any sound sequence that expresses it, has not yet been shown to exist, and in the absence of evidence to the contrary will be presumed nonexistent.

We may ask now whether it is possible to determine whether a sequence is a member of Set A without considering Set B. Consider the following examples:[3]

E9. (a) Bronson$_i$ hated him$_j$.
   (*b) Bronson$_i$ hated himself$_j$.

---

[2] See Chomsky (1957).

[3] The subscripts that appear on the words in the sentence in the text are simply a device to indicate that two (or more) words bearing the same subscripts are to be interpreted as referring to the same person or object. They are said to be *referential indices,* or in the case that the indices are identical, the words are said to be *coreferential.*

E10. (*a)   Bronson$_i$ hated him$_i$.
    (b)   Bronson$_i$ hated himself$_i$.

E11. (a)   He$_i$ hated Bronson$_j$.
    (*b)   Himself$_i$ hated Bronson$_j$.

E12. (*a)   He$_i$ hated Bronson$_i$.
    (*b)   Himself$_i$ hated Bronson$_i$.

The point of E9 through E12 is to demonstrate that while in some cases one can decide whether a particular sound sequence is a member of Set A without making any reference to information contained in its meaning (information from Set B), in general such a procedure is not possible. Thus E11(b) and E12(b) would under no circumstances be considered well-formed sound sequences of English. A comparison of E9(a) with E10(a), E9(b) with E10(b), and E11(a) with E12(a) reveals, however, that whether a particular sequence is a well-formed sound sequence in English may depend sometimes on whether or not it is intended to express a particular proposition.

So far in this chapter we have been blithely making various judgments about the classification of sound sequences and meanings. We have been making these judgments as if they were self-evident, without referring to any rules or theories. In so doing, we have been making use of the same tool that every linguist employs in accepting or rejecting sequences as well-formed with respect to Set A or Set B—namely, our intuitions as native speakers of English.

Now, although we are accustomed to thinking of a thermometer or a pressure gauge or an electron microscope as a scientific measuring device, and are also accustomed to accepting the information received from such a device as reliable under normal conditions, the idea of "intuition" in such a role is more difficult to accept. The basic data of linguistics can only be the membership and structure of various sequences, and yet the only instrument available for the evaluation of that data is the human mind, which is notoriously lacking in gauges and dials.

The objections that have been raised against the methods of linguistics on these grounds—that is, that they are "unscientific"—cannot be easily answered. However, even if it were possible for us to construct a workable mechanical device to judge linguistic data for acceptability and the like, we would still be no better off, since the only standard against which we could measure the performance of such a device would remain the native speaker's intuition.

Compare, for example, the bubble-chamber electron detection experiment conducted by a physicist, with the Set A membership judgments made by a linguist.

BUBBLE CHAMBER ELECTRON
    DETECTION

Phenomenon: movement of particles

Sensing device: ionization traces
    in the chamber

Observer: the physicist

SET MEMBERSHIP JUDGMENT

Phenomenon: a sound
    sequence

Sensing device: the head of
    the linguist, that is, in-
    tuition

Observer: the linguist

In both cases there exists the possibility of human error. The significant difference between the two is that in the physics experiment the possibility of human error enters at only one point, while in the linguistics experiment it enters at two. In the physics experiment we have a nonhuman sensing device; in the linguistics experiment, a human one. Chomsky described the situation as follows:

> There are, in other words, very few reliable experimental or data-processing procedures for obtaining significant information concerning the linguistic intuitions of the native speaker. It is important to bear in mind that when an operational procedure is proposed, it must be tested for adequacy (exactly as a theory of linguistic intuition—a grammar—must be tested for adequacy) by measuring against the standard provided by the tacit knowledge that it attempts to specify and describe. (Chomsky, 1965a:19.)

Since the subject matter of linguistics is human language, and only humans produce human language, this situation should not be a surprise to anyone.

Naturally, the linguist employs any means he can to increase the stability of his data. In the case of research in the language of which the linguist is himself a native speaker, he will make use not only of his own intuitions but also of the intuitions of other native speakers. If he is working with a language other than his own, he will work closely with more than one native speaker of that language. The concept upon which this procedure is based is called *the intersubjective criterion*. It guarantees that whatever the actual facts may be with regard to the phenomenon being observed, that phenomenon is at least being validly detected in more than one human being.

The process of determining set membership—whether a particular linguistic object is or is not a member of Set A or Set B—must be sharply distinguished from the actual construction of the grammar, which is the statement of the relationship between the two sets. The set membership determination process corresponds to the use of the sensing device in the preceding paradigm showing the physics experiment contrasted with the linguistics experiment. The data so obtained must then be referred for interpretation to the observer; in both cases the observer is a human being and therefore it is impossible to eliminate the factor of human error. The explicit statement of the relation of Set A and Set B is, of course, subject to the same requirements of simplicity, internal consistency, and elegance that are asked of the theory of any other body of phenomena.

It is necessary to point out that the actual utterances produced by native speakers of a language are not to be looked upon as necessarily constituting part of Set A. If you will spend half an hour conscientiously eavesdropping, you will discover that there are differences between what people produce in ordinary discourse and what they would be willing to accept as English. If you listen to yourself speaking for a while, you will be amazed at the things that come out of your mouth, many of which you would have sworn you would never say. (This sort of linguistic self-consciousness, in which you find yourself listening to yourself speaking, observing yourself listening to yourself, and so on, ad infinitum, is an occupational hazard of linguistics.)

Various factors—such as the amount and type of drugs or stimulants in the body, the interest which the speaker has in both the person being spoken to and the subject being discussed, the physical position of the people engaged in the conversation, the structure of the memory system, the amount and intensity of emotion being experienced by the speaker—will obviously affect speech production. The distortions introduced by such factors are in themselves of interest to the psychologist in developing a model of actual speech production, but they have little significance for the model of linguistic competence, the grammar. The deliberate rejection of certain types of data as being irrelevant to the construction of the grammar follows naturally from the simplifying assumption known as the Competence-Performance distinction, first expressed by the French linguist de Saussure, and perhaps most effectively expressed by Chomsky as follows:

> Linguistic theory is concerned primarily with an ideal speaker-listener, in a completely homogeneous speech-community, who knows its language perfectly and is unaffected by such grammatically irrelevant conditions as memory limitations, distractions, shifts of attention and interest, and errors (random or characteristic) in applying his knowledge of the language in actual performance. (Chomsky, 1965a:3.)

It might seem safe to assume that the decision as to whether a sound sequence contains distortions introduced by grammatically irrelevant factors would be an easy one to make. In fact, there are many cases in which this is indeed true. For example, it is obvious that such things as hiccups, screams of pleasure, cries of rage, delirium, and the like can be immediately disregarded by the linguist as belonging to some behavioral system outside the framework of linguistics. But to conclude that such judgments are ordinarily easy to make is not accurate, despite its surface appeal.

Consider the following sentence taken from the work of Bever (1970):

E13. The girl pushed through the door laughed.

The sequence represented by E13 is often understood by listeners as being E14:

E14. The girl pushed through the door and laughed.

When the sequence is repeated and it is pointed out that there is no conjunction "and" present, most speakers will reject the sentence as non-English. They will do so, that is, until the suggestion that E13 has a structure parallel to E15 is presented to them.[4]

E15. The girl thrown through the door laughed.

The question then arises as to whether E13 ought to be included as a member of Set A for English. Most linguists agree that it should be, and attribute the difficulty of interpretation which is characteristic of such sentences to factors irrelevant to the grammar itself. Notice that it is quite easy to see the differences between E13 and E15 even though they have the same structure. One can predict which sequences having the structure of E13 and E15 will have a low comprehensibility (like E13) and which ones will be readily understood (like E15).

The structure represented by E15 and E17 follows the formula

F1. NOUN PHRASE   VERBAL FORM
    The girl   pushed/thrown
    PREPOSITIONAL PHRASE   VERBAL FORM
    through the door   laughed.

We can predict that any sequence that fits the requirements specified by F1, and which in the second position contains a verbal form whose past participle and simple past tense are the same, will have the same level of comprehensibility as did E13. No such difficulties will be experienced with

---

[4] Notice that there are sequences which one would obviously want to relate to the sequences E13 and E15 in the text:
    (i)   The girl who was pushed through the door laughed. (Parallel to E13)
    (ii)   The girl who was thrown through the door laughed. (Parallel to E15)
Sequences such as *who was pushed/thrown through the door* are usually referred to as *relative clauses*. Sequences such as *pushed/thrown through the door* in the sequences E13 and E15 are usually referred to as *reduced relative clauses*. Critically, note that the paraphrase relationship holds between E13 and (i) and between E15 and (ii); that is, E13 means the same thing as (i) and E15 means the same thing as (ii). The device for explicitly stating this relationship—the transformation—will be discussed in Chapter 4.

sequences that satisfy F1 but which have unlike past participles and simple past tense forms for the verbs. For example, the simple past and past participle forms of the verbs in column A are phonetically identical, but this is not so for the verbs in column B.

A	B
pushed	seen saw
hurried	taken took
rushed	blown blew
shoved	drawn drew

We predict that the substitution of any one of the verbal forms of column A into F1 will result in a comprehensibility problem like that exhibited by E13; the substitution of forms from column B will cause no such difficulty. For example:

E16. (a) The girl shoved through the door laughed.
     (b) The girl seen through the door laughed.

It has been argued by Bever (1970) that comprehensibility difficulties such as the one under discussion are the result of a perceptual strategy employed by native speakers of English. Bever suggested that whenever such a speaker encounters a sequence of the form Noun Phrase—Verbal Form—Prepositional Phrase—Verbal Form, if the first three positions in the formula are themselves a grammatical sentence of English, he will assume that they constitute the entire sentence. Then, when he hears the verbal form in the fourth position, he is forced to reinterpret the entire sequence, and this causes the low comprehensibility situation.

We can distinguish between the two claims, that of Bever and the one that we first outlined, with an example such as E17:

E17. The girl carried through the door laughed.

A sequence like E17 has the structure that we predicted will cause low comprehensibility. It also meets the condition that the first verbal form is one whose past participle and simple past are identical. Therefore, the conditions we have set up predict that it should cause a difficulty of interpretation. Bever's hypothesis, however, which states that the phenomenon will occur only if the first three elements of the formula constitute a grammatical sentence, correctly predicts that no such difficulty will occur.

This is important for two very good reasons: First, it makes clear the fact that a linguist cannot just accept an apparently plausible solution; he must search for other evidence, counterexamples, alternate explanations, and so on. Second, it is important because, as Bever suggests, this perceptual constraint is an example of the general cognitive principal of *Closure,* operating within the speech perception system.

Consider Figure 2.1. If you look at it from the top, you will see it as an arch; if you look at it from the bottom, you will see it as a three-columned structure. Such visual confusions are believed to follow from the same principle of closure. This principle says simply that the first coherent structure encountered by the perceptual system of the human being will be accepted as constituting the complete structure. Consider E17 once again. Since the sequence *the girl carried through the door* does not constitute a coherent and complete English sentence, no closure occurs until the verbal form *laughed* is reached.

The point of all this discussion is that there are many sound sequences about which judgments are exceedingly subtle. In some of these cases it is not clear to the linguist whether it is the grammar itself or some related behavioral system that is to characterize the properties of the sequence. Therefore, the sets A and B are not well defined—that is, there is no specific mechanical procedure or algorithm that can be employed to decide whether a particular sequence is a member of either of these sets. The linguist is again forced to rely upon his major tool, the intuitions of the native speaker, and the relationship between the grammar and other behavioral systems remains an open issue for research.

Let's look at one more example of a type of sound sequence that requires subtle distinctions and creates difficulties of the kind we have been describing.

E18. (a)   The soldier shot 73 birds.
     (b)   The soldier the president honored shot 73 birds.
     (c)   The soldier the president the students visited honored shot 73 birds.

A sentence like E18(c) again presents us with the question of whether the interpretation difficulty is a grammatical one or one caused by some related but presumably independent system.

The grammatical phenomenon that allows the situation described in E18 to arise is the *recursiveness* of natural language. That is, while any particular sentence of English is finite in length, the set of all well-formed sentences in English is infinite (can be matched one-to-one with the set of positive integers). There can be no "longest possible sentence." To any given sequence constituting a grammatical English sentence, you can add another relative clause,[5] and no natural limit can be set at which such structures become incomprehensible.

---

[5] This is not strictly true. In sequences such as (i), there is no possibility of attaching a relative clause.
    (i) It's raining.
In general, it is possible to attach a relative clause just in case the original sequence contains a common (as opposed to a proper) noun.

Fig. 2.1.   Roger Hayward's "undecidable" monument. (From "Mathematical Games" by Martin Gardner. Copyright © May 1970 by Scientific American, Inc. All rights reserved.)

The process of inserting relative clauses into sentences in this way is called *embedding,* sequences like those in E18 being examples of *center-embedded* sequences. Consider the following examples:

E19. (a)   The hunters shot the ducks.
(b)   The hunters shot the ducks that were swimming against the current.
(c)   The hunters shot the ducks that were swimming against the current which was carrying the poor birds out to sea.

In E19 the new relative clauses do not cause the same sort of difficulty that occurs in E18 because the embedding is not center-embedding. In center-embedded structures the new relative clauses are inserted in such a way that they interrupt and break up elements of the original sequence. Consider the following such sequence:

E20.   The National Guardsmen the governor the people the students had tried to talk to had elected ordered to the campus milled about in the quadrangle clutching their canteens.

You will see at once that it is difficult if not impossible to understand E20 without writing it out, even though it is produced by the same process as the sentences in E19; that is, by adding new relative clauses to Noun Phrases in the sentence.

Notice that with each inserted relative clause in E20, the distance between the Noun Phrase subject (the *National Guardsmen* in the original sequence) and the verbal form that belongs with that Noun Phrase (*milled about in the quadrangle clutching their canteens*) increases. Thus, in order to understand the sentence, the listener must hold in his memory the series of Noun Phrases encountered in the first half of the sequence until each is paired up with its proper Verb form. We can diagram this situation as follows: [6]

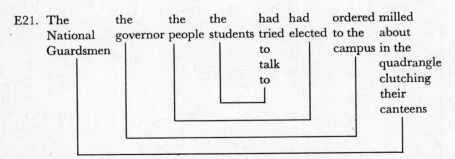

E21. The National Guardsmen   the governor   the people   the students   had tried to talk to   had elected   ordered to the campus   milled about in the quadrangle clutching their canteens

---

[6] Such a construction is called a *properly nested dependency.*

The suggestion has been made that it is the structure of short-term memory (that memory system used to retain a telephone number from the time you look it up in the book until you dial it) that causes the low intelligibility of sequences like E21, and that such differences in comprehensibility are outside the concern of the linguist.[7] Whether such an explanation will prove to be ultimately satisfactory is unknown.

We have considered in some detail what the basic data of linguistics are and how the linguist typically approaches his field of investigation. We have tried to give the flavor of the linguist's attitude toward certain data with regard to its relevance for his task.

Chapter 3 will deal with the kinds of linguistics that led up to transformational grammar. Then we will take up the explicit problem of the linguist's primary task—the construction of the statement (the grammar) that accounts for the specific way in which Set A and Set B are to be related.

EXERCISES

1. Make a list of five examples that are members of Set A but not of Set B; that is, they are well-formed sound sequences but are ill formed semantically.

Example: Mary's only son talked to his brother.

2. Make a list of five examples that are members of Set B but not of Set A; that is, they are well-formed semantic sequences, but not well-formed sound sequences.

Example: Those boys is silly.

3. It has been claimed that each of the following five sentences is ambiguous:

   (a) This pig is ready to eat.
   (b) Don't forget how low Leonard is.
   (c) Benjamin told Michael that it would be difficult to shave himself.
   (d) They fed her dog biscuits.
   (e) I know a taller man than Doug.

Write down each of the possible meanings of these sentences.

4. Now that you have worked through the examples in Exercise 3, you probably have noticed that there seems to be more than one type of ambiguity. Consider the ambiguity of 3(a) as compared to that of 3(b). In the case of 3(b), it can be accurately said that the ambiguity resides in the single lexical item *low*. Make a list of three lexical ambiguities and a list of three nonlexical ambiguities.

---

[7] See Chomsky (1965b).

5.   Break the class into small groups. Using the ambiguities that you found in Exercise 4, check your intuitions against the intuitions of the other students, noting differences. Look for systematic differences in intuitions; it is likely that these differences will be correlated with factors such as area of the country where the first six years of life were spent, social habits, and the like.

6.   The text presented two conditions that a sequence must meet in order to be perceptually difficult:

(b)   The verbal form in the second position must be one whose past + PREPOSITIONAL PHRASE + VERBAL FORM.

(b)   The verbal form in the second position must be one whose past participle and simple past tense are the same.

Try to find an additional example of a grammatically well-formed but perceptually difficult construction in English. Determine what conditions it must meet in order to exhibit the perceptual difficulty.

ANSWERS

1.   No answer necessary, the text gives an example.

2.   No answer necessary, the text gives an example.

3.   (a)   This pig is ready to eat something.
        This pig is ready for someone to eat.

     (b)   Don't forget how low (on the side of the mountain) Leonard is.
        Don't forget how low (untrustworthy, immoral) Leonard is.
        Don't forget how low (miserable and unhappy) Leonard is.

     (c)   Benjamin told Michael that it would be difficult for Michael to shave himself.
        Benjamin told Michael that it would be difficult for Benjamin to shave himself.

     (d)   They fed biscuits to her dog.
        They fed dog biscuits to her.

     (e)   I know a man who is taller than Doug is.
        I know a taller man than Doug does.

4.   Lexical ambiguities:
     (a)   At last Algernon has *arrived*.
     (b)   Melanie is rather *weak*.
     (c)   How many *functions* does it have?
     Nonlexical ambiguities:
     (d)   Mary's murder amazed us.
     (e)   I was hit by the girl with a brick.
     (f)   The chair was carried by the girl.

5.   Depends on individual student.

6.   An additional example of this phenomenon is demonstrated by the following sentences:

(a)   The boy [who left] laughed → The boy laughed who left.

(b)   The table [that was cracked] fell apart → The table fell apart that was cracked.

(c)   The boy [who was happy] kissed the girl → The boy kissed the girl who was happy.

(d)   The table [that was cracked] fell on the chair → The table fell on the chair that was cracked.

In order to cause the perceptual problem indicated by the sentences (a) to (d), a sequence must have the following two characteristics:

(i)   It must be of the form NOUN PHRASE + RELATIVE CLAUSE + VERBAL FORM + NOUN PHRASE.

(ii)   When the relative clause is moved to the end of the sentence, the resulting sequence of Noun Phrase + Relative Clause can itself be a well-formed constituent.

Chapter 3

The Historical Antecedents of Transformational (Generative) Grammar

It is possible, if you go around talking to linguists today, to receive the impression that transformational linguistics simply sprang into existence in a void, and that nothing of any significance had ever happened in linguistics before. This is, of course, completely untrue. The Greeks, for example, had well-developed schools of philosophy that dealt with the subject matter of linguistics. The Indian grammarian Panini, working in 300 B.C., produced what is considered by many to be the most accurate and complete grammar of any language written to date. The medieval philosophers and the French Port Royal grammarians developed systems of grammatical analysis that even by present standards were extremely sophisticated. The work conducted by non-Indo-European linguists has not yet even been researched—the usual situation—but undoubtedly contains many valuable efforts in this field.

Unfortunately, the scope of this text does not allow us to review this vast body of work in even the most elementary way. The Bibliography lists texts that do just that, if you should wish to go into the history of linguistics more fully.

What we do is begin in this chapter, quite arbitrarily, with the work of the man whose philosophy of grammar dominated the field of linguistics in the United States until recently, Leonard Bloomfield.

Bloomfield (1926) wrote his most influential works while he was struggling in the throes of the philosophy of a science called Positivism. In particular, he was greatly influenced by the reflex of Positivism upon the field of psychology that was known as Behaviorism. Behaviorists contended that all experimentation, all discussion, all research, and in effect all work of any kind done by behaviorists must be restricted to those phenomena that are directly observable. This approach had a therapeutic effect as a reaction against metaphysical reasoning and vague mentalistic philosophy. However, it now seems clear that if the demands made by Bloomfield's model were strictly adhered to, there would be little or no content left in science, and no work could be done at all.

Besides this purely practical objection, there have been a number of deeper objections, made primarily on logical grounds,[1] to such a concept of the limits of science. However, Bloomfield did attempt to work out his philosophy of grammar within the behaviorist boundaries, and those boundaries had very definite effects, both positive and negative, upon Bloomfield and therefore upon the development of linguistics in this century.

We will return to the negative effects later; but first we examine the positive ones. If one were asked to choose the most significant and valuable contributions made by Bloomfield, it is probable that the following two would be the ones most frequently selected:

1. The object to be described is not the written language but the spoken one, and the relation of the linguist to the language must be that of a nonmanipulating observer.

2. The set of structures that the linguist discovers in the language he is studying must be characterized in an absolutely explicit manner, without any overt or covert appeal to the general cognitive or linguistic abilities of the individuals using the description.

The first statement means that the explicit statement of the structure of the language must describe that language as it is actually used by native speakers, not as the linguist or some formal body like a language academy has decided that it should be used. Grammars, in other words, are not supposed to be prescriptive or normative. They are supposed to reflect the real structure of the language for the real people who use it. As Bloomfield expressed it:

> An unfortunate outgrowth of the general-grammar idea was the belief that the grammarian or lexicographer, fortified by his powers of reasoning, can ascertain the logical basis of language and prescribe how people ought to speak. In the eighteenth century, the spread of education led many dialect-speakers to learn the upper-class forms of speech. This gave the authoritarians their chance: they wrote normative grammars, in which they often ignored actual usage in favor of speculative notions. Both the belief in "authority"

---

[1] See Hempel (1948) and Popper (1968) for a general treatment of Positivism. For a criticism of the behavioristic attempt to account for various aspects of linguistic phenomena, see Chomsky's scathing review of B. F. Skinner (Fodor and Katz, 1964).

> and some of the fanciful rules (as, for instance, about the use of *shall* and *will*) still prevail in our schools. (Bloomfield, 1933:6; Holt, Rinehart and Winston, Inc.)

(What is perhaps even more unfortunate is that this situation *still* prevails in our schools.) Bloomfield went on to distinguish between what he felt are the proper interests of a linguist and the interests of specialists working in related disciplines, as follows:

> The student of literature observes the utterances of certain persons (say, of a Shakespeare) and concerns himself with the content and with the unusual features of form. The interest of the philologist is even broader, for he is concerned with the cultural significance and background of what he reads. The linguist, on the other hand, studies the language of all persons alike; the individual features in which the language of a great writer differs from the ordinary speech of his time and place interest the linguist no more than do the individual features of any other person's speech, and much less than do the features that are common to all speakers. . . . The discrimination of elegant or "correct" speech is a by-product of certain social conditions. (Bloomfield, 1933:22.)

By "turning at once to the observation of normal speech" (Bloomfield, 1933:22), the linguist was able to avoid dealing with the pseudosystems of language set up on ethnic or class bases.

Bloomfield's second statement, that the linguistic structures must be explicitly formulated without appeal to the intuitions of speakers, is extremely important to linguistics.

For example, in traditional grammars of English one can find statements similar to the following:

> In English the subject and the predicate must agree in person and in number. For example, one says "I see," "he sees," but not "I sees," "he see."

Such a statement, supplemented perhaps by a paradigm showing the forms for the irregular English verbs, like *to be* and *to do,* normally exhausts the information presented by the text with respect to the topic. It may strike you that this amount of information is all that is necessary. The reason that you feel that way, however, is because you are yourself a speaker of English, and you already know exactly how to manage the language.

It is easy to show, however, that such statements are in no sense complete or explicit, but are in fact simply relying upon an assumption that the reader will know what is meant, that is, relying upon the linguistic abilities and the intuition of the reader as a native speaker of English. Consider the following sentences:

E1. There was an attempt made by the liberals to limit the number of U.S. troops located in foreign countries.

E2. There were attempts made by the liberals to limit the number of U.S. troops located in foreign countries.

The subject of both E1 and E2 is the word *there*. Notice, however, that while the subject is the same, the verb forms are different. They do not "agree with the subject in person and in number," as we have been told that they should.

However, any native speaker of English can tell you that the phenomenon is not random. Thus, for most speakers, the following are not acceptable sequences of English:

E3. *There were an attempt made by the liberals to limit the number of U.S. troops located in foreign countries.

E4. *There was attempts made by the liberals to limit the number of U.S. troops located in foreign countries.

When a traditional grammar is forced to deal with such data as E3 and E4, it can only fall back upon the universal grammatical catchall, the "exception." Such a grammar must say either that there is a special class of sentences like E1 through E4, where the normal rule of Subject-Predicate agreement is suspended, or that if the subject of the sentence is *there,* then the predicate must "agree" with the first Noun Phrase or nominal expression that follows it. Neither of these alternatives does anything more than set up sentences with *there* subjects as exceptions to the postulated rule of Subject-Predicate agreement.

But if the notion of "subject"—the notion of the grammatical entity that is the focus or theme of the sentence—has any real value, then one must surely maintain that the subject of sentences like E1 through E4 cannot be the empty word *there*. Notice, for example, the structural and semantic relationships between sentences E1 through E4 on the one hand and E5 and E6 on the other:

E5. (a) An attempt was made by the liberals to limit the number of U.S. troops located in foreign countries.

(b) Attempts were made by the liberals to limit the number of U.S. troops located in foreign countries.

E6. (*a) An attempt were made by the liberals to limit the number of U.S. troops located in foreign countries.

(*b) Attempts was made by the liberals to limit the number of U.S. troops located in foreign countries.

An examination of these sentences (E1 through E6) will show you that the relationships that hold among them are systematic rather than random. If it were possible to state these relationships in such a way that the Subject was constant, then it is conceivable that the principle about Subject-Verb agreement could be salvaged with an accompanying deeper and more explicit understanding of the traditional notion of Subject.[2]

The statement of such a relation involves rather sophisticated notions about the structure of these particular sequences and, more importantly, about the structure of language systems in general. The formal devices necessary for this statement form the subject of later chapters of this book; the point of the above examples is to show that the traditional rules of grammar, while appearing to be quite general and explicit, are neither, but rather rely on one's intuitions and knowledge of the language being represented. It was this deficiency of the traditional treatment of grammatical phenomena that Bloomfield wished to eliminate when he suggested the following:

> The method of postulates (that is, assumptions or axioms) and definitions is fully adequate to mathematics: as for other sciences, the more complex their subject-matter the less amenable they are to this method, since under it every descriptive or historical fact becomes the subject of a new postulate. Nevertheless, the postulational method can further the study of language, because it forces us to state explicitly whatever we assume and to decide what things may exist independently and what things are interdependent. Certain errors can be avoided or corrected by examining and formulating our (at present tacit) assumptions and defining our (often undefined) terms. (Bloomfield, 1926:153.)

These two clearly formulated, if not original, theses issued by Bloomfield were also characteristic of his students. Unfortunately, there was one other dictum that Bloomfield's students accepted as a foundation upon which they could erect an entire theory of language.

As we mentioned earlier in this chapter, Bloomfield was strongly influenced by the particular brand of psychology known as Behaviorism. This influence is apparent in the following description:

> Suppose Jack and Jill are walking down a lane. Jill is hungry. She sees an apple in a tree. She makes a noise with her larynx, tongue, and lips. Jack vaults the fence, climbs the tree, takes the apple, brings it to Jill, and places it in her hand. Jill eats the apple. (Bloomfield, 1933:23.)

Bloomfield discussed this curious passage at length. He began by designating the following terms:

---

[2] The device for relating these sequences in a completely explicit way is the Transformation, which we will introduce in Chapter 4. Specifically, the transformation known as THERE INSERTION has been proposed (McCawley, 1970a) to account for these relationships.

sight of the apple in the tree = stimulus (S)
movement toward acquisition
  of the apple   = reaction (R)

Bloomfield pointed out that one way for Jill to secure the apple was to move toward the tree, climb it, and pick the apple herself. This situation is symbolized as

S   → R

Alternatively, Jill might make a noise "with her larynx, tongue, and lips." These vocal movements are simply a speech or substitute reaction for the act of getting the apple herself, the R. This substitute reaction is symbolized by *r*. Similarly, Jack could have performed the actions (R) described in Bloomfield's description on the basis of the sight of the apple alone (S). But actually he reacted to the reaction of Jill (*r*). Thus, we can call Jill's vocal output, with relation to Jack, an *s*. The entire passage can now be (or at least, for Bloomfield, could be) symbolized as follows:

S   → r . . . s   → R

The importance of the entire description for Bloomfieldians becomes obvious when we find that S is equated with the "practical events preceding the act of speech" (A) and R is equated with the "practical events following the act of speech" (C) and that

> . . . we say that speech-utterance, trivial and unimportant in itself, is important because it has a *meaning:* the meaning consists of the important things with which the speech utterance (B) is connected, namely the practical events (A and C). (Bloomfield, 1933:27.)

The seriousness of Bloomfield's intent in this cannot be doubted, and is perhaps more explicitly presented in his famous article *A Set of Postulates for the Science of Language,* where he presented the following definitions:

> The vocal features common to same or partly same utterances are *forms;* the corresponding stimulus-reaction features are *meanings.*
>
> Thus a form is a recurrent vocal feature which has meaning, and a meaning is a recurrent stimulus-reaction feature which corresponds to a form. (Bloomfield, 1926:55.)

Bloomfield thus committed himself to a theory of the meaning of the linguistic forms of language which was based on the behaviorist model of stimulus-response. Linguistic productions, that is, speech, are viewed as reactions substituted for the direct nonspeech action that could have been taken in the situation—for example, Jill's getting the apple herself.

The objections raised against Behaviorism, then, are themselves objections to Bloomfield's conception of the meaning of linguistic forms. Rather than attempt to summarize the various arguments against this philosophy, we can simply demonstrate by an example that such an approach places the study of meaning outside the scope of linguistics.

Assume that the vocal productions made by Jill were the sounds represented by E7(a):

E7. (a) Get me an apple, man.

It is quite possible that such a linguistic production in the vicinity of an apple tree would result in the actions ascribed to Jack. It is also quite possible that any one of the following would have had exactly the same effect:

E7. (b) I'm dying of hunger.
   (c) I thought you said that you were going to bring something to eat.
   (d) I just love apples.
   (e) Bring me an example of the symbol that appears on the label of the Beatles' records.
   (f) An apple a day keeps the doctor away.
   (g) So please me, love.

The list could be extended indefinitely. The point, however, is that the meaning of linguistic forms cannot, in general, be identified with the activities they elicit.[3] If this were the case, all vocal productions listed under E7 would be equivalent in meaning. While it is certainly true that all sequences (a) through (g) of E7 could well have the same result under certain circumstances, most linguists would not be willing to claim that they are equivalent in meaning. It is important to realize that it is just that claim that is implicit in the concept of linguistic forms and their meanings proposed by Bloomfield. Since in such a system the meaning of any particular sequence will vary as a function of the context in which it is uttered, it becomes questionable that any coherent account of the meanings of linguistic forms is possible. And it is certain that if such an account could indeed be made, it would not be made within the scope of what is usually understood to be the field of linguistics.

This stifling concept of linguistic meanings, coupled with the general contention of Behaviorism that the observable aspect of language behavior must constitute the entire domain of linguistic research, caused linguists to avoid nearly all but the phonological and morphological aspects of language

---

[3] This would appear to be the extreme functional view of linguistic meaning (often attributed to Wittgenstein, for example).

systems. In the writings of the descriptivists (the successors and students of Bloomfield) it is typical to find the nature of the subject matter to be entirely phonological and morphological; little or no work was done on the syntactic or semantic systems. Such work, in the terms we have previously established, concerned itself with the rules for the enumeration of Set A, the set of permissible sound sequences. The structure and the regularities of Set B and the relation of the set of well-formed meanings to Set A were ignored. The history of linguistic research carried on by Bloomfield and his followers is, then, largely a history of the development of the principles and methodology of phonology; in fact, it is largely the history of the development of the sound system concept of the phoneme. (We will take up this material in Chapter 12.[4])

The standard of rigor exhibited by linguists during this period was particularly high, and there was much concern with the methodology. The goal of these men has been called the construction of a *discovery procedure*.[5] Simply put, a discovery procedure is a mechanical device or method that accepts as input a set of data and yields as output a grammar. We might think of a discovery procedure, for example, as a program for a computer that, if given enough data from some language, would construct a fully explicit and accurate grammar for that language. Analogously, if such a discovery procedure existed in the physical sciences, it would accept as input the measurements of density, radioactivity, and behavior in the presence of a magnetic field of a certain strength of the naturally occurring elements; and it would present as a result of the action of the program upon this input a unified theory of the physical world. It seems obvious at this point that such a goal, however seductive, was a totally misleading one.

It was a natural outgrowth of the advances in the procedures of analysis employed in the research and description of the phonological systems that linguists should try to extend these procedures into the higher-order systems of morphology and syntax. One of the first problems encountered was that of classification of the material being dealt with, and it was approached by means of an attempt to formalize the traditional imprecise notions of "parts of speech." This effort, the division of words and phrases into Noun, Noun Phrases, Verbs, Adjectives, and so on, was called "immediate constituent analysis." The situation facing the linguist interested in doing such analysis was well described by Harris:

> One of the chief objectives of syntactic analysis is a compact description of the structure of utterances in the given language. The paucity of explicit

---

[4] See Teeter's article (1969) for a somewhat different view of the contributions made by Bloomfield. It must be pointed out that while Bloomfield was consistently positivistic in his theoretical statements, he did not allow such constraints to ruin his own linguistic descriptions.

[5] See Chomsky (1957: 50–51).

methods in this work has made syntactic analysis a tedious and often largely intuitive task, a collection of observations whose relevance is not certain and whose inter-relation is not clear. Partly as a result of this, many grammars have carried out little or no syntactic description. (Harris, 1946:161.)

Harris then went on to describe what he regarded as the major tool to be used in the syntactic description of utterances:

The procedure to be indicated below consists essentially of repeated substitution: e.g., *child* for *young boy* in *where did the* _____ *go?* To generalize this, we take a form A in an environment C _____D and then substitute another form B in the place of A. If, after such a substitution, we still have an expression which occurs in the language concerned, i.e., if not only CAD but also CBD occurs, we say that A and B are members of the same substitution class, or that both A and B fill the position C _____ D, or the like. The operation of substitution is basic in descriptive linguistics. Not only is it essential in phonemics, but it is also necessary for the initial setting up of morphemes, for the recognition of morpheme boundaries. (Harris, 1946:163.)

As the preceding passage indicates, the procedure of analysis referred to as "repeated substitution" was first developed as a method of analysis in the phonological research being conducted. Its extension into the field of descriptive syntax provided linguists with an explicit method with which to attack the problems of the higher-order system of syntax. The development of the techniques of analysis in phonology and their subsequent extension into syntax assisted in motivating the attitude held (apparently) by the majority of descriptive linguists, the attitude referred to as the concept of "separation of levels." Hockett expressed this methodological assumption quite succinctly:

There must be no circularity; phonological analysis is assumed for grammatical analysis, and so must not assume any part of the latter. The line of demarcation between the two must be sharp. (Joos, 1963:107.)

This statement merely expresses the attitude taken by nearly all linguists of that period regarding the use of information from a higher level of analysis (syntax) to assist in arriving at an analysis of a lower level (phonology). Pike, himself an exception to this dictate, characterized the attitude as follows:

In recent years various phonemicists seem to have set as an ideal of phonological description and analysis the elimination of all reference to or reliance upon facts about the grammatical structure of the language being investigated. (Pike, 1947:155.)

He opposed this thesis, stating his position as follows:

The present article holds that it is impossible for such claims to be realized completely, and that even if it were possible it would at times prove undesirable. . . . To eliminate the facts of grammatical relationship and structure from the analysis and presentation of phonological structure is frequently undesirable because many of the phonological facts are inextricably interwoven with grammatical facts and structural relationships; avoiding the portrayal of this relationship means omitting, completely or at least temporarily, an important part of the total structure of the language. (Pike, 1947:155.)

The notion of the substitution class and the mechanical procedure for establishing it motivated Rulon Wells, a contemporary of Harris, to attempt a unified treatment of the procedures for determining the syntax structures of the utterances of a language. Wells cited Zelig Harris's work in the introduction to his article entitled "Immediate Constituents":

Zellig S. Harris, in his article "From Morpheme to Utterance" [1946], makes explicit an operation of substituting one sequence of morphemes for another; by somewhat elaborating this operation and defining some auxiliary terms, we arrive at a conception of *expansion*. This characterizes one special variety of patterning; two sequences of morphemes, insofar as one is the expansion of the other, pattern alike. (*Language,* 1947:23; 81.)

Wells then described the notion of expansion and its importance in analysis:

Now the simple but significant fact of grammar on which we base our whole theory of ICs is this: that a sequence belonging to one sequence-class A is often substitutable for a sequence belonging to an entirely different sequence-class B. By calling class B entirely different from the class A we mean to say that A is not included in B, and B is not included in A; they have no member sequences in common or else relatively few. . . . For instance *Tom and Dick* is substitutable for *they,* wherever *they* occurs: *They wanted me to come* is a grammatical sentence, and so is *Tom and Dick wanted me to come.* . . . We may roughly express the fact under discussion by saying that sometimes two sequences occur in the same environments even though they have different internal structures. When one of the sequences is at least as long as the other (contains at least as many morphemes) and is structurally diverse from it . . . we call it an *expansion* of that other sequence, and the other sequence itself we call a *model.* (*Language,* 1947:23; 82.)

An example will help to clarify the procedure. Wells analyzed the sentence "The king of England opened Parliament" as follows:

Our general principle of IC [immediate constituent] analysis is not only to view a sequence, when possible, as an expansion of a shorter sequence, but also to break it up into parts of which some or all are themselves expansions. Thus in our example it is valuable to view *The king of England opened Parliament* as an expansion of *John worked* because *the king of England* is an expansion of *John* and *opened Parliament* is an expansion of *worked*. On this basis we regard the IC's of *The king of England opened Parliament* as *the king of England* and *opened Parliament*.

The king of England is in turn subject to analysis, and *John* is no help here because it is a single morpheme. *The king* will serve; *the king of England* is an expansion of *the king*, and in turn, *king of England* is an expansion of *king*. *The king of England* is accordingly analyzed into *the* and *king of England*. The reasons for analyzing the latter into *king* and *of England* (rather than *king of* and *England*) will be given later.

As for the second half of the sentence, *opened Parliament,* besides the obvious analysis into *opened* and *Parliament* there is another, instantly rejected by common sense but yet requiring to be considered, into *open* and *-ed Parliament*. The choice between the two analyses is dictated by . . . the principle that word divisions should be respected. (*Language,* 1947:23; 83.)

The principle of expansion, itself a derivative from the principle of substitution, in effect allowed the syntactician to escape the often questionable and highly intuitive task of determining which classes of linguistic objects were involved in any particular construction or sequence. By using this procedure, the linguist was able to arrive at an abstract structural formula that represented relationships present in the sequence under consideration. By repeated application of this technique on a number of superficially dissimilar strings, he was able to capture the intuitively detected similarities in a formal way. Given the class abbreviations that suggest their relation to traditional terms such as N(oun), V(erb), A(djective), T(Article), the analysis of sequences like E8 resulted in structural formulas such as F1.

E8. The kids have broken the window.
F1.   T N_1 v   V   T N_2

The structural formula F1 represents not only the structure of E8 but also of any sequence that can be broken into the sequence of classes that the formula lists. F1 therefore can represent all the sequences of E9.

E9. (a)   The authorities were laughing at the situation.
(b)   The girl had sung the mantra.
(c)   The ecologists didn't mention the source of the pollution.
(d)   The girl has bought the grapes.

The major conceptual breakthrough, which seems to have been the proximate cause of the development of transformational grammar, was made by Harris. In his article "Co-occurrence and Transformation in Linguistic Structure," Harris said:

This paper defines a formal relation among sentences, by virtue of which one sentence structure may be called the transform of another sentence structure (e.g., the *active* and the *passive,* or in a different way *question* and *answer.*) The relation is based on comparing the individual co-occurrences of morphemes. By investigating the individual co-occurrences, we can characterize the distribution of certain classes which may not be definable in ordinary linguistic terms (e.g., pronouns). More important, we can then proceed to define transformation, based on two structures having the same set of co-occurrences. (Harris, 1957:283.)

Harris first determined the classes on the basis of their co-occurrences of patterns of distribution:

. . . Some morphemes have very similar (though not identical) sets of co-occurrents. Thus, the set of co-occurrents for *cloth*—e.g., *The (   ) tore, The (   ) was torn, Get me a (   ) quick*—may have many morphemes in common with the set for *paper,* certainly more than with the set for *diminish.* This suggests that morphemes can be grouped into classes in such a way that members of a class have rather similar sets of co-occurrents, and that each class in turn occurs with other classes to make a sentence structure. . . . (Harris, 1957:284.)

Finally, Harris presented the notion of *transformation* itself as follows:

. . . we can compare the co-occurrences of two different constructions which contain the same classes. In many such constructions, as in *N's N* [*George's cat*—J.T.G.] and *N is a N* [*Bill is a guru*—J.T.G.] the co-occurrences are different. In some constructions the co-occurrences are about the same, and it is for these that transformation will be defined. . . .
    For example, every triplet of N_1, V, and N_2 in the N_1 v V *active* sentence (with some exceptions discussed below) can also be found in reverse order, in the N_2 v be Ven by N_1 *passive* sentence: *The kids broke the window, The window was broken by the kids; The detective will watch the staff, The staff will be watched by the detective.* . . . N_1 v V N_2—N_2 v be Ven by N_1. . . . (Harris, 1957:287.)

The now relatively well-defined notion of transformation and in particular the so-called PASSIVE Transformation may, of course, be applied to any sequence that has the structure F1, or equivalently, by substitution, the structure specified by F2:

F2. N_1 v V N_2

For example, all the sequences of E9 are of the required structure. If we apply the transformation that Harris proposed, we have the derivative transforms in E10:

E10. (a)   The situation was being laughed at by the authorities.
 (b)   The mantra was sung by the girl.
 (c)   The source of the pollution wasn't mentioned by the ecologists.
 (d)   The grapes have been bought by the girl.

In Chapter 4 we will see how the notion of *transformation,* as presented by Harris, was revised and refined by his student and collaborator, Noam Chomsky. Both men acknowledged their mutual intellectual debt to one another. The monograph *Syntactic Structures* (Chomsky, 1957), usually considered to be the document that initiated the field of transformational grammar, was published in the same year as the article written by Harris, from which we have been quoting.

We have attempted in this chapter to present a rational reconstruction of the line of thought and research that began with Bloomfield and culminated in the first presentation of the concept of transformation as the formalized relation between sets of sentences. A brief review may be of help at this point.

Bloomfield, setting the tone for the research that was to be the standard of descriptive linguistics in the United States until the advent of transformational grammar, was very much influenced by the behaviorist climate in psychology. The behaviorist demanded that the individual doing research restrict himself to observables. The most observable feature of language systems is the sound system, or phonology. The high standard of rigor proposed by Bloomfield survived as a characteristic of the work of his successors in their research on phonological systems. There was a great deal of emphasis on methodology, which culminated in a continuing attempt to specify a discovery procedure that could guarantee a unique solution, given the relevant data. One feature of this discovery procedure was the principle that levels of analysis must be kept separate in order to avoid circularity.[6] Another feature of the discovery procedure was the development of explicit, formal tools of analysis. These tools or procedures were extended into the analysis of the higher-order system of syntax. The notion of substitution and expansion made possible the development of what we regard as the primary conceptual advance—the notion of formal relations between sentences, the *transformation.*

We will examine in Chapter 4 the document that launched the field of transformational syntax.

---

[6] There were linguists who resisted this methodological assumption. See Pike (1947).

EXERCISES

In the text, we identified a common "rule" of grammar as presented by traditional textbooks. We showed that the formalization of the rules was anything but obvious. Further, we showed that there exist glaring surface counterexamples to this "rule."

1. Write down a list of five "rules," either from memory or from your favorite traditional textbook.

2. Show by discussion of each of the five "rules" you have selected that it makes an appeal to your linguistic intuitions as a speaker of English in order to decide whether a particular case falls under the "rule." That is, the "rule" uses ill-defined and nonexplicit terms.

As an example of the choices to be made, consider the following so-called rule from a typical traditional textbook:

The English adjective must always precede the noun it modifies.

Now consider the following counterexample:

I have some oregano green as grass.

It is obvious that the "rule" applies only when you are dealing with just the two lexical items representing the Noun + Adjective. So the "rule" correctly predicts the following:

    a.   green oregano
           Adj N
*b.   Oregano green
           N   Adj

It is equally obvious that the "rule" does not cover the counterexample sentence. The grammar of English derives a sentence like "I have a green hat" as follows:

from:
I have a hat [hat is green] →
    RELATIVE FORMATION
I have a hat which is green →
    RELATIVE REDUCTION
I have a hat green →
    ADJECTIVE PREPOSING
I have a green hat.

3. Using the class abbreviation given in F1 (T, N, v, V), construct another sentence formula and give three examples of sentences that fit it.

4. Select an additional class abbreviation of your own devising and apply it to the answers you gave to Exercise 3 to produce new sentences.

ANSWERS

1. Depends on individual student.
2. Depends on individual student.
3. v T N_1 V
   Did the man leave?
   Can the girl sing?
   Has the pig eaten?
4. Q-interrogative word
   Q v T N_1 V
   When did the man leave?
   How can the girl sing?
   Who has the pig eaten?

Chapter 4

The Beginning of Generative Grammar—Noam Chomsky's Syntactic Structures

In Chapter 3 we examined a number of characteristics of the intellectual background from which transformational grammar sprang. We saw that the discipline of linguistics in the mid-1950s was still dominated by what is often called "American Structuralism," or "descriptive linguistics." This approach was the natural outgrowth of the positivist approach to the analysis of natural language systems proposed by Bloomfield. Now we are going to move on to an examination of the book that marks the beginning of the field known as transformational grammar—Chomsky's *Syntactic Structures*.

For a new approach or theory to replace an older established model, there appear to be two things necessary. First, the new model must account for roughly the same amount of data[1] as did the old one. Second, there must be some reason—other than simple novelty—for preferring the new theory to the old. That is, if the new theory is nothing more than a set of new terminology for the old theory, there is no reason for making the change.

The question is: What sorts of things can be called legitimate reasons for preferring a new theory, given the assumption that the first condition is fulfilled? The following are usually considered to be examples of such reasons:

[1] Notice that the data themselves constitute a variable in the sense that the phenomena regarded as the core of what is to be explained are not necessarily constant.

1. The new model can solve with relative ease problems that were put in the "exceptions" bag in the previous system.

2. The new system is able to combine under a single explanatory principle phenomena that required separate explanations under the old system.

3. The new model is able to provide a formal demonstration that the old model is unable to account for certain classes of data considered to be an essential part of the subject matter of the discipline.

The last argument listed is, of course, the strongest and the most telling of the three.

Now, this set of reasons—or some subset of it—is said to be *necessary* before one theory can replace another. This is not to say that the presence of the total set of such reasons is *sufficient* to guarantee the success of the new theory. It may not even be sufficient to ensure that the new model will constitute a serious challenge to the old. This is true because the overthrow of an established system and its replacement by a new one in an event that takes place in the heads of the people involved. Whether a set of arguments will or will not prove to be compelling is not necessarily a function of the quality of those arguments, but is likely to be a function of the personalities of the individuals involved. (Since a study of the more human aspects of this revolution[2] in linguistics would entail the study of materials far outside the intended scope of our text,[3] we will not attempt to do more than to point out that such human factors exist.)

Syntactic Structures (Chomsky, 1957) represents the classic document on the subject of the *necessary* conditions. Written in a persuasive non-technical style, it offers a model of language that appears to cover the full range of phenomena accounted for by the old model. In addition, and most impressively, the book presents a formal demonstration that, for a certain class of grammars, there exist grammatical phenomena beyond the descriptive power of these grammars. We will consider the latter demonstration first.

Chomsky (1957) began by pointing out that natural languages have certain properties. One such property, as we have ourselves observed earlier, is that there exist in English, for example, an infinite number of grammatical sentences. Obviously, the device that we are to construct—the grammar—which will generate all and only grammatical sentences of English, must contain some sort of recursive mechanism. The simplest[4] and most constrained grammar, which is itself finite, is an object known as a Finite State Grammar. Chomsky described such a grammar as follows:

[2] Kuhn (1967) characterized revolution in science as major events which occur in the social system of scientists.

[3] For example, in the field of social change, the recent study of Gandhi by the well-known psychoanalyst Erickson.

[4] The term "simplest" here is used to present the idea of "the least powerful."

Suppose that we have a machine that can be in any one of a finite number of different internal states, and suppose that this machine switches from one state to another by producing a certain symbol (let us say, an English word.) One of these states is an *initial state;* another is a *final state.* Suppose that the machine begins in the initial state, runs through a sequence of states (producing a word with each transition) and ends in the final state. We call the sequence of words which has been produced a "sentence." Each such machine thus defines a certain language; namely, the set of sentences that can be produced in this way. Any language that can be produced by a machine of this sort we call a *finite state language;* and we call the machine itself a *finite state grammar.* A finite state grammar can be represented graphically in the form of a *state diagram.* (Chomsky, 1957.)

Figure 4.1 is a graphic representation[5] of a Finite State Grammar. This particular Finite State Grammar will generate the following sequences:

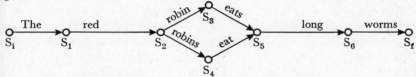

E1. (a)   The red robin eats long worms.
  (b)   The red robins eat long worms.

The property of recursion can be represented in state diagrams in the form of a loop. Notice, for example, the addition of the loop in Figure 4.2, which is otherwise identical to Figure 4.1.

Fig. 4.2.

The language generated by Figure 4.2 differs essentially, of course, from the language generated by Figure 4.1. While Figure 4.2 represents all the sequences enumerated by Figure 4.1, there is not any finite list of

[5] The symbol → in this system is usually referred to as an operator.

the sequences enumerated by Figure 4.2. The form of the language (Figure 4.2) can be suggested by the sequences in E2.

E2. (a)   The red robin(s) eat(s) . . . very . . . long worms.

The dots on either side of the word *very* are intended to represent the fact that the number of "very's" that may occur is unlimited. Each time the grammar reaches the state at which the loop appears in Figure 4.2, in other words, it is possible for the grammar to "go around the loop" any number of times. Thus, the device in Figure 4.2 generates an infinite number of sequences.

Chomsky (1957) next turned to artificial languages, as follows:

A language is defined by giving its "alphabet" (i.e., the finite set of symbols out of which its sentences are constructed) and its grammatical sentences. Before investigating English directly, let us consider several languages whose alphabets contain just the letters *a,b* and whose sentences are as defined in (10 i–iii):

(10)   i—ab, aabb, aaabbb, . . . , and in general, all sentences consisting of *n* occurrences of a followed by *n* occurrences of b and only these;

ii—aa, bb, abba, baab, aaaa, bbbb, aabbaa, abbbba, . . . , and in general, all sentences consisting of a string X followed by the "mirror image" of X (i.e., X in reverse), and only these;

iii—aa, bb, abab, baba, aaaa, bbbb, aabaab, abbabb, . . . and in general, all sentences consisting of a string X of a's and b's followed by the identical string X, and only these.

Let us consider the first of Chomsky's artificial languages in some detail. Notice that the language 10(i) consists of sequences of the form

F1. $a^n b^n$

where the two superscripts are understood as being identical.

The only restriction on the number of a's and b's that may occur in the language in question is that they be equal. Thus, for example, while the sequences in the preceding quote are "grammatical" in the language, 10(i), the following are not:

E3. *aaabb
    *aaaaaaaaaaaaabbb
    *bba

The task, then, is to construct a Finite State Grammar that will produce all the sequences represented by E3 but none of the sequences of E4. Notice that it is trivial to construct such a machine if some arbitrary limitation is placed on n. Let n be ≤ 10. The ladder-shaped state diagram represented by Figure 4.3 correctly generates 10(i) for $n \leq 10$.

Fig. 4.3.

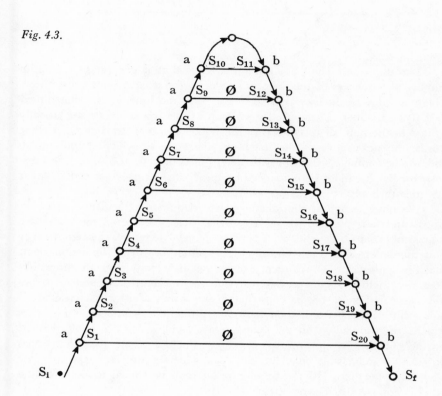

Notice in Figure 4.3 that the number of states internal to the machine required to generate the language correctly is 21. Using the "ladder" approach to the construction of a machine for the language, we see that in general the number of states internal to the machine which are required to generate the language represented by the formula $a^n b^n$ is systematically related to the value of n in the formula. Specifically, $N_s = 2n + 1$, where N_s is the number of internal states of the machine and n is the value of n in F1.

Obviously, for the language $a^n b^n$, where n is not arbitrarily restricted and, in particular, where n is infinite, there is no finite state machine that can generate the language in question. Now we must consider the alternative; that is, where we use the recursive device, the loop, to allow for the fact that n is not arbitrarily restricted. Consider the machine represented by Figure 4.4.

Fig. 4.4.

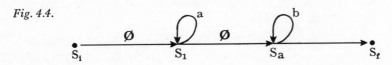

The important point about Figure 4.4 is that it generates an infinite number of sequences of the form $a^n b^n$, where n and m are not constrained. There is no way, however, for a finite state machine to be constrained so that the number of times that the b loop will be traversed is systematically related to the number of times that the a loop has been traversed. In other words, the next move of the machine (the state to which it will move, and correspondingly, its output) is determined only by the state it is presently in; but it cannot be influenced by the "path" or previous states that it has gone through.

We have seen that the language $a^n b^n$ demands a recursive device (a loop), and it is possible for us to provide such a device. However, there is no way to set up dependencies between loops. Therefore, the requirement that the superscripts in F1 be identical cannot be met. The requirement that the superscripts be identical can be met in a finite state machine that does not include recursive devices; but such a machine cannot, as we have seen in Figure 4.3, be constructed unless n is arbitrarily restricted. If n is arbitrarily restricted, then there are an infinite number of sequences which are grammatical in the language $a^n b^n$, but which are not generated by the machine so constrained. We may conclude, then, that there does not exist a finite state machine that can generate the language $a^n b^n$, or Chomsky's language [10(i)]. Similar results can be shown to hold for the other languages [10(ii) and 10(iii)].

The characteristic that places all three of the languages listed by Chomsky beyond the generative power of the class of grammars referred to as Finite State Grammars is the fact that there exists in each a dependency between noncontiguous elements. The language 10(i) can be regarded as either of two kinds of dependencies, which are called *properly nested* and *improperly nested*. Graphic representations of these two types of dependencies are shown in E4 and E5.

E4 and E5 show that there exist artificial languages for which there exists no Finite State Grammar. We now want to extend our discussion to English, as an example of a natural language.

The fact that English contains structures exhibiting noncontiguous dependencies (as shown in E6) and is an essentially recursive language (as shown in Chapter 2 of this text) guarantees the accuracy of E6.

E4. (a)   aaaaa . . . bbbbb . . .   (PROPERLY NESTED DEPENDENCY)

(b)   aaaaa . . . bbbbb . . .   (IMPROPERLY NESTED DEPENDENCY)

The languages 10(ii) and 10(iii) have the property of including a noncontiguous dependency, as shown in E5:

E5. (a)   aabbabab . . . babababba   [language 10(ii) properly nested]

(b)   aabbabab . . . aabbabab   [language 10(iii) improperly nested]

E6. (a)   If S_1, then S_2 . . .
(b)   Either S_3 or S_4 . . .
(c)   The man who said that [S_5] is arriving today . . .
(where each S_i is a sentence of English)

R1.   English is not a Finite State language.

To make R1 clearer, consider E7:

E7.   (a)   If Max sees the moon, either he'll howl or he'll read Ginsberg; then Sue will freak out.
(*b)   If Max sees the moon, either he'll howl, then Sue will freak out, or he'll read Grinsberg.

That these sequences in E7 contain noncontiguous dependencies as listed in E6 can be shown by the following schema, thus paralleling E4 and E5:

E8.   If Max sees the moon either he'll howl or he'll read Ginsberg; then Sue will freak out.

E7(a) was constructed by correctly embedding one properly nested English dependency E6(b) within another E6(a), thus yielding a grammatical sequence. Example E7(b), on the other hand, was constructed by incorrectly embedding one properly nested dependency within another. Additional examples using different combinations of these three properly nested English dependencies listed can be obtained mechanically by substituting one properly nested dependency for another. Such structures are, of course, not restricted to English. In fact, R1 should be replaced by the more general and more accurate statement

R2. Human languages are not Finite State languages.

The proof of R2 will have to wait until analysis has been made of the full range of human languages. However, no human language examined so far has disproved it.

Remember that Chomsky's objective was a demonstration in principle that human languages were beyond the descriptive power of the types of theory acceptable to the descriptivists. In a footnote (1957:20), he notes that Hockett's model of language in *A Manual of Phonology* was "essentially" a Finite State Grammar.

The demonstration of the inadequacy of finite state models for the description of natural languages was accomplished by Chomsky in a formal, rigorous way. The same set of arguments would not do, however, for the next most powerful class of grammars, the *Phrase Structure Grammar,* or PSG.

The PSG systems are said to have greater "generative capacity." That is to say, PSG are able to generate all the languages that Finite State Grammars can generate and, in addition, they are able to generate languages that cannot be generated by the Finite State Grammars. We saw above (R2) that there exists no Finite State Grammar that can generate the language $a^n b^n$. It is trivial to construct a PSG for this language, however.

First, we need to define some terminology. PSG rules can be represented by the following rule schema:

R3. $X \ Y \ Z \rightarrow X \ a \ Z$

The symbol $\rightarrow$ is to be understood as meaning "is to be rewritten as." The rule schema R3 may then be paraphrased by the statement: The sequence of symbols X Y Z is to be rewritten as the sequence of symbols X a Z. Equivalently, it can be rewritten as: The symbol Y is to be rewritten as the symbol *a* if Y is immediately preceded by the symbol X and immediately followed by the symbol Z.

There are usually two classes of PSGs distinguished: They are called Context-Free (CF) and Context-Sensitive (CS) Phrase Structure Grammars. We can most easily distinguish between them by referring again to R3. CF-PSG have the restriction that the symbols X and Z must be null ($\emptyset$) elements; that is, the symbol Y is to be rewritten as *a* no matter where or under what circumstances it occurs. The following rule schema represents the form that rules must take in CF-PSG's:

R4. $XYZ \rightarrow XaZ$ *or* $Y \rightarrow a$
where X and Z are null

The fact that the symbol Y is rewritten as *a* without regard for the context in which it appears is responsible for the term *context free*.

There are no such restrictions on the symbols X and Z in the rule schema for Context-Sensitive PSGs. That is, in a CS-PSG it will not always be the case that Y is rewritten as *a*. Compare R5, which are CF rules, with those in R6, which are CS rules:

R5. $F \rightarrow f$ **R6.** $XFZ \rightarrow XfZ$
     $I \rightarrow i$ $XCZ \rightarrow XcZ$
     $T \rightarrow t$ $XKZ \rightarrow XkZ$
     $S \rightarrow s$ $XEZ \rightarrow XeZ$

Just as Finite State Grammars are a special subset of PSG, so CF-PSG may be thought of as a special subset of CS-PSG, a subset distinguished by the condition given by R4.

R5 says that the symbol F is to be rewritten as the symbol *f* wherever it appears, without regard for the symbols that surround it, if any. R5 is applicable in all cases, regardless of environment or context—that is, everywhere. R6, however, being context-sensitive, must meet an additional requirement: F must be immediately preceded by X and immediately followed by Z in order to be rewritten as "*f*." In E9, then, R6 applies only to (b) and (d).

E9. (a)   F
     (b) $X \ F \ Z \rightarrow X \ f \ Z$
     (c)   W X F Y Z
     (d) $W \ X \ F \ Z \ Y \rightarrow W \ X \ f \ Z \ Y$

Now we may return to the question of the generative capacity of PSG as opposed to Finite State Grammars. CS-PSG's are capable of generating languages like F1, which contain noncontiguous dependencies. Obviously, since CF-PSG's are included as a special case of CS-PSG, they, too, are capable of generating languages like F1. Consider R7:

R7. (a) $S \rightarrow a \ X$
     (b) $X \rightarrow a \ X \ b$
     (c) $X \rightarrow b$

This set of rules is said to "generate" or enumerate the language of F1, $a^n b^n$, and is thus said to be the *grammar* of F1. If this set of rules is followed, it will generate all and only the grammatical sequences of language $a^n b^n$ and no others, which is precisely what a grammar is supposed to do.

The "vocabulary" of the language $a^n b^n$ is the following set of elements:

[S, X, a, b]. It is customary to divide the vocabulary of a grammar into two parts: the terminal vocabulary and the nonterminal vocabulary.[6] The terminal vocabulary is the set of all elements of the vocabulary which never appear on the left-hand side of the rewrite symbol →. In the $a^n b^n$ language, the symbols *a* and *b* constitute the total inventory of terminal symbols, and the terminology used to express this fact is the following: The symbols *a* and *b* *exhaust* the terminal vocabulary. (If you notice at this point that all these terms and symbols also exhaust *you,* you may take this to be perfectly normal.)

The remaining symbols, which constitute the nonterminal vocabulary of the language, are defined as the Complement of the terminal vocabulary.

We can now examine the manner in which a PSG functions.

1. Write down the initial symbol S (that is, the symbol that appears only on the left-hand side of the arrow).

    S   Initial symbol

2. Find the rewrite rule in which that initial symbol appears on the left side of the arrow.

    R7(a)

3. Write down the sequence of elements that appears on the right-hand side of the rule just identified, immediately below the last line of symbols.

    S
    a X   Initial symbol R7(a)

4. Search the sequence just written for the presence of a nonterminal symbol(s). If one is present, find the rewrite rule in which it appears on the left side of the arrow.

    R7(b)

5. Now rewrite the last sequence of symbols, replacing the nonterminal symbol(s) with the sequence that appears on the right side of the arrow in the rule you have just identified.

    S   Initial symbol
    a X   R7(a)
    a a X b   R7(b)

6. Repeat 4 and 5 until no nonterminal symbols remain.

    S   Initial symbol
    a X   R7(a)
    a a X b   R7(b)
    a a a X b b   R7(b)
    a a a b b b   R7(c)

The result of the preceding operation is called a Derivation with respect to a particular set of rules or a particular PSG. The object "derivation" is a well-defined, explicit notion.

[6] It is customary to distinguish, in addition, the symbol S in R7 as the Initial symbol. Obviously, it functions simply to allow one to initiate a derivation.

There are several properties that are characteristic of E9 which should be noted. First, notice that we have restricted ourselves to a CF-PSG. Second, note that R7 contains a rule whose form is of particular interest, repeated here for convenience.

$$X \rightarrow a\,X\,b \qquad [R7(b)]$$

The rule is of the general form

R8. $A \rightarrow \ldots A \ldots$
where . . . may contain any symbol(s) in the vocabulary.

The important point about rules of this form is that they function in rewrite systems exactly as loops function in Finite State Grammars; namely, they represent the property of Recursion. Since there is no constraint on the number of times that R7(b) may be applied, given the nonterminal symbol X appearing in the last line of the derivation, the PSG generates an infinite number of strings. The form of those strings is the form $a^n b^n$ specified by F1.

Perhaps this last point is not immediately obvious. To begin the construction of the derivation, one writes down the initial symbol S. Only one rule may now "apply," namely, R7(a). R7(a) produces one terminal symbol a and the nonterminal symbol X. There are now two possibilities for rewriting the symbol X, R7(b) and R7(c). If R7(c) is selected and "applied," then the derivation is terminated, resulting in the sequence ab. This sequence is, of course, grammatical in the language $a^n b^n$, specifically where $n = 1$. If R7(b) had been selected, it would have resulted in the sequence $aaXb$, which is of the form $a^n\,X\,b^{n-1}$, where n $= 2$. Repeated applications of R7(b) will produce sequences of the same general form, $a^n\,X\,b^{n-1}$. The application of R7(c) is necessary to terminate every derivation, as it is the only rule that contains only terminal symbols on the right side of the rewrite symbol. But the application of R7(c) to a sequence of the form $a^n\,X\,b^{n-1}$ results in a sequence of the form $a^n b^n$, as the rule replaces the nonterminal symbol X with a b. Thus, we see that for PSG, R7 will generate the language F1, which is beyond the descriptive power of the class of grammars first considered, the Finite State grammars. PSG can be constructed for each of the three languages identified by Chomsky as being outside the generative capacity of Finite State grammars. These languages therefore constitute no difficulty for the class of grammars known as PSG. The arguments concerning the inadequacy of PSG as models for human, rather than artifical, languages are not so rigorous, but rely on other considerations that we will turn to in a moment.

The fragment of the PSG grammar of English presented by Chomsky in *Syntactic Structures* was very much like the following set of PSG rules:

R9.   (a)   S(entence)   → # N(oun) P(hrase) V(erb) P(hrase) #
     (b)   NP   → (Det(erminer))N
     (c)   VP   → V (NP)
     (d)   Det   → the, a, . . .
     (e)   N   → ball, girl, boy, . . .
     (f)   V   → saw, kiss, fly, . . .

Given this set of PSG rules, where parentheses are used to indicate optional elements, and the concept of a derivation that we illustrated above, we can show the derivation of a sample string of English.

E10.
	Initial Symbol
# S #	Initial Symbol
# NP VP #	R9(a)
# Det N VP #	R9(b)
# Det N V NP #	R9(c)
# Det N V Det N #	R9(b)
# The N V Det N #	R9(d)
# The girl V Det N #	R9(e)
# The girl saw Det N #	R9(f)
# The girl saw the N #	R9(d)
# The girl saw the boy #	R9(e)

The derivation E10 can also be represented as a *tree structure,* or a Phrase Marker, as demonstrated in E11. There exists a mechanical procedure, or algorithm, for relating PSG derivations to tree structures.[7]

E11.

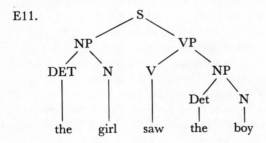

Tree structures are more frequently used in the literature than any other illustrative device and will also be used in the subsequent material in this text.

One of the most important relations commonly defined on tree structures is the *is a* relation. Using E11 as an example, we can see that the

---

[7] There exists a possible ambiguity in the PSG derivations which will allow more than one tree representation, or Phrase Marker, for particular derivations. See Postal (1964), Bach (1964), or McCawley (1968a) for discussion.

sequence *"the girl"* is a NP, in the sense that the point or node in the tree that exhaustively dominates the sequence *the girl* is labeled NP. The *is a* relation is the formal counterpart of the notion of constituent structure, which occupied the attention of many linguists prior to *Syntactic Structures* (Chomsky, 1957). Several empirical claims are implicit in the notion of the *is a* relation or constituent structure. The relation predicts that native speakers of English will agree that the sequence *the girl* is the same kind of structural unit as the sequence *the boy*. This intuition is reflected by the fact that the first set of nodes that exhaustively dominates each of the phrases bears the same label, NP. The *is a* relation claims further that while there exist constituents such as *the girl, the boy, saw the boy,* and *the girl saw the boy,* with their accompanying labels, there exist no constituents *girl saw, saw the,* and *the girl saw*. This intuition is captured by the tree structure, in that for each of the former sequences there is a single labeled node that dominates it exhaustively, but that for the latter sequences no such node exists.

The derivation of the sequence E10 is misleading, as we have looked at only a portion of the derivation of a sequence of English, specifically the derivation of a sequence with respect to a PSG component similar to the one that appeared in the system developed by Chomsky (1957) in his presentation of the fragment of the grammar in *Syntactic Structures*. The example was deliberately chosen so that it appears unnecessary for any further processes to apply to it in order to produce a grammatical string of English. This is not really the case. The actual system developed by Chomsky in his work contained two distinct mechanisms. There was the PSG, which we have already seen, and the transformational component. The PSG enumerated sequences of English morphemes with their accompanying tree structure in just the manner we have discussed; these structures, which appeared in the output of the PSG, constituted the input to the transformational component. Suppose some expansion of the rule R9(f) other than *saw* had been selected. As E12 shows, the results would not have been grammatical.

E12. *The girl kiss the boy.

The difficulty with E12 is obvious to every native speaker of English; in traditional terms, the predicate or verb and subject do not agree in number. The problem did not occur with the sequence considered previously because the simple past tense in English is not inflected for number.[8] This well-known syntactic phenomenon demonstrates clearly the inadequacy of the less powerful class of PSGs, the CF-PSG. An examination of the PSG

---

[8] That is, the verbal forms for third person singular and third person plural are identical, both phonologically and orthographically.

rules in R9 will show that all the rules are within the class of CF-PSG.
Consider the problem of producing a grammatical sequence of English, given
the rule for the expansion of V (V → saw, kiss, fly . . .) and a fully developed tree such as E13 except for the expansion of the symbol V.

E13.

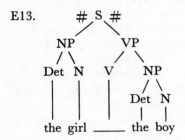

If the expansion *saw* is chosen for V, there is no difficulty. But what of the
case where *kiss* is selected? Is there some method of constraining the
expansion of V in R9(f) so that only grammatical strings of English are
enumerated? Notice that, in addition to the grammatical sequence E14(a),
we have also in English the grammatical sequence E14(b) :

E14. (a) The girl kisses the boy.
       (b) The girls kiss the boy.

In our attempt to solve this difficulty within the limits of CF-PSG,
it might be pointed out that the expansion of V [R9(f)] should include
both the words *kiss* and *kisses,* and that the grammaticality of both sequences
listed in E14 is evidence of this. If such asuggestion were adopted, then
the device would generate all four of the sequences listed under E15.

E15.   (a) The girl kisses the boy.
        (b) The girls kiss the boy.
       (*c) The girl kiss the boy.
       (*d) The girls kisses the boy.

All such suggestions will prove to be futile, given the definition of
CF-PSG presented with R4. The defining characteristic of a CF-PSG rule
is that the symbol to be rewritten (V) is to be rewritten without reference
to the context in which it occurs (in this case *the girl* or *the girls.*) Thus,
by definition, one cannot write a CF-PSG rule that will expand the symbol
V into *kiss* in the context of being immediately preceded by the sequence
the girls and that will expand the symbol V into *kisses* in the context of
being immediately preceded by the sequence *the girl.* In other words, any
set of CF-PSG rules that generate (correctly) the sequences E15(a) and

E15(b) will also generate (incorrectly) the sequences E15(c) and E15(d). The grammatical phenomenon of Subject-Predicate agreement is sufficient to guarantee the accuracy of R10:

R10. English is not a CF-PSG language.

The more powerful class of PSG, the CS-PSG cannot be eliminated from consideration by the same argument. CS-PSG are, in fact, eminently suitable for the statement of such grammatical phenomena as Subject-Predicate Number agreement in English. The CS-PSG rules R11 would capture the correct dependencies and, if substituted for R9(e) and (f), would give us the appropriate results.

R11. (a) $N \rightarrow \begin{Bmatrix} N_{singular} \\ N_{plural} \end{Bmatrix}$

(b) $N_{singular} \rightarrow$ boy, girl, toad, . . .

(c) $N_{plural} \rightarrow$ boys, girls, toads, . . .

(d) $N_{singular} V \rightarrow N_{singular} V_{singular}$

(e) $N_{plural} V \rightarrow N_{plural} V_{plural}$

(f) $V_{singular} \rightarrow$ saw, kisses, flies, . . .

(g) $V_{plural} \rightarrow$ saw, kiss, fly, . . .

Now, given R11 as PSG rules and the tree fully developed except for the expansion of V, as in E16,

E16.

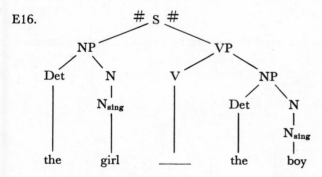

we see that only R11 (d) and R11 (f) are applicable, as the other expansions of V require that the immediately preceding element be a node labeled N_{plural}; but, in fact, the immediately preceding N-node is labeled "singular," the context required by R11 (d) and R11 (f). Therefore, *kisses* but not *kiss* will be selected, and the results are in accordance with the native speaker's judgments of grammaticality. It is therefore shown that the addition of such rules to the grammar is sufficient to capture the dependencies in terms of number agreement between subjects and predicates in English.

While the grammatical phenomenon of Subject-Predicate Number agreement in English presents no difficulty for a CS-PSG, it has been argued that there exist similar syntactic processes for which CS-PSG rules are inadequate.[9] Consider, for example, the relations between the two versions of E17:

E17. (a) The boy threw out the explosives.
     (b) The boy threw the explosives out.

E17(a) and (b) versions will be judged by native speakers of English to be synonymous; that is, there is no situation that one can imagine in which one version of E17 is true and the other false. Obviously, both versions of E17 are composed of the same set of English words, the difference between the two lying in the left-to-right order of the words involved. How, then, are the relations between the two versions of E17 to be captured in a grammatical description of English?

First consider how a set of PSG rules might attempt to capture the relations. We begin by noting the fact that there are sequences such as "throw out." "pick up." "call up," "look over" "pass out," . . . , which shows that our set of PSG rules will have to be amended in order to allow the introduction of this type of sequence. Such constructions are usually labeled Verb + Particle (V + Prt). R12 accomplishes this change.

R12. (a) VP → V (Prt) (NP)   [Replaces R9(c)]
      (b) Prt → in, out, over, . . .

Given this change, we see that the tree representing the derivation of E17(a) would be E18:

E18.

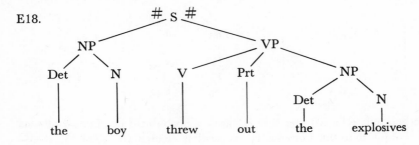

---

[9] See Postal (1964) for an excellent discussion. See Harmon (1963) for an objection to the claim made here. The dispute seems largely, if not entirely, terminological. The point is that coding devices that incorporate the power of transformations can be built into what appears *superficially* to be a CS-PSG.

Further, it seems clear that the tree that represents E17 (b) should be E19. Our problem is how the two should be related.

E19.

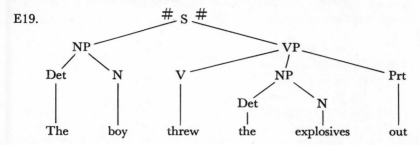

There appear to be two logical approaches to the solution of this problem. First, we might consider the introduction of a PSG rule like R13 in addition to R12:

R13. VP → V (NP) (Prt)

There are two objections to this proposal: (1) any grammar that contains both R12 and R13 fails to capture the intuition that the two versions of R12 or R13 must necessarily be made prior to the expansion of the selected as an expansion of VP is not free in American English,[10] as E20 shows:

E20. (*a)   The boy threw out it.
   (b)   The boy threw it out.

That is, if the NP object is a pronominal element, the particle obligatorily appears on the right-hand side of it. It is important to notice that it will not do to introduce rules like R14:

R14. (a)   N → N$_{pronominal}$
   (b)   N → N$_{regular}$

and then select either R12 or R13 on the basis of the information as to whether R14(a) or R14(b) was selected. This is futile because the choice of R12 or R13 must necessarily be made prior to the expansion of the node NP into N, which in turn is expanded into either N-pronominal or N-regular. The point is that the *information* as to whether or not the NP object is pronominal is *not* available until after the "decision" to use R12 or R13 has been made.

[10] As it is, say, in British English.

CS-PSG rules can overcome this difficulty. The way that they do so is itself the argument that they are not the correct mechanism to capture the dependencies involved in the process. The set of rules in R15 is adequate to accomplish the desired result.

R15. (a) VP → V (Prt) (NP)
    (b) NP → N_{pron}
    (c) NP → N_{reg}
    (d) Prt N_{pron} → N_{pron} Prt
    (e) N_{pron} → he, she, it, . . .

With this set of rules we have overcome the two deficiencies that the first solution contained. We can now illustrate the derivation of the two sequences in E20.

E21.

Derivation	Initial Symbol
# S #	*Initial Symbol*
# NP VP #	R9(a)
# Det N VP #	R9(b)
# Det N_{reg} VP #	R15(c)
# Det N_{reg} V Prt NP #	R12(a)
# Det N_{reg} V Prt N_{pron} #	R15(b)
# Det N_{reg} V N_{pron} Prt #	R15(d)
# The N_{reg} V N_{pron} Prt #	R9(d)
# The boy V N_{pron} Prt #	R9(e)
# The boy threw N_{pron} Prt #	R9(f)
# The boy threw it Prt #	R15(e)
# The boy threw it out #	R12(b)

The tree structure, or phrase marker, that corresponds to this derivation is shown in E22:

E22.

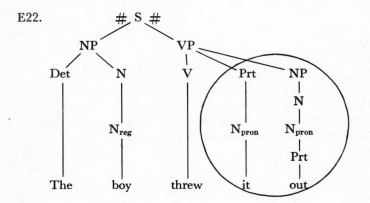

The inadequacy of the CS-PSG solution should be apparent from the derivation and the tree in E22. Consider specifically the portion of the tree circled and its corresponding portion of the derivation. It is precisely at this point that the CS-PSG rule has "applied," ensuring that only the grammatical version of E20 will be generated, that is, E20(b). The proposal actually fails for two reasons. First, notice the claim being made by the *is a* relation in tree E22. The claim is that *is a* relation holds between the Prt and the N_{pron} elements. That is, the claim is that, in English, particles are pronominal nouns, and vice versa. Such a claim is surely absurd, running counter to the very facts that the grammar is designed to capture, the native speaker's intuitions. Second, while it is true that E20(b) will be generated (correctly) and that E20(a) will be excluded (correctly), it is also true that the following sequences will be generated by the same rules.

E23. (a)   The boy threw it up.
      (*b)   The boy kisses it up.
      (c)   The boy threw it over.
      (*d)   The boy kisses it over.

The reason that the sequences of E23 are enumerated is because the following two rules are independent of one another:

R16. (a) $V_{sing} \rightarrow$ saw, kisses, flies, threw, . . .   [Same as R11(f)]
      (b)   Prt $\rightarrow$ in, out, over, . . .   [Same as R12(b)]

In other words, the choice of verb and particles is context-free. In order to capture the dependencies, one is required to write CS-PSG rules that contain the actual English words, as in R17:

R17.   threw NP Prt $\rightarrow$ threw NP $\left\{ {out \atop up} \right\}$

By writing such rules, however, one gives up all hope of starting the general process. What is needed is some way of stating that, in American English, when the sequence Verb Particle is succeeded by a Pronominal, the Particle must appear on the right-hand side of that Pronominal. This must be done without mentioning any particular verb sequences. Transformations are designed expressly to state such phenomena formally.

Transformations may be represented by the following schema:

R18.   Structural Index $X_i, \ldots, X_j, \ldots, X_n$
      Structural Change $X_i, \ldots, X_k, \ldots, X_n$
      where X_i, X_j, and X_k, X_n, are elements of the vocabulary of the language and $X_j \neq X_k$ for some j and k.[11]

[11] The form of R18 could just as easily be made to conform to the rewrite schema, as follows:
$X_i, \ldots, X_j, \ldots, X_n \rightarrow X_i, \ldots, X_k, \ldots, X_n$
where X_i, X_j, X_k, and X_n are elements of the vocabulary of the language and $X_j \neq X_k$ for some j and k.

Specifically, consider the transformation that has been proposed to handle the phenomenon under consideration, PARTICLE MOVEMENT.[12]

E24. PARTICLE MOVEMENT   #   X   V   Prt   NP   Y   #
Structural Index   1,   2,   3,   4,   5,   6,   7
Structural Change   1,   2,   3, $\varnothing$,   5 + 4,   6,   7
where + means that the moved element is placed under the node that dominates the stationary symbol that it crosses.

The structural index of a transformation specifies what the structure of a sequence must be in order for it to be eligible to undergo that transformation. The formula that appears as the structural index of a transformation must partition (divide exhaustively) the sequence of terminal elements. If a sequence is so partitioned by the structural index, then it is said to be *properly analyzable* with respect to that transformation. Notice that the structural index of the transformation partitions the sequences E17(a) and E20(a).

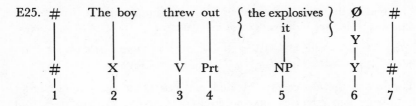

We see the same thing in tree representation:

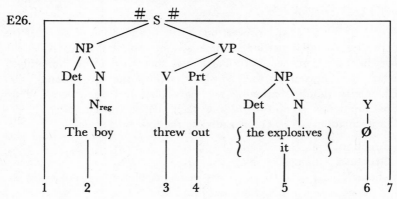

[12] You will remember the additional condition on this transformation. While the transformation is optional (may or may not be applied without affecting the grammaticality of the result) if the term 5 is a lexical noun, it becomes obligatory in American English if term 5 is a pronominal form.

Notice that although it is a requirement that the sequence of terminal elements be partitioned, they are in fact partitioned in terms of a formula that mentions only higher-level nodes (nonterminal vocabulary symbols), ensuring the most general statement—that is, ensuring that all sequences of English that have the structure specified by the structural index will be eligible to undergo this process. This feature is sometimes referred to as the property of *variable reference*. The effect of the transformation is specified by the structural change. The resulting tree is therefore analyzable with respect to the structural change shown in E27. Note that the two nodes Prt and NP have permuted under the node VP.

E27.

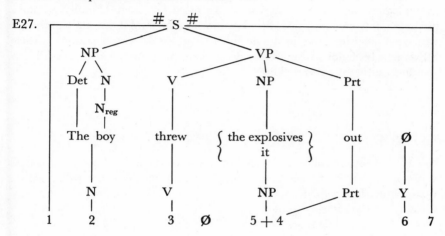

Tree structures E26 and E27 are said to be *transforms* of one another; more commonly, E27 is said to be *derived* from E26. This latter terminology reminds us of the issue alluded to earlier—that there were two syntactic mechanisms proposed by Chomsky in his early work, the PSG and the transformational component. Thus, one may speak of the derivation of some sequence with respect to either set of rules or both.

Transformations, we have seen, formally relate, or map, tree structures into tree structures (or, equivalently, Phrase Markers into Phrase Markers.) This device states the formal analog of the intuitions of native speakers with regard to the intimate relation between pairs of sequences such as E17 and E20, thus accurately reflecting these judgments. It does so while avoiding the inaccurate claims made by CS-PSG rules.

This chapter has presented portions of the arguments developed by Chomsky to show the inadequacy of the previously proposed systems of grammatical description. We have seen the outline of the formal demonstration of the inadequacy of one class of grammars, the Finite State Grammars. Similarly, we have shown that there exists at least one grammatical process that is beyond the generative capacity of the next most powerful class of grammars, the CF-PSG.[13] While the formal arguments fail to hold in the case of CS-PSG, we have noted what seem to us quite cogent arguments, suggesting the clumsiness and the inaccurate structural claims of such systems in the description of certain syntactic phenomena. Thus, although the process used as an example (PARTICLE MOVEMENT) does not lie outside the generative capacity of CS-PSG, it is obvious that if the grammar is to faithfully mirror the intuitions that native speakers have about the structure of their language, then CS-PSG cannot serve as an adequate model of human language. The failure of CS-PSG is an empirical failure as opposed to the logical failure of the previously discussed grammars. Finally, we have presented the device called the Transformation, and have shown that it accurately registers the intuitions of native speakers concerning Particle Movement behavior in English while at the same time avoiding absurd and counterintuitive structural claims.

EXERCISES

1. In each of the following examples, we have made up a set of sequences that constitute a language. Your task is to design an FSG that will generate all and only these sequences.

(a) Vocabulary—(a,b)
Permissible sequences—aaab, aabb, abbb, aaaa, bbbb
(b) Vocabulary—(a,b)
Permissible sequences—aaba, aaaaaaba, ba, aaaba, aaaaaba, aaaaba

2. List the sequences(s) generated by the following machine, following the states indicated.

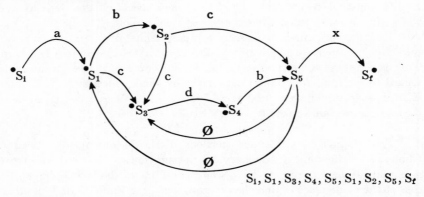

$S_1, S_1, S_3, S_4, S_5, S_1, S_2, S_5, S_f$

---

[13] Chomsky used different phenomena in his book to make the same point.

3. How many ways can the sequence abcdbx be generated, using the machine in Exercise 2? List them.

ANSWERS

1(a)

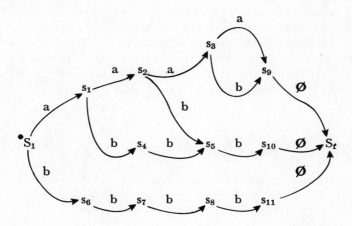

1(b)

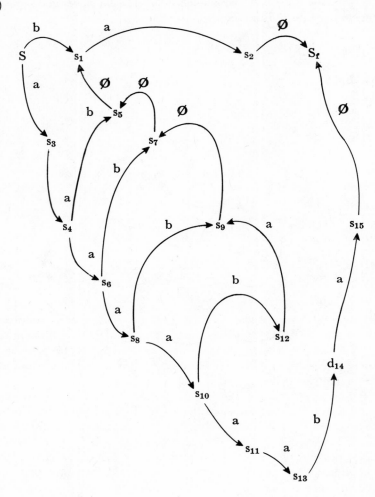

2. Sequences enumerated by the states listed:

a b c x

a b c d b x

a b c b c d b x

a b c b c x

3. There are two ways to generate the sequence *abcdbx,* using the machine in Exercise 2: s_i s_1, s_2 s_3, s_4, s_5, s_f and s_i, s_1, s_2, s_5, s_3 s_4, s_5 s_f.

Chapter 5

Early
Transformational Syntax

In this chapter we consider some of the work done by the early transformationalists. In doing so, we have two purposes in mind: (1) to present some of the grammatical phenomena that they uncovered; (2) to provide the background necessary to make the more recent developments in transformational grammar intelligible.

It is important that we have clearly in mind just what the theory of language proposed in *Syntactic Structures* (Chomsky, 1957) was. To begin with, there was a Context-Free Phrase Structure grammar that enumerated[1] an infinite number of Phrase Markers. These Phrase Markers were the tree representations, the structural representations of the basic underlying syntactic objects that make up the inventory of basic sentence patterns in a particular language. The constituent structure of phrasal grouping internal to the sentential unit was given by the branching patterns in the tree (the *is a* relation). The nodes dominating the terminal symbols of the tree indicated by their labels which categories in the language these terminal symbols belonged to. The bottom line of the tree structure was composed

---

[1] The term *enumerated* as used in this and similar contexts within transformational grammar is perhaps best understood as *specified*. One can imagine, for example, an actual machine that produces tree representations from a set of PSG rules. The PSG rules could then be said to enumerate the tree structures—the shape and labeling of the trees are fully determined by the set of PSG rules.

of terminal symbols—in this model, a series of actual words.[2] The next component in this system was a series of transformations, to which the set of trees enumerated by the CF-PSG was subjected. These formal objects, the transformations, mapped one tree structure into another if certain formal conditions were met; namely, that the terminal symbols of the tree could be partitioned (divided exhaustively) by an abstract formula associated with the transformation in question. This formula was called the Structural Index of the transformation with which it was associated. If the tree could be partitioned by the Structural Index, it was said to be properly analyzeable with respect to that transformation. The structure of the resultant or derived tree was specified by a second abstract formula associated with the transformation: the Structural Change. The final derived tree representation was called the Surface Structure, an actual sentence of the language.[3] This entire object, from the CF-PSG to the Surface Structure, was called a Derivation. F1 is a schema representing such a derivation.

$$\textbf{F1.} \quad \text{CF-PSG} \rightarrow \begin{Bmatrix} T_1 \\ T_j \\ \cdot \\ \cdot \\ \cdot \\ T_n \end{Bmatrix} \rightarrow \text{Transformations} \rightarrow \begin{Bmatrix} T_1 \\ T_j \\ \cdot \\ \cdot \\ \cdot \\ T_n \end{Bmatrix} = \text{Surface Structure}$$

where T is a Phrase Marker produced by the CF-PSG and T′ is a final derived Phrase Marker.

This much we have seen in Chapter 4. There are several additional distinctions proposed by Chomsky (1957) in the model presented in *Syntactic Structures* which are worth noting.

Transformations were considered to be of two basic types: Obligatory and Optional. The set of obligatory transformations was just that set of transformations whose application was necessary in *every* derivation of the sentences of the language if the resulting sequence was to be grammatical. For example, in English, every grammatical sequence must undergo the Number Agreement transformation, the transformation whose function it is to ensure Subject-Verb agreement. Since this transformation must apply

----

[2] The model in *Syntatic Structures* allowed elements other than actual words in the terminal vocabulary. In general, the terminal vocabulary elements that were not actual words were markers of the tense and number, and markers that identified the limits of clauses.

[3] This is not, of course, accurate. The final derived trees, the output of the transformational component, are actually the input to the phonological component where they receive a phonological interpretation (their pronunciation value). The inaccuracy does not affect the validity of the arguments.

in every derivation,[4] it is said to be obligatory. In other words, one can predict that failure to apply this transformation will always result in a sequence that is ungrammatical, as, for example, in E1:

E1. (*a)   The boy see the ball.
     (*b)   The attack disrupt the class.

The set of remaining transformations, those that were not obligatory, constituted the set of optional transformations. The (a) and (b) versions of E2 would be related to each other by an optional transformation in this system.

E2. (a)   The people proposed a joint function.
     (b)   The people didn't propose a joint function.

E3. (a)   The real question is whether there is any intelligent life in the universe.
     (b)   Is the real question whether there is any intelligent life in the universe?

E4. (a)   Timothy never said that it was entirely a question of spacing.
     (b)   Never did Timothy say that it was entirely a question of spacing.

Notice that the (a) versions of E2, E3, and E4 are grammatical; that is, the sequences are grammatical without the application of the optional transformations.

Given this distinction between obligatory and optional transformations, the notion of *kernel sentence* can be defined as follows: A kernel sentence is any surface structure to which only the set of obligatory transformations has applied.

The remaining feature of *Syntactic Structures* to be discussed is the way in which the property of Recursion is represented. You will remember from Chapter 2 that the process of sentence embedding, or more specifically the process of Relative Clause Formation, has no natural limit. No grammar can be seriously considered unless it accounts for this process. E5 illustrates sentence embedding.

E5. (a)   The man raised the flag.
     (b)   The man who was laughing raised the flag.

---

[4] The distinction between Obligatory and Optional transformations is one of the distinctions originally proposed which seems to have received little attention in the subsequent work. It does not appear to be a well-defined notion within the present systems. Most likely, its present interpretation would be: A transformation is obligatory if it must apply in every derivation of a Phrase Marker in which its structural index is met.

(c)   The man who was laughing raised the flag which his mother had given him.

In the system of grammar presented in *Syntactic Structures* (Chomsky, 1957), which formed the model for research in the seven years following its publication, recursion was represented in the transformational component by a special set of transformations called double-based or generalized transformations.

E6. (a)   The man$_i$ raised the flag.
    (b)   The man$_i$ was laughing.

Notice that each of E6(a) and (b) sequences has a Noun that is indexed *i*, indicating that it refers to the same object.[5] We may combine these two sequences by embedding one into the other by means of the GENERALIZED RELATIVIZATION transformation, which has the following form:

F2. $[_S$X   N$_i$ Y$]_S$ $[_S$X′   N$_i$ Y$]_S$

Structural Index	1	2	3	4	5
Structural Change	1	2 + 4	3	Ø	5

where N$_i$ is coreferential with N$_i$:

The structural index of F2 partitions the sequences E6(a) and (b), as E7(a) shows; the result of the "application" of F2 to these sequences is E7(b):

The grammar, then, represents the process of recursion by means of transformations that receive as input two sentences independently generated by the CF-PSG and, subject to the condition that each contains an occurrence of a co-referential Noun, place one within the other. The sentence that occupies the left position in F2, the one into which the other is inserted, is called the Matrix sentence. This process is iterative and may, of course, "apply" as many times as there are pairs of sentences that are properly analyzable with respect to the structural index in E7. Subsequent transformations will replace the second occurrence of the coreferential N with a relative pronoun, yielding the Surface Structure:

E8.   The man who was laughing raised the flag.

[5] In the original formulation, and in most of the early work, the coreference condition (indexing of Nouns or Noun Phrases in the structural indices of transformations) was not allowed, but rather only formal identity conditions (that is, the shape of the two terms must be identical) were acceptable. This was consistent with the avoidance of reference to any semantic facts (Set B) while specifying the syntax of a language, the separation of levels constraint.

E7. (a)

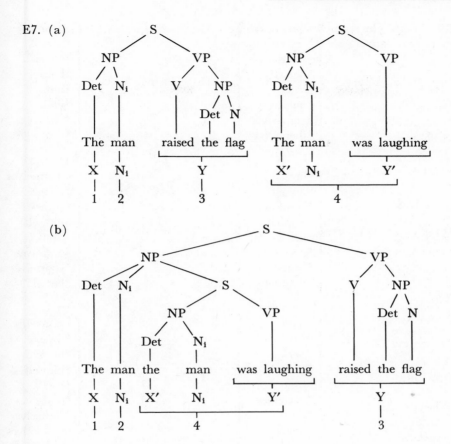

(b)

We have now examined the essential characteristics of the model pre-sented by Chomsky in *Syntactic Structures*. It is important to understand exactly what this system was intended to do. It should be obvious that the task of this system was to generate all and only the members of Set A—the set of well-formed sound sequences of the language. It was to accomplish this without making reference to the information in Set B, the set of well-formed semantic representations, and it was to make no reference or appeal to the relation between Set A and Set B.

With both the model and its purpose clear in our mind, we can now proceed to examine what may be regarded as a classic example of argu-mentation in the early transformational work.

The data displayed in the sequences of E9 illustrate the phenomenon in English called REFLEXIVIZATION.

E9.

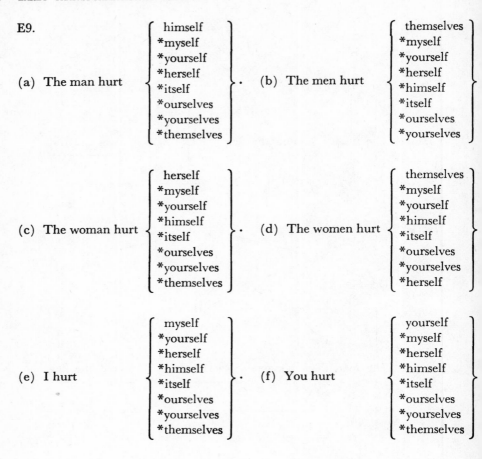

(a) The man hurt
{
himself
*myself
*yourself
*herself
*itself
*ourselves
*yourselves
*themselves
}
.
(b) The men hurt
{
themselves
*myself
*yourself
*herself
*himself
*itself
*ourselves
*yourselves
}

(c) The woman hurt
{
herself
*myself
*yourself
*himself
*itself
*ourselves
*yourselves
*themselves
}
.
(d) The women hurt
{
themselves
*myself
*yourself
*himself
*itself
*ourselves
*yourselves
*herself
}

(e) I hurt
{
myself
*yourself
*herself
*himself
*itself
*ourselves
*yourselves
*themselves
}
.
(f) You hurt
{
yourself
*myself
*herself
*himself
*itself
*ourselves
*yourselves
*themselves
}

Suppose we agree to the following terminology: We will refer to the *-self* forms as reflexive anaphors and to the subjects of the E9 sequences as antecedents (in particular, as antecedents of the reflexive anaphors). We may then state what appears to be the correct generalization.

R1. Reflexive anaphors must agree with their antecedents in number and person.

It is important to realize that R1 is only a statement of fact about the distribution of English reflexives; it tells us nothing about the mechanism of English grammar that must account for this fact.

The second relevant piece of information comes from the grammaticality patterns in sequences that contain the word *own,* the sequences of E10, for example:

E10.

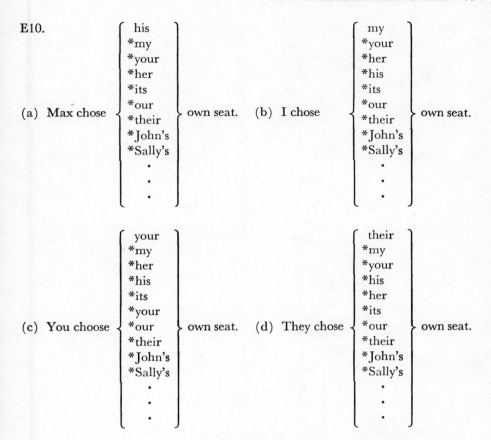

(a) Max chose { his, *my, *your, *her, *its, *our, *their, *John's, *Sally's . . . } own seat. (b) I chose { my, *your, *her, *his, *its, *our, *their, *John's, *Sally's . . . } own seat.

(c) You choose { your, *my, *her, *his, *its, *your, *our, *their, *John's, *Sally's . . . } own seat. (d) They chose { their, *my, *your, *his, *her, *its, *our, *their, *John's, *Sally's . . . } own seat.

The generalization here seems to be that stated in R2.

R2. The possessive anaphor that immediately precedes the word *own* in the structure $NP_i + V + Possessive\ Anaphor + own + N$ must agree in number and person with its antecedent NP_i.

A third bit of information, which will be useful in determining what the processes involved must be like, is displayed by the sequences of E11:

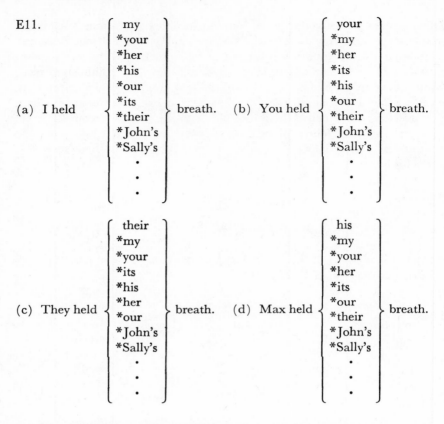

E11.

(a) I held $\left\{ \begin{array}{l} \text{my} \\ \text{*your} \\ \text{*her} \\ \text{*his} \\ \text{*our} \\ \text{*its} \\ \text{*their} \\ \text{*John's} \\ \text{*Sally's} \\ \cdot \\ \cdot \\ \cdot \end{array} \right\}$ breath. (b) You held $\left\{ \begin{array}{l} \text{your} \\ \text{*my} \\ \text{*her} \\ \text{*its} \\ \text{*his} \\ \text{*our} \\ \text{*their} \\ \text{*John's} \\ \text{*Sally's} \\ \cdot \\ \cdot \\ \cdot \end{array} \right\}$ breath.

(c) They held $\left\{ \begin{array}{l} \text{their} \\ \text{*my} \\ \text{*your} \\ \text{*its} \\ \text{*his} \\ \text{*her} \\ \text{*our} \\ \text{*John's} \\ \text{*Sally's} \\ \cdot \\ \cdot \\ \cdot \end{array} \right\}$ breath. (d) Max held $\left\{ \begin{array}{l} \text{his} \\ \text{*my} \\ \text{*your} \\ \text{*her} \\ \text{*its} \\ \text{*our} \\ \text{*their} \\ \text{*John's} \\ \text{*Sally's} \\ \cdot \\ \cdot \\ \cdot \end{array} \right\}$ breath.

The restriction displayed by the data in E14 can be stated as follows:

R3. In the structure NP_i *hold Possessive Anaphor's breath,* the possessive anaphor must agree in number and person with its antecedent NP_i.

We now have three statements (R1, R2, R3) describing restrictions on the distribution of different types of anaphors in English; that is, nothing more than a collection of descriptions of grammatical facts. We will return to these in a moment.

Most traditional grammar books contain a statement to the effect that every English sentence must have a subject. There is, however, a set of counterexamples to this claim; namely, the set of imperatives or commands, such as those in E12:

E12. (a) Cut it out.
(b) Forget it.
(c) Bring your stuff with you.

As with many of the claims to be found in traditional grammar, the claim that every sentence has a subject is somehow intuitively satisfying. Grammar books often attempt to account for this set of counterexamples, the imperatives, by saying that they have an "understood" subject. Within the framework of transformational grammar, we are able to give an explicit account of this intuition concerning an "understood" subject. Suppose we claim that every sequence output by the CF-PSG has an overt subject. We want, then, to claim that the original tree structure of E12(a), (b), and (c) (output of the CF-PSG) is that represented by E13(a), (b), and (c), respectively:

E13. (a) NP cut it out.
    (b) NP forget it.
    (c) NP bring your stuff with you.

That is, all sequences of E12 are to be regarded as surface realizations of underlying structures of the form E14:

E14.

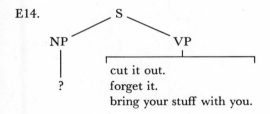

We have now made the claim; our task now is to find support for it. In particular, the symbol ? must be replaced by a *motivated* NP. Because the word *motivated* is of such importance in Generative Grammar, we must state clearly what we intend to convey by its use. Remember, there exists an infinite number of linguistic objects that belong to the category Noun Phrase in English. Any one of them might be the one that should replace the symbol ? in the E14 tree representation. Our task is to select one of these NP's and show why it, as opposed to any one of the others, is to replace the ? symbol. If we can select an NP based on facts (particularly distributional facts) unrelated to the phenomenon being considered and independent of the problem of selecting an NP to replace the symbol ?, we have succeeded in motivating the choice of NP. Thus, we can formulate the problem as: Are there distributional facts in English in independent linguistic phenomena which force us to choose one NP over the others to serve as the underlying subject of English Imperative sentences? The answer is yes; consider the grammaticality pattern in the sequences of E15:

E15.

(a) Pull $\left\{\begin{array}{l}\text{yourself}\\ \text{*myself}\\ \text{*herself}\\ \text{*himself}\\ \text{*itself}\\ \text{*ourselves}\\ \text{*themselves}\end{array}\right\}$ together. (b) Expand $\left\{\begin{array}{l}\text{yourself}\\ \text{*myself}\\ \text{*herself}\\ \text{*himself}\\ \text{*itself}\\ \text{*ourselves}\\ \text{*themselves}\end{array}\right\}$.

The pattern displayed by the sequences of E15 should immediately bring to mind our generalization about the distribution of Reflexive Anaphors in English, namely, R1. Thus, if the symbol ? were to be replaced with the NP *you* in the underlying tree for the English Imperative, the pattern of grammaticality would be perfectly explicable with reference to R1. This proposal receives further support from the pattern in E16:

E16.

(a) Choose $\left\{\begin{array}{l}\text{your}\\ \text{*my}\\ \text{*his}\\ \text{*her}\\ \text{*our}\\ \text{*its}\\ \text{*their}\\ \text{*John's}\\ \text{*Sally's}\\ \cdot\\ \cdot\\ \cdot\end{array}\right\}$ own seat. (b) Roll $\left\{\begin{array}{l}\text{your}\\ \text{*my}\\ \text{*his}\\ \text{*her}\\ \text{*its}\\ \text{*our}\\ \text{*their}\\ \text{*John's}\\ \text{*Sally's}\\ \cdot\\ \cdot\\ \cdot\end{array}\right\}$ own cigarettes.

Once again we note that if it were the case that the arbitrary symbol ? were to be replaced with the NP *you,* the fact that R2 exists as a statement necessary in the grammar on independent grounds would explain the fact that only the Possessive Anaphor *your* can occur grammatically in the Imperative structure $V + Possessive\ Anaphor + own + N$. Finally, we can predict, given R3 and provided we are correct that the missing subject NP in English Imperatives is the term *you,* that in the Imperative expression *hold Possessive Anaphor's breath,* only the Possessive Anaphor *your* may occur grammatically. E17 shows that our prediction is accurate.

Thus we see that the three distributional phenomena R1, R2, and R3 conspire to provide us with a motivated answer to the question of what the arbitrary symbol ? should be replaced with—that is, a motivated answer to the question as to what the underlying NP subject of English Imperatives is. This, in turn, allows us to make explicit the syntactic phenomenon that reflects the traditional claim that every English sentence has a subject;

E17. Hold 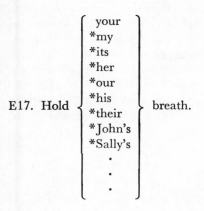 breath.

$$\text{E17. Hold} \left\{ \begin{array}{l} \text{your} \\ \text{*my} \\ \text{*its} \\ \text{*her} \\ \text{*our} \\ \text{*his} \\ \text{*their} \\ \text{*John's} \\ \text{*Sally's} \\ \cdot \\ \cdot \\ \cdot \end{array} \right\} \text{breath.}$$

in particular it allows us to give substance to the claim regarding an "understood" subject for the English Imperative. Notice that if it were not the case that the subject of the Imperative were the NP *you*, the grammaticality patterns displayed in E15, E16, and E17 would have to be accounted for by some set of statements other than those of R1, R2, and R3, which would still be needed to account for the data we used to introduce them.

In the argument we have just presented, we were able to find evidence to support an analysis that maintained that English Imperatives have a subject in their underlying tree representations. In effect, we argued for a deeper level of syntactic structure in which there existed a subject NP for the Imperative, even though the Surface Structures of the sequences being considered were without any subject NP. This subject NP, this nonsurface-structure-occurring element, turned out to be an actual English word. Arguments for the existence of elements that do not occur in the Surface Structure of a particular type of sentence, but which must be present at some deeper syntactic level, do not always result in support for the existence of some actual natural language element such as the *you* mentioned above. It is sometimes the case that such arguments lead one to postulate the existence of an abstract element that never itself occurs in any Surface Structure of the language being analyzed. The following argument is one such case.

The following material is in large part taken from one of the classic articles in early transformational grammar, E. S. Klima's "Negation in English" (1964). We will adopt the terminology employed by Klima in his article. The English word *not,* including its contracted form in words such as *didn't* and *isn't,* will be referred to as the Negative Particle. The term Negative Preverbal Adverbs will be used to identify the set of adverbs in E18:

E18. never, scarcely, hardly, rarely, seldom, barely, little

As the title of his article suggests, Klima attempted to present a unified treatment of the entire system of negation in English. More specifically, one of the tasks that he set for himself in the article was to show decisively that while the two sets of elements, the Negative Particles and the Negative Preverbal Adverbs, had been considered distinct, both were in fact different surface realizations of the same underlying element, the same abstract element NEG. The demonstration hinges mainly on showing that the syntax of the two sets of elements is identical. We will present a number of the arguments that he used to establish this claim.

The EITHER Argument

We begin by noting that the distribution of the operator *either* is not totally free in the surface structures of English.

E19.   (a)   Publishers will usually reject suggestions, and writers will not accept them either.
       (*b)   Publishers will usually reject suggestions, and writers will reject them either.
       (*c)   Publishers will usually reject suggestions, but writers will reject them either.

In the three examples given, it is relevant to note that the only well-formed sequence is the one in which the Negative Particle *not* occurs in the second clause, the one immediately preceding the term *either*. Example E20 shows that it is indeed necessary that the Negative Particle occur in the clause *immediately* before the *either*.

E20.   *Writers will not accept suggestions, and publishers will usually reject them either.

Now, if the hypothesis regarding the deeper identity of the set of Negative Preverbal Adverbs and the Negative Particle is correct, it must be the case that replacing the Negative Particle in any of its occurrences in the E19 surface strings of English will not change the grammaticality of that sequence. By selecting a Negative Preverbal Adverb from the list E18, we may test our hypothesis by making the substitution in the cases of E19(a) and E20.

E21.   (a)   Publishers will usually reject suggestions, and writers will rarely accept them either.
       (*b)   Writers will rarely accept suggestions, and publishers will usually reject them either.

We see, in fact, that the parallelism is perfect; E21(a), the counterpart of E19(a), is well formed, while E21(b), the counterpart of E20, is ill formed.

The TAG Argument

In sequences such as those of E22, one finds short, apparently elliptical clause fragments tagged onto the end of an otherwise complete sequence.

E22. (a) He's been to another planet, hasn't he?
     (b) She wears her shoes inside out, doesn't she?
     (c) Her space suit isn't in that bottle, is it?
     (d) He doesn't often interrupt himself, does he?

Notice that the positiveness or negativity of the tag is systematically related to the positiveness or negativity of the clause to which it is appended. We see this clearly by reversing the positive-negative value of the tags for E22 while maintaining the positive-negative value of the main clause.[6]

E23. (*a) He's been to another planet, has he?
     (*b) She wears her shoes inside out, does she?
     (*c) Her space suit isn't in that bottle, isn't it?
     (*d) He doesn't often interrupt himself, doesn't he?

We can state the condition for well-formedness for sequences with such tags by saying that if the main clause contains the Negative Particle, then the tag must not, as in E22(c) and (d). Conversely, if the main clause does not contain the Negative Particle, then the tag must, as in E22(a) and (b). Now notice the structure of the sequences of E24:

E24. (a) He's never been to another planet, has he?
     (b) She rarely wears her shoes inside out, does she?
     (c) Her space suit is never in that bottle, is it?
     (d) He hardly interrupts himself, does he?

If our hypothesis is correct, and the Negative Preverbal Adverbs are a surface reflex of the same abstract element as the Negative Particle, then the pattern of grammaticality displayed by E24 as well as that displayed by E25 is explicable.

---

[6] It appears that one must distinguish between regular negation (*not* and the Preverbal Adverbs) and what we will call lexical negation. For example the lexical item *refuse* is a near-paraphrase of *not accept*. However, the syntax of *refuse* and *not accept* with reference to the distributional facts mentioned in the text are different.

E25. (*a)   He's never been to another planet, hasn't he?
     (*b)   She rarely wears her shoes inside out, doesn't she?
     (*c)   Her space suit is never in that bottle, isn't it?
     (*d)   He hardly interrupts himself, doesn't he?

The generalization is that if the main clause of a sequence containing a tag contains a surface representation of the underlying element NEG, the tag must not. And conversely, if the clause contains no instance of the abstract element NEG, then the tag must.[7]

The *Not Even* Fragment Argument

The fragment *not even* differs radically in a distributional sense from the tags we considered in the preceding section.

E26. (a)   Max won't come, not even if you beg him.
     (b)   Tina can't stand excitement, not even if she is enjoying herself.

Thus we see that one of the conditions necessary for a sequence containing the fragment *not even* to be acceptable is that the clause preceding the fragment contain the Negative Particle. If the preceding clause does not, then the entire sequence is ill formed, as in E27:

E27. (*a)   Max will come, not even if you beg him.
     (*b)   Tina can stand excitement, not even if she is enjoying herself.

Of course, as predicted by our hypothesis, if the preceding clause contains one of the Negative Preverbal Adverbs, then the sequence is grammatical:

E28. (a)   Max will seldom come, not even if you beg him.
     (b)   Tina can never stand excitement, not even if she is enjoying herself.

The NEITHER Fragment Argument

The distribution of the element *neither* contributes to the motivation of the claim we are discussing.

---

[7] The fact that not just any one of the list of Negative Preverbal Adverbs is substitutable into the environment is a fact not accounted for. For most dialects of English, the sequences of E23 are acceptable with a special intonation. Klima identified the tags that he was interested in (1964b:263) "by the absence of a particular intonation to which are associated incredulous or sarcastic overtones." Notice, however, even with this special intonation, the sequences of E25 are impossible.

E29. (a)   George can't leave and neither can Tillie.
    (b)   Martha won't stop shouting and neither will John.

The dropping of the Negative Particle in the clause preceding the Neither Clause results in an ill-formed sequence.

E30. (*a)   George can leave and neither can Tillie.
    (*b)   Martha will stop shouting and neither will John.

The introduction of one of the members of the list of Negative Preverbal Adverbs restores the sequences to grammaticality.

E31. (a)   George never can leave and neither can Tillie.
    (b)   Martha will rarely stop shouting and neither will John.

The *Some* → *Any* Shift Argument

For many speakers of English, the sequences of E32 are unacceptable.[8]

E32. (*a)   Sam talked to anyone.
    (*b)   Horace wanted to talk about anything.

E32(a) and (b), however, are well formed if the Negative Particle is introduced into the sequence before the verbal form:

E33. (a)   Sam didn't talk to anyone.
    (b)   Horace didn't want to talk about anything.

E32(a) and (b) are also acceptable without the introduction of the Negative Particle if the words *any* are replaced by the words *some:*

E34. (a)   Sam talked to someone.
    (b)   Horace wanted to talk about something.

Considerations such as these have led generative grammarians to the view that the presence of the Negative Particle causes (transformationally) a shift of all terms containing the element *some-* to their corresponding element containing the element *any-*. Stated differently, the presence of the Negative Particle is a necessary condition for a sequence containing *any-* compounds to be grammatical.[9] Parallelly, we see in E35 that the Negative Preverbal Adverbs also allow the occurrence of the *any-* compounds.

[8] Once again, the sequences of E32 are possible with special intonation.
[9] There are obvious counterexamples to this; for instance, *Anyone can read.*

E35. (a) Sam rarely talked to anyone.
     (b) Horace seldom wanted to talked about anything.

The UNTIL Argument

As a first approximation, the presence of the term *until* in a Surface Structure of English renders that sequence ungrammatical unless the Negative Particle is also present.[10]

E36. (*a) Bill fell until yesterday.
     (b) Bill didn't fall until yestedray.
     (*c) Kathleen finished drawing until yesterday.
     (d) Kathleen didn't finish drawing until yesterday.

As we would expect if our hypothesis were correct, the presence of the Negative Preverbal Adverb is also adequate to allow the occurrence of the term *until*:

E37. (a) Bill never fell until yesterday.
     (b) Kathleen scarcely finished drawing until yesterday.

We have presented above six different instances in the grammar of English where the Negative Particle and the Preverbal Adverbs display an identical syntax—that is, where their presence allows the occurrence of other elements whose distribution is otherwise highly restricted. The force of these observations is that if there existed an abstract underlying element common to these actually occurring English words (*not* and the members of E18), then its presence in the underlying tree structures of all the preceding examples could be used to explain all the above restrictions as a unified phenomenon. To avoid postulating such an element is tantamount to missing the obvious regularities presented above, or minimally, to being required to make the identical statement twice in each of the cases given, once for the Negative Particle and one for the set of Negative Preverbal Adverbs.

We have attempted in this chapter to make clear the methods and goals of early transformational research. We have shown how the early work uncovered the existence of elements (the subject NP of the Imperative

---

[10] The accurate account of the restrictions involved with *until* is much more complex and seems to include the notion of duration. Notice that if we have a situation such as the one described in the beginning of *Alice in Wonderland*, we can perfectly well say *Alice fell until she could no longer see the top of the hole*. The analysis would have to distinguish these cases from the actual NEG elements if the argument were to be fully acceptable.

you) which by analysis could be shown to belong to the derivation of a Surface Structure of English even though the element itself did not appear in that specific structure. We then showed the perhaps more startling fact that by parallel analysis we could demonstrate the desirability of postulating an underlying abstract element (Neg), which never itself occurred in *any* Surface Structure of English.

It is important to understand that this work was done with the specific purpose of accounting for the shape—the formal syntactic structure—of the surface structures of English. As Klima expressed it,

> By stressing shape, I mean to emphasize that the aspect of language of concern to grammar, as the term is used here, consists of differences in the form of sentences (varying restrictions on the occurrence of elements with respect to one another) and not similarities and differences in the meaning of sentences. (Klima, 1964b:247.)

In other words, the express purpose of the early research was to specify the formal regularities of the languages or, in our terms, to specify Set A. As is obvious from the Klima quotation, appeals to meaning similarities and differences were unacceptable for establishing such regularities. There was to be no reference made to the set of regularities existing in Set B or to the interaction of the two sets.

EXERCISES

One of the more important considerations looked for by linguists in constructing relations between sentences or phrases in the grammar is that of distribution. In general, if the distribution of some terms "x" is restricted to some set of environments $e_1, \ldots, e_n$, and one finds another term "y" that is also confined in its appearance to $e_1, \ldots, e_n$ (or perhaps to some subset of $e_1, \ldots, e_n$), one immediately attempts to find a deeper relation between x and y.

1. Determine what the restriction on the Noun Phrase that may occur in the blank is. Attempt to make the most general statement possible.
Noun Phrase brought Noun Phrase to [_____]'s senses.

2. The phrase *at all* is restricted in its distribution. For example,
*He hoped to come *at all*.
He didn't hope to come *at all*.
Find a general statement of the set of environments in which it occurs.

3. The word *budge* exhibits severe distributional restrictions on its use. Attempt a general statement of its set of possible environments.

4.   Find verbs or verb pairs that may not occur in the blank in the structure:
Noun Phrase forced Noun Phrase to _____.
Example: John forced Mary to leave.
Is there any general characterization of the set of elements that may not occur?

5.   Break up the class into small groups and work through the arguments presented in the text (or in Exercises 1–4). Be sensitive to dialect variation, and especially to systematic differences in dialects. That is, if an individual has restricted environments *a* and *b* in his dialect with regard to the occurrence of some item, then can you predict whether he will or will not accept its use in another environment "c"?

ANSWERS

1.   Begin by considering strings like

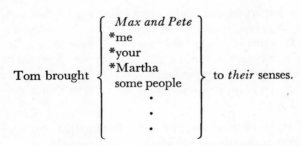

$$\text{I brought } Sam \text{ to } \left\{ \begin{array}{l} his \\ *\text{my} \\ *\text{your} \\ *\text{Martha's} \\ \bullet \\ \bullet \\ \bullet \end{array} \right\} \text{ senses.}$$

or

$$\text{Tom brought } \left\{ \begin{array}{l} Max \text{ and } Pete \\ *\text{me} \\ *\text{your} \\ *\text{Martha} \\ \text{some people} \\ \bullet \\ \bullet \\ \bullet \end{array} \right\} \text{ to } their \text{ senses.}$$

After considering a number of such strings, it will become obvious that the constraint will specify that the elements appearing in the blanks in the following formula must refer to the same individual(s).

Noun Phrase bring _____ to _____'s senses.

2.   The phrase *at all* is sometimes referred to as a Negative Polarity (Baker, 1970a) item. Essentially, this means that the item may appear in some string just in case there is a negative element also present. For example:

*John wanted to come at all.

John did*n't* want to come at all.

Seldom did John want to come at all.

John *never* did want to come at all.

I did*n't* expect John to come at all.

I was *surprised* that John came at all.

*I think that John will come at all.

I *doubt* that John will come at all.

I persuaded John *not* to come at all.

I *dis*suaded John from coming at all.

*I am able to believe that John came at all.

I am unable to believe that John came at all.

Notice that in the examples with *surprise, doubt,* and *dissuade,* the negative polarity item occurs grammatically. This suggests that the lexical items mentioned above include a NEG element at some point in their derivation.

3. The lexical item *budge* is also a negative polarity item; thus, it should parallel the phrase *at all* and its environments should be the same.

4. Begin by identifying some members of the set of grammatical strings of that form and some of the members of the set of ungrammatical strings of that form.

John forced Ned to leave
{ *be tall
  *weigh fourteen pounds
  *know the answer }

I forced Sue to talk to me
{ *be alive
  *grow quickly
  *manage to succeed }

The Verb/Adjectives that appear in the blank and render the string ungrammatical are usually referred to as Stative Verb/Adjectives. Semantically, they seem to be descriptions of things over which the animate object of the predicate *force* has no control.

Chapter 6

Families
of Transformations

In this chapter we examine in somewhat more detail the mechanism called a Transformation. We have already discussed in Chapter 4 the arguments that motivate the inclusion of such powerful devices in the grammar of natural languages. Their acceptance as an indispensable element in linguistic description is assumed for the following discussion. We have already seen an example of a transformation, namely, PARTICLE MOVEMENT. We approach the discussion of transformations by means of a taxonomy of the transformations that have actually been proposed in the literature. We begin, however, with a brief review.

A transformation maps tree structures (Phrase Markers) into tree structures. It consists of two parts: a structural index and a structural change, which can be represented by the following schema.

R1. Structural Index $\quad X_1, X_2, \ldots, X_i, \ldots X_n$
Structural Change $\quad X_1, X_2, \ldots, X_j, \ldots X_n$
where $X_i \neq X_j$ for some i and j

The purpose of the transformation in natural language research is to state explicitly the relations judged by native speakers to exist between distinct Surface Structures. If, for example, there exist two distinct Surface Structures of English, S_i and S_j, which are felt by native speakers of English to be closely related structurally, then the structural relation intuitively identified may be formally stated as a Transformation. More specifically, say we represent the two hypothetical surface structures by the schema.

R2. $S_i >=< t_1, t_2, \ldots, t_i, \ldots, t_n$

$S_j >=< t_1, t_2, \ldots, t_j, \ldots, t_n$

where $>=<$ is to be understood as *is composed of the ordered sequence of* and t is to be understood as *term*.

That is, R2 may be paraphrased as: S_i is composed of the ordered sequence of terms, $t_1, t_2, \ldots, t_i, \ldots t_n$ and S_j is composed of the ordered sequence of terms, $t_1, t_2, \ldots, t_j, \ldots, t_n$. Notice that S_i differs from S_j only in that S_i contains the term t_i and not the term t_j, while S_j contains the term t_j and not the term t_i. In other words, S_i and S_j differ in one term. The obvious parallelism between R1 and R2 should be examined. R2 says, in effect, that there are two surface structures that differ in one term. R1 says that if there is a sequence of elements $X_1, \ldots, X_n$ which is grammatical, then there is another sequence of elements $X_1, \ldots, X_n$ that differs from the first sequence in one term and is derived from the first, and is also grammatical. Thus, the Transformation is the explicit statement of the structural relation, the formal analog of the intuition of the relation identified by the native speaker.

The question quite naturally arises as to what sorts of transformations are necessary to capture the processes found in natural languages. The answer to this question provides us with the taxonomy or system of classification mentioned above. Two perfunctory remarks are in order before attacking the taxonomy itself. First, any serious claim about an adequate taxonomy must, of course, wait upon the results of research in a greater variety of human languages than is at present available.[1] Second, and more important for our present purposes, it must be clearly understood that absolutely nothing in the definition of the formal device itself (the Transformation) renders impossible the statement of the most absurd relations imaginable. Consider R3:

R3. (a) Structural Index $X_1, X_2, \ldots, X_i, \ldots, X_{n-1}, X_n$

         Structural Change $X_n, X_{n-1}, \ldots, X_i, \ldots, X_2, X_1$

    (b) Structural Index X_1, X_2, X_3, X_4, X_5

         Structural Change X_5, X_2, X_1, X_4, X_3

The effect that R3(a) would have would be to reverse the order of elements of the sequence to which it applied; that of R3(b) would be to identify the odd-numbered elements and move each of them one odd-number position to the right, the last odd-numbered position element being moved to the front of the string. The difference between E1(a) and (b) and (E2(a)

---

[1] See Joseph Greenberg (1966). The only difficulty with the work reported in Greenberg's study is that similarities and differences reported among the languages are confined to Surface Structure differences.

and (b), respectively, is an illustration of the effect of these two Transformations.

E1.   (a)   John just picked the bottle of ink. ⎫
      (*b)   Ink of bottle the picked just John. ⎬ *Transformation, R3(a)*
                                               ⎭

E2.   (a)   Timothy climbed over the fence. ⎫
      (*b)   Fence climbed Timothy the over. ⎬ *Transformation, R3(b)*
                                             ⎭

The fact that the statement of processes such as those indicated by the transformations of R3 is possible and is no more complex than the statement of PARTICLE MOVEMENT is at present one of the most serious obstacles to an interesting theory of language. One surely demands from such a theory the characterization of what a possible transformation is. Such a characterization would provide part of the answer to the question as to how much of the structure of human language is built into the human being. We will return to a discussion of this point in Chapter Thirteen, "Universal Grammar." It is sufficient for the moment to point out that the device itself, the Transformation, does nothing to guide or limit the research that will eventually determine the question of what a possible transformational process is.

We have at several points in the previous chapters presented formulas of the general form of R4:

R4. X A B C [E Y] Z
              D   D

where the letters A, B, C, D, E, represent members of the set of possible node labels such as NP, VP, V, N, . . . , and the letters X, Y, Z represent variables.

Before beginning our survey of examples of the different types of transformations, we will discuss briefly the interpretation of these symbols. R4 represents an infinite number of possible tree structures, all of which can equivalently be represented by[2] the schema E3:

E3.

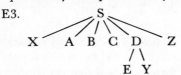

Notice that the schema E3, since it includes variables (or equivalently R4), truly represents an infinite number of trees. It is precisely the function of

---

[2] By *equivalent* we mean that there is an algorithm or mechanical procedure that converts material appearing in labeled brackets into a tree representation preserving the relations involved.

the variables to allow any set of nodes to occur in just the place where the variable occurs; for example, the trees of E4 are instances of E3. Equivalently, R4 or the tree schema E3 may be said to accurately represent each of the tree structures of E4.

E4. (a)

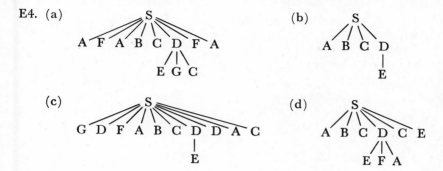

In the tree E4(a), the variable X includes the nodes A and F; in E4(b), the variable X includes only the null element; while in E4(c), it includes G, D, and F; and in E4(d), once again, includes the null element. The composition of all three of the variables is given in E5:

E5.

Tree	Variable	Constituents
(a)	X	A F
	Y	G C
	Z	F A
(b)	X	Ø
	Y	Ø
	Z	Ø
(c)	X	G D F
	Y	Ø
	Z	D A C
(d)	X	Ø
	Y	F A
	Z	C E

As the tree E4(b) illustrates, variables are understood to include the null element.

The only symbols that are used in formulating transformations which we have yet to discuss are those occurring in the structural change of transformations. These symbols serve as instructions to show how the terms that appear on either side of them are to be related in the tree structure in which they occur. They are usually referred to as *adjunction symbols*. The one most commonly found in the literature is called Sister Adjunction, the symbol $+$. In effect, it specifies that the symbols that occur on both sides of the symbol $+$ are to be "sister" nodes; that is, they are to be dominated by the same node. As an example, given the transformation E5 which specifies sister adjunction and the input string E6, the tree structure E7 is the result.

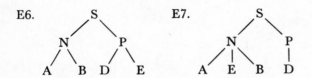

E5. WHOOPEE	X	A	B	Y	E	Z
Structural Index	1	2	3	4	5	6
Structural Change	1	2	5 $+$3	4	Ø	6

E6.   E7.

The other two adjunction operators that have been proposed are called Daughter (&) and Mother ($\sqrt{}$) Adjunction. The names are suggestive of the structural relations. E8 is the result of the application of the transformation WHOOPEE, with Daughter Adjunction being the structural relation that is specified between the nodes E and B in the structural change instead of the Sister Adjunction relation. E9, on the other hand, results from the application of WHOOPEE to E6, with Mother Adjunction replacing Sister Adjunction. Note that transformations may adjoin moving modes either to the left or to the right.

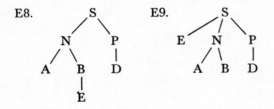

E8.   E9.

The remainder of the chapter is concerned with the taxonomy of transformations and the presentation of examples of each type. The three types of transformations that seem to encompass the entire range of transformations proposed thus far are Permutation transformations, Substitution transformations, and Insertion transformations.[3]

[3] The category to which any particular transformation belongs can be determined by a simple inspection of the Structural Index and Structural Change.

Permutation Transformations

We have already examined in some detail (in Chapter 4), an example of the Permutation transformation—PARTICLE MOVEMENT. PARTICLE MOVEMENT is the transformation that relates the sequences of E10(a), (b), and (c) to the sequences of E11(a), (b), and (c), respectively.

E10. (a) Benjamin scribbled down the telephone number.
    (b) Alden revved up his bike.
    (c) Sidney put across her point.

E11. (a) Benjamin scribbled the telephone number down.
    (b) Alden revved his bike up.
    (c) Sidney put her point across.

E11(a), (b), and (c) make it clear that the "effect" of the transformation is to move the particle (*down, up, across*) from its position, immediately to the right of the verb with which it is associated, to a position immediately to the right of the NP that originally succeeded it. Schematically,

R5. X V Particle NP Particle Y
    where X and Y are variables covering any stretch of elements including the $\emptyset$ element.

The transformation PARTICLE MOVEMENT can be written as

E12. PARTICLE MOVEMENT	X	V	Particle	NP	Y
Structural Index	1,	2,	3,	4,	5
Structural Change	1,	2,	$\emptyset$,	$4 + 3$,	5

Next consider the structural relations between the sequences of E13 and E14:

E13. (a) That Marsha was indisposed irritated John.
    (b) That the book budget was in question distressed the librarians.
    (c) That the reference books had exceeded the predicted figure for the year reassured many students.

E14. (a) It irritated John that Marsha was indisposed.
    (b) It distressed the librarians that the book budget was in question.
    (c) It reassured many students that the reference books had exceeded the predicted figure for the year.

The structure of the sequences of E13 may be represented by E15(a) and those of E14 by E15(b):

E15. (a)

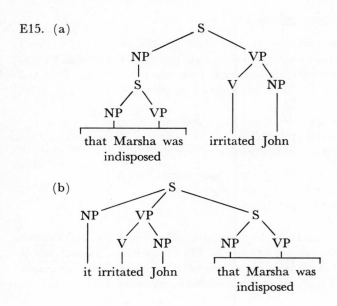

(b)

Apparently, when one finds surface structures in which the subject is a complete clause in itself, there are related forms for them; namely, forms in which the subject is the term *it* and the original full-clause subject occurs at the extreme right end of the structure. Thus, we might suggest R6 as the correct formulation of the transformation that relates the pairs listed above.

R6. EXTRAPOSITION	X	$\begin{matrix}[S]\\ \text{NP NP}\end{matrix}$	Y
Structural Index	1,	2,	3
Structural Change	1,	Ø	$3 + 2$

(The empty grammatical term *it* is to be introduced by a later rule.)

The trees that represent E13 are properly analyzeable with respect to the structural index of EXTRAPOSITION and the resultant trees (representing E14) are of the form specified by the structural change of EXTRAPOSITION.

E16.

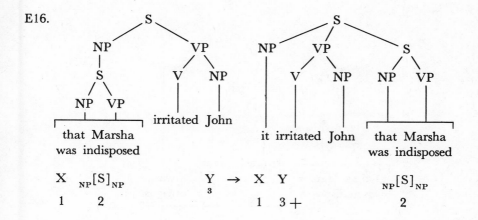

$$X \quad {}_{NP}[S]_{NP} \quad Y \rightarrow X \quad Y \quad {}_{NP}[S]_{NP}$$

$$1 \qquad 2 \qquad 3 \qquad 1 \quad 3 + \qquad 2$$

The formulation of the EXTRAPOSITION transformation R6 is adequate to handle the relation between the pairs of E13 and E14. But consider now what the effect of R6 on the strings of E17 (represented by the tree structure E18) would be.[4]

E17. (a) That that Marsha was indisposed irritated John was obvious.

(b) That that the book budget was in question distressed librarians was clear to everyone.

(c) That that the reference books had exceeded the predicted figure for the year reassured many students alarmed the faculty.

---

[4] The structures in E17 are considered grammatical as they stand, the difficulty they present in comprehension being attributed to performance.

E18. (a)

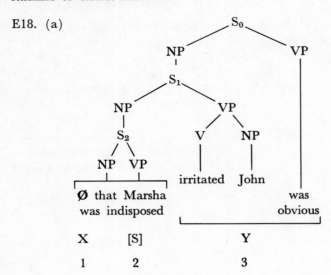

(b)

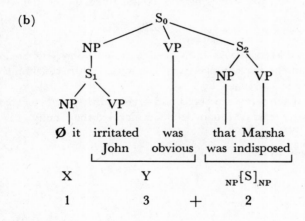

The structure E18(b) represents the result of application of the EXTRA-POSITION transformation as proposed in R6. The results of this application are seen in E19:

E19. (*a) That it irritated John was obvious that Marsha was indisposed.

   (*b) That it distressed librarians was clear to everyone that the book budget was in question.

(*c)   That it reassured many students alarmed the faculty that the book count had climbed above the predicted figure for the year.

Clearly, the formulation R6 was incorrect. The examples of E13 make it easy to see that when the operation EXTRAPOSITION applies correctly, moving the subject clause, it is sensitive to the material over which the subject clause moves. More accurately, it is sensitive to the distance (structurally) that it may move. The grammatical surface structures related to E17 by a single application of EXTRAPOSITION are those listed in E20 with the tree structure of E21.

E20.   (a)   That it irritated John that Marsha was indisposed was obvious.
       (b)   That it distressed librarians that the book budget was in question was clear to everyone.
       (c)   That it reassured many students that the book count had climbed above the predicted figure for the year alarmed the faculty.

E21.

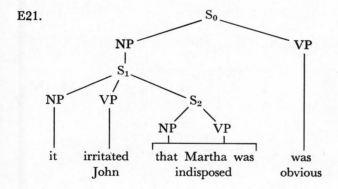

A comparison of the structural difference between the grammatical sequences derived from E17 (that is, E20) and the ungrammatical sequences derived from E17 (that is, E19)—and especially their representative trees— provides the information necessary for a proper formulation of the rule of EXTRAPOSITION. What is needed is the restriction that when the subject clause is moved by EXTRAPOSITION, it may move only to the end of the clause in which it originates. We may then rewrite the EXTRAPOSITION rule properly as

R7.   EXTRAPOSITION   X $[S]_{NP\ NP}$ VP   Y

      Structural Index   1,   2,   3,   4
      Structural Change   1, $\emptyset$ 3 + 2,   4

A careful comparison of the incorrect rule first written as R6 and the corrected rule R7 will show that they they differ only in the presence of the fourth term on the right, which serves to place a right boundary on the moved term, term 2. The reformulated rule properly derives the grammatical sequences of E20 but not, of course, the ungrammatical sequences of E19.[5]

As a final example of the class of transformations known as Permutation transformation, we will briefly consider the process referred to as Wh-Q Movement.[6] By a series of arguments (many of which were parallel to those we have seen in the case of the postulation of the abstract underlying element NEG by Klima), Katz and Postal (1964:89–95) argued for the derivation of so-called Wh-questions, such as those of E22, from an underlying structure of the form E23.

E22. (a)   Who did Sonya see?
      (b)   What did the iguana eat?

E23. (a)   Q   Sonya saw Wh + someone.
      (b)   Q   the iguana ate Wh + something.

The simplest formulation of the Wh-Q Movement transformation is R8:

R8.	Wh-Q Movement	Q	X	Wh + N	X
	Structural Index	1	2	3	4
	Structural Change	1 + 3	2	Ø	4

---

[5] Ross (1967b) has argued persuasively that all rules that move constituents to the right are restricted so that they may not move elements farther than the end of the clause containing those elements. If this is true, the particular transformation EXTRAPOSITION in the grammar of English need not include the refinement presented here, as it will be true of all right movement transformations, a fact that will be stated but once in the general theory of language and will be applicable to all right-movement transformations. (See Chapter 13 for discussion.)

[6] We will return to a more complete discussion of the source and meaning of the abstract elements WH and Q in Chapter 9. For the moment, they should be viewed as abstract underlying elements that have multiple surface realizations, elements parallel to the NEG element presented in Chapter 8.

The transformation R8 will alter tree structures in the manner suggested by E24. Using E22 as an example, we have

E24. (a)

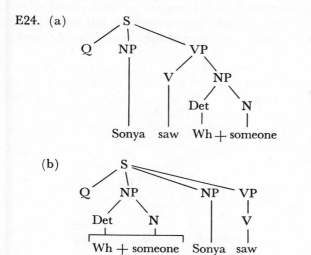

(b)

Later rules will convert the *Wh + someone* to *Who* and insert the element *do* to give the sequence its final form; namely, E22(b).

Substitution Transformations

There are two types of Substitution transformation: type A, those that substitute the null element for some term in the Structural Index; and type B, those that substitute some non-null element for one of the terms in the Structural Index. Type A is more commonly called Deletion transformations. We consider an example of type B first.

It is recognized by transformational as well as traditional grammarians that natural languages contain a small set of terms, the so-called Pronouns, whose function it is to stand for or take the place of Nominals in the surface structures of the language in question. Consider, for example, the difference in the following pairs:

E25. (a)   Norris hurt Norris.
     (b)   Norris hurt himself.

E26. (a)   Norris said that Norris was sick.
     (b)   Norris said that he was sick.

The sequence E25(b) is unambiguous; the only interpretation is that the two terms *Norris* and *himself* refer to the same person (are coreferential).

E25(a) cannot be understood in a similar way. Similar considerations hold for the differences in possible interpretations for E26(a) and (b). In addition, however, in E26(b) the pronominal element *he* is not necessarily coreferential with the term *Norris;* it may be so understood, but it may also be understood as referring to any male. The structures underlying E25 and E26 are E27 and E28, respectively.

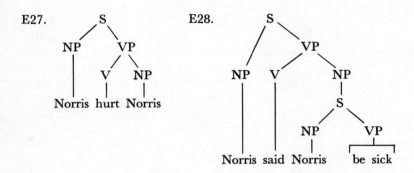

In the case of E25(a) and (b), the transformation that relates them is called REFLEXIVIZATION.

R9. REFLEXIVIZATION

	U	[X	NP	Y	NP	Z]	W
		s				s	
Structural Index		1,	2,	3,	4,	5	
Structural Change		1,	2,	3,	4,	5	
					[+ reflex]		

where $2 = 4$

There is a feature of R9 which should be noted: The transformation has a condition upon it, the statement "where $2 = 4$." That is, the transformation is contingent upon the second and fourth terms being coreferential.[7] Therefore, in addition to it being necessary that the terminal string of a particular sequence be partitioned with respect to the structural index of the REFLEXIVE transformation, the added requirement exists in this case that the coreference relation hold between certain members of the terminal string.

----

[7] *Coreferentiality* or any such notion of *reference* would seem to be semantic in nature and therefore it is not indisputable that the transformations should be able to make use of this information to determine whether a string is properly analyzable. This is one of the controversial issues in linguistics at present.

49651

The process which has been claimed to relate *Norris said that Norris was sick* to *Norris said that he was sick* when the two "Norrises" are the same is called PRONOMINALIZATION.[8]

You will notice from examination of the two tree diagrams E27 and E28 that although both occurrences of "Norris" are directly under the same S-node in E27, they are each under a separate S-node in E28. It is primarily this structural difference that determines whether the transformation of REFLEXIVIZATION or of PRONOMINALIZATION applies. The two processes are very alike in that if two terms ("Norris" and "Norris" in E27) are in a certain structural relation and are coreferential, one of them is changed to the appropriate pronoun.[9] The PRONOMINALIZATION transformation itself is subject to complications that are far beyond the scope of this introductory text, and therefore we will not discuss it in more than this superficial way.

Those substitution operations in which the null element is substituted are known as Deletion transformations. They are well-attested language phenomena. We have already seen one of them in operation in our discussion of the English Imperative. Another such operation is the transformation called EQUI-NP DELETION. Consider the pairs of sequences in E28 and E29 and the two tree diagrams in E30, which represent the (a) members of E28 and E29.

E28. (a) $John_i$ hoped [$John_i$ leave].
    (b) John hoped to leave.

E29. (a) Barry convinced $Nancy_i$ [$Nancy_i$ run].
    (b) Barry convinced Nancy to run.

---

[8] There is some dispute at present as to whether PRONOMINALIZATION is to be considered a transformational process.

[9] The word *appropriate* appeals to the reader's linguistic intuitions and therefore must be replaced by some explicit statement.

Lincoln Christian College

E30. (a)

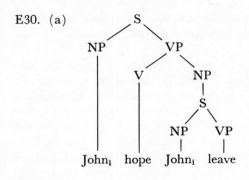

John$_i$ hope John$_i$ leave

(b)

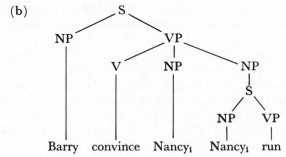

Barry convince Nancy$_i$ Nancy$_i$ run

The transformation EQUI-NP DELETION is formulated as follows:

R10. EQUI-NP DELETION   X   NP   Y   [NP   Y]$_S$ Z

Structural Index	1,	2,	3,	4, 5,		6
Structural Change	1,	2,	3,	Ø, 5,		6

where 2 = 4

Examination of the tree diagram in E30(a) will make it obvious that the effect of this transformation is to delete the subject NP of an embedded sentence when that NP is co-referential with an NP higher in the tree.

Another example of a Deletion transformation is COMPARATIVE REDUCTION, the operation of which can be seen by examining the pairs of sequences in E31 and E32.

E31. (a)   George is happier than Sam is.
     (b)   George is happier than Sam.

E32. (a)   David is happier than the man who hates him is.
     (b)   David is happier than the man who hates him.

As a final example of the Deletion class, there is the transformation known as GAPPING, which removes the second of two identical verbs in compound sentences.

E33. (a) Gertrude ordered beer and Mildred ordered schnitzel.
    (b) Gertrude ordered beer and Mildred schnitzel.

R11. GAPPING X' [X V Y]$_S$ Conj.   [W V Z]$_S$ U

Structural Index	1,	2,	3,	4,	5
Structural Change	1,	2,	3,	Ø,	5

The Insertion Transformations

The Insertion transformations are characterized, as their title suggests, by the fact that a comparison of the Structural Index and the Structural Change of these transformations will show that there is in the Structural Change at least one more term than in the Structural Index. The transformation THERE INSERTION is perhaps the best known member of this class of transformations.

E34. (a) A boy is in the garden.
    (b) There is a boy in the garden.

E35. (a) A storm is coming tonight.
    (b) There is a storm coming tonight.

The essential characteristics of the process are captured by

R12. THERE INSERTION   X   [NP V Y]$_S$ Z

Structural Index	1,	2, 3, 4,	5
Structural Change	1,	THERE + 3, 2, 4,	5

In R12 the variables X and Z appear at the extremes of the Structural Index; this is equivalent to the claim that the process may occur even where the clause into which the item *there* is inserted is preceded and followed by other material. This claim is accurate, as E36 (where the clause involved is embedded) demonstrates.

E36. (a) Mary thought that Sam knew that some friends were coming.
    (b) Mary thought that Sam knew that there were some friends coming.

It has been argued by Klima (1964a) that the element which occurs in E37(b), but not in E37(a), is inserted in dialects of American English to allow the expression of tense when the order in the Surface Structure is required to be Verb-Initial.

E37. (a) *Want you me to leave?
    (b) Do you want me to leave?

More recent attempts to handle this phenomenon have disputed the inserted nature of the element *do,* and have argued that the element is present in Deep Structure (Ross, 1966).

Another class of elements that has been argued to be inserted post-Deep Structure in a derivation are the so-called Complementizers: the elements *for-to,* poss-*ing,* and *that* as they occur in the following strings (Rosenbaum, 1965–1967).

E38.   (a)   Max resents it *for* Sue *to* kiss Sam continually.
     (b)   Max resents Sue's kiss*ing* Sam continuously.
     (c)   Max resents it *that* Sue kisses Sam continually.

The analysis that argues for the insertion of these complementizers claims that it is the verb of the immediately dominating clause that determines which of the complementizers is inserted. Thus, in E38 the lexical entry for the verb *resent* will allow any of the three types of complementizers, while the entry for the verb *notice* will allow the poss-*ing* and *that* complementizers, but not *for-to,* as E39 shows:

E39.   (a)   The reader has probably noticed that I am ripped.
     (b)   The reader has probably noticed my being ripped.
  (*c)   The reader has probably noticed for me to be ripped.

More recent treatments of Complementizer systems tend to analyze the complementizers as being present in the Deep Structure rather than being inserted (for example, see Bresman, 1971).

We have concerned ourselves in this chapter with a rather shallow survey of the types of transformations that have been proposed in the research literature to date. The original arguments for the existence of the transformations discussed in this chapter have not been presented, but they can be found in the Bibliography. It is important to note that, thus far, there has been no serious successful attempt to constrain the power of the device called the Transformation, the central mechanism proposed for the transformational analysis of language. Until heavy constraints are formalized, the characterization of possible transformational processes in natural language (and concomitantly, serious claims about the structure of the portion of the human mind concerned with language acquisition) is not possible.

EXERCISES

Transformations are formal statements that relate sets of tree structures. The following exercises are designed to increase your facility in handling these objects.

1. In the text, the following conventions regarding derived tree structures were presented (the symbols used here are not standard in the literature) :

+ = sister adjunction
& = mother adjunction
√ = daughter adjunction

For each of the following trees, apply the transformation indicated three times, using the three types of adjunction; write out the resultant tree structures.

(a)

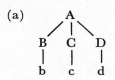

B	C	D
1	2	3
1	Ø	3 β 2

where the symbol β is to be replaced by +, &, √

(b)

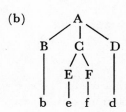

B	E	F	D
1	2	3	4
1	4 β 2	3	Ø

(c)

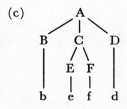

B	E	F	D
1	2	3	4
Ø	2	1 β 3	4

2. For each of the following pairs of trees, write the transformation that captures the relation shown. Capital letters are the nonterminal vocabulary.

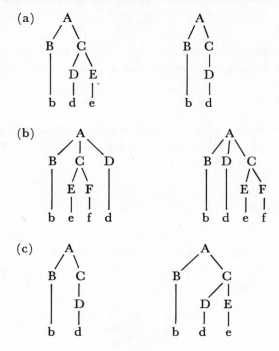

What is the relation between the transformation that relates the tree structures of (a) and the one that relates the tree structures of (c)? Specifically, consider the relation between the Structural Index of (a) and the Structural Change of (c).

3. Write the transformation that will relate the sets of sentences of which (a) and (b) are representatives.

    (a)   Mary gave the stuff to Big Nurse.

    (b)   Mary gave Big Nurse the stuff.

Use your intuitions to find other examples that will assist you in determining the proper structural requirements.

4. Write the transformation that will relate the sets of sentences of which (a) and (b) are representatives.

    (a)   Max tried to swim and George tried to swim, too.

    (b)   Max tried to swim, and George, too.

Use your intuitions to find other examples that will assist you in determining the proper structural requirements.

ANSWERS

1. (a)

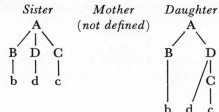

Sister   Mother   Daughter

        (not defined)

(b)

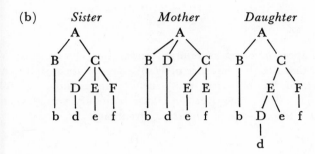

Sister   Mother   Daughter

(c)

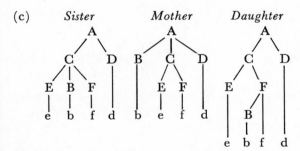

Sister   Mother   Daughter

2. (a)

B	D	E	or making use of variables	X	E	Y
1	2	3		1	2	3
1	2	$\emptyset$		1	$\emptyset$	3

(b)

B	C	D
1	2	3
1	$3+2$	$\emptyset$

X	C	D	Y	or	B	E	F	D	(with variables)
1	2	3	4		1	2	3	4	
1	$3+2$	$\emptyset$	4		1	$4+2$	3	$\emptyset$	

(c)

B	D	(with variables)	X	D	Y
1	2		1	2	3
1	$2+E$		1	$2+E$	3

The transformation (a) and the transformation (c) have inverse relationship: Transformation (a) deletes a node E when it immediately follows the node D, while transformation (c) inserts a node E immediately after the node D.

3. The transformation involved in these strings is usually referred to as INDIRECT OBJECT MOVEMENT (see Chapter 10 for a brief discussion). The following formulation is adequate:

$$
\begin{array}{cccccc}
X & [\underset{\text{VP}}{V} & NP & NP & \underset{\text{VP}}{Y}] & Z \\
1 & 2 & 3 & 4 & 5 & 6 \\
1 & 2 & 4+3 & \emptyset & 5 & 6
\end{array}
$$

4. The transformation involved is referred to in the literature as VP DELETION. The fact that the (b) sequence of 4(a) is grammatical shows that the structural index of VP DELETION must include an essential variable, since the deletion has taken place over the clause boundary symbol S, the recursive symbol. One formulation for the transformation is:

$$
\begin{array}{ccccc}
X & VP & Y & VP & Z \\
1 & 2 & 3 & 4 & 5 \\
1 & 2 & 3 & \emptyset & 5
\end{array}
$$
where $2 = 4$

Chapter 7

Early Semantics

We have pointed out several times in earlier chapters that the initial assumptions of the researchers in transformational grammar included the deliberate avoidance of any consideration of generalizations that might be present at the semantic level of language. It is very clear from Chomsky's remarks in *Syntactic Structures* (1957) that he was restricting his attention to the formal aspects of language (that is, the syntax) and that the assumption that syntax was completely autonomous and separate from semantics was not only an acceptable part of his methodology but also a necessary one.

We have suggested that this reluctance to consider semantics in the development of the grammar of a language stemmed from the structuralists' insistence that the various "levels" of language be kept completely separate in analysis. You will have noted that nowhere in any of the transformational work that we have discussed up to this point in the text has the idea of the "meaning" of a sequence been allowed to figure in analysis.

As a result of this separation of levels of analysis principle, all descriptions and specifications of the device that would generate Set A proceeded without consideration of any regularities within Set B. In this chapter we survey the first attempt that was made to construct a system that would both capture a nontrivial portion of the regularities and relations present within Set B and simultaneously mesh with the system of syntactic insights characteristic of early transformational syntax.

The first step in the construction of such a system would be to decide what are the minimum requirements that could be expected of it.

As was pointed out in Chapter 2, the relation between Set A and

Set B will not be one-to-one. Consider the following pair of sentences:

E1. (a) Martha picked up the trash.
    (b) Martha picked the trash up.

E1 is an example of a single member of Set B having two corresponding members of Set A. When two Surface Structures may have the same semantic representation, we refer to the relation between them as the Paraphrase Relation. One of the requirements of a theory of grammar that concerned itself with Set B would be to deal with this relation adequately and clearly.

Next, we would require of such a theory that it be able to cope with the relation of Ambiguity, which is shown by the following sentence:

E2. The chickens are ready to eat.

This sentence, which can mean either that the chickens are ready to eat something or that they are ready for someone else to eat them, is an example of a single Surface Structure that must have two semantic representations.

Further, we should expect a semantic theory to predict and describe the relation of Contradiction that holds between the two following sentences:

E3. (a) The boy left home.
    (b) The boy did not leave home.

And the single mechanism that is doing all these things will also have to operate in stating that E4 is not well formed.

E4. *The boy who left home did not leave home.

The first attempt to construct a theory that could meet these minimum requirements and at the same time make use of the theory of transformational grammar was that of Katz and Fodor (1964). There can be no doubt as to their objective. They wanted a semantic theory that was fully compatible with the outline of the grammar suggested by the early work of Chomsky, Lees, Klima, and a few other writers. This compatibility requirement forced them to accept the methodological restriction to which we referred earlier as the constraint of separation of levels. This acceptance is explicit in the now well known formula proposed by them (1964:483):

F1. Linguistic description minus grammar equals semantics.

The authors of this theory characterize the minimum requirements for a serious semantic theory as describing and explaining

. . . the interpretive ability of speakers: by accounting for their performance in determining the number and content of the readings [meanings] of a sentence; by detecting semantic anomalies; by deciding upon paraphrase relations between sentences; and by marking every other semantic property or relation that plays a role in this ability. (Fodor and Katz, 1964:483.)

To understand what this means, consider a single English sentence that offers semantic difficulties and see just how the Fodor and Katz theory would propose to handle it. Look at sentence E5:

E5. The suit is light.

Native speakers of English will find this sentence to be ambiguous, since two meanings of E6 are possible:

E6. (a) The suit is light enough to carry.
    (b) The suit is light enough to make that tie look dark.

Fodor and Katz (1964) point out that the ambiguity of E5 cannot be structural, however, because the syntax will assign to both possible meanings of E5, as expressed in E6, the same underlying tree representation, E7.

E7. The suit is light.

When a single sentence has two possible meanings in this way, transformationalists say that it has two "readings," that is, it can be read, or understood, in two ways. It is, of course, possible to find instances where sentences have more than two meanings. The fact that more than one reading exists for a sentence may be caused by a number of different factors; in the case of E7, we have an example of *lexical ambiguity,* that is, an example in which the two readings are a result of the lexical item itself (the word *light*) having more than one possible meaning, both of which can occur in the structure of E7. The authors of this semantic theory take the position that

The basic fact that a semantic theory must explain is that a fluent speaker can determine the meaning of a sentence in terms of the meanings of its constituent lexical items. To explain this fact, a semantic theory must contain two components: a dictionary of the lexical items of the language and a system of rules (which we shall call projection rules) which operate on fully grammatical descriptions of sentences and on dictionary entries to produce semantic interpretations for every sentence of the language. (Fodor and Katz, 1964.)

The dictionary that contained all meanings of the words in the language was called a *lexicon*. The material that represented the word in the lexicon was called a *lexical entry*. A lexical entry would have the following parts:

1. Phonological markers
2. Syntactic markers
3. Semantic markers

The phonological markers contained information adequate to determine the proper pronunciation of the word. The syntactic markers specified such things as the part of speech or syntactic category to which the word belonged. The semantic markers specified the meaning(s) of the word.

It was proposed that there existed some set of semantic markers for the language, a finite set, that contained items like the following:

1. ± Human
2. ± Female
3. ± Physical object

Thus, an entry for the word *woman* would contain the markings for both [+ Human] and [+ Female]; the entry for *rock* would contain neither one. The entry for *man* would of course have [+ Human], but not [+ Female].[1]

If a particular lexical item was itself ambiguous it would be found in the lexicon with a series of conjunctions of these semantic markers. Each member of these conjunctions specified one of the meanings of the word. Such an entry can be represented by the following diagram:

F2. (word) [phonological markings]
[syntactic markers]
$[SM_i, SM_{i+1}, \ldots SM_{i+n}]$ v $[SM_j, SM_{j+1}, \ldots SM_{j+n}]$

---

[1] There are, of course, relations that hold between the various features proposed. For example, one can predict that any lexical entry marked [+ Human] will also be marked [+ Animate], as the set of objects that are Human are wholly contained within the set of objects that are Animate. The fact that this relation holds would be captured in the lexicon by a lexical redundancy rule. Entries that are [+ Animate], [+ Human] are marked only as [+ Human]. We then have the lexical redundancy rule [+ Human] → [+ Human], [+ Animate].

(where SM stands for some Semantic Marker, and the symbol "v" stands for the English word *or*)

A single entry will have as many conjunctions of semantic markers as it has possible meanings. Now, within the set of semantic markers, Fodor and Katz (1964) proposed that there were special markers referred to as Distinguishers, and it was these distinguishers that made it possible to characterize a case of lexical ambiguity. The purpose of the distinguishers was to specify the semantic environments in which that particular meaning of the word could occur.

For example, the fact that E5, but neither of the pairs in E6, is ambiguous could be accounted for by ensuring that the distinguishers will show that there are two possible semantic environments for *light,* one in which it serves to contrast with the word *dark* and one in which it contrasts with the word *heavy*. The distinguishers would mark on the entry the fact that the word *light* with the meaning associated with color could not be used in the semantic environment where the attribute of weight was the quality desired, and that the converse was also true. These distinguishers were designed by Fodor and Katz (1964) to capture the fact that native speakers will agree that the word *light* is ambiguous in isolation but will deny that it is ambiguous in contexts such as those of E6.

Now consider the following sentence:

E8. The suit is too light to wear.

That this is still ambiguous is shown by E9:

E9. (a)   The suit is too light to wear in this cold weather.
    (b)   The suit is too light to wear with that tie.

It is obvious, therefore, that it is not enough to say that *light* is unambiguous in context, as there are many contexts in which it remains ambiguous. In E9(a) and (b) we would have to be certain that the distinguishers on the verb *to wear* interacted with the distinguishers on the word *light* in such a way that it would be possible to characterize the ambiguity of E8. As you can see, this sort of interaction and overlapping of markings would make the actual construction of the lexicon extremely complex.

In addition to the lexicon itself, Fodor and Katz stated that it would be necessary to have some mechanism that could make use of the information contained in the lexicon and also of the structure specified by the syntax, and which could associate meanings of English words with sequences of English words. This mechanism was to be the Projection Rules referred to in the Fodor and Katz quotation. The projection rule accepts as input the tree representation specified by the PSG, including the terminal elements of the tree (the sequences of English words) and the lexicon, and produces readings (or meanings). The projection rules were to begin with the conjunctions of semantic markers present in the most deeply embedded constituent(s) of the tree representation. These rules worked their way up the tree, combining the sets of conjunctions of semantic markers (minimally one for each constituent present) until the entire tree had been traversed (the topmost S-node had been reached). The end result was called an Amalgamated Path. This type of operation reflects directly the claim that the meaning of the entire sentence is a function of the meaning of its individual constituents. Consider E10(a) and (b):

E10. (a)   The cat ate the rat.
      (b)   The rat ate the cat.

Obviously, the two sequences are understood by native speakers of English to mean different things. Since they contain the identical set of English words, it is equally obvious that the Amalgamated Path for E10(a) contains precisely the same set of semantic markers that the Amalgamated Path for E10(b) contains. Therefore, the difference between the two versions of E10 cannot be attributed to the meaning of any particular lexical item or set of lexical items.

The point of the examples E10(a) and (b) is to show that structural relations, as specified by the syntax, are a necessary part of the input to the projection rules. In other words, the structural position occupied by some lexical item in the tree may contribute to the meaning of the entire sentence. Thus, the projection rules must be sensitive to the tree representations on which they are operating. This fact provides part of the motivation for the presence of syntactic information in the determination of meaning. Let's refer to this fact as the Argument Position Problem. We will need to adopt the following terminology for the discussion of this problem.

R1. Each clause of English has a verb and some n number of noun positions. The verb is called a Relation and the NP's are called Arguments.[2]

If we agree to refer to NP's such as *the rat* and *the cat* as Arguments of the verb or Relation *eat,* then we can say that the Argument Position that an argument occupies for a particular relation may have semantic impact. More specifically, using the example E10, we notice that while the Amalgamated Paths for E10(a) and (b) are identical, the terms occupying Argument Positions of the relation *eat* are not. If we call the NP argument position

---

[2] The analogy to standard first-order predicate calculus will be apparent to readers familiar with that system.

that is directly before the verb the Subject Argument Position, we can simply note that the NP occupying those positions in the two versions are different. Notice now that we can attempt a more general statement: If we have two sequences S_i and S_j such that each element of S_i is also an element of S_j (equivalently, for the present purposes, the Amalgamated Path of S_i contains the same set of semantic markers as does the Amalgamated Path of S_j) and the same elements occupy the same argument position in both S_i and S_j, then S_i and S_j mean the same thing. Now consider the meaning of E4(a) and (b).

E11. (a)   The rat was eaten by the cat.
  (b)   The cat was eaten by the rat.

Once again the two sequences of E11 involve the same set of semantic markers, yet differ one from the other just as the two sequences of E10 do. Apparently, this is explicable in the same way as the difference between the two sequences of E10 was characterized; namely, by appealing to the fact that the argument positions are occupied by different terms. What is more interesting for our present purposes is that while neither the pair E10(a) and (b) nor the pair E11(a) and (b) have the same meaning, any native speaker of English will judge the pairs E10(a) and E11(a) and E10(b) and E11(b) to have the same meaning. Let's isolate one such pair for consideration, say E10(a) and E11(a), repeated here as E12(a) and (b).

E12. (a)   The cat ate the rat.
  (b)   The rat was eaten by the cat.

Evidently, since the semantic theory we are discussing accepts as a reasonable task the explication of the relation of paraphrase between sentences of natural language, we must entertain two distinct projection rules; one that operates on the tree representation of E12(a)—that is, E13(a)—and the other that operates on the tree representation of E12(b)—that is, E13(b):

E13. (a)   (b)

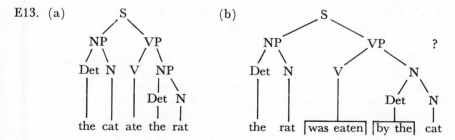

The solution is, at best, an unhappy one, as a moment's reflection will reveal that the so-called logical relations that are understood to exist between the relation *eat* and the arguments *the cat* and *the rat* are constant.[3] Yet, if the projection rules are sensitive to the syntactic position of each of the NP arguments in order to determine its semantic contribution (as we have already seen is necessary to distinguish between E10(a) and (b)), and if the projection rules accept as input the distinct tree representations E13(a) and (b), two such rules must be included in the grammar. The alternative solution to this problem (the one proposed by the authors of the theory) avoids this unhappy claim by making use of one of the more striking features of the transformational approach to language analysis; namely, that the tree representations E13(a) and (b) are related to each other by the formal mapping operation, the transformation. In other words, the sequences E12(a) and (b) are simply two distinct Surface Structures resulting from two distinct derivations from the same underlying tree. These two derivations differ only in that in the case of the derivation that results in the surface tree E13(a), there has been no application of the transformation known as the PASSIVE, whereas the derivation that results in the surface tree E13(b) has had an application of the PASSIVE transformation. Schematically,

F3. $\text{CF-PSG} \rightarrow \text{TS}_i \rightarrow \text{T}_i \rightarrow \text{TS}_{i+1} \rightarrow \text{T}_{i+1} \rightarrow \text{TS}_{i+2}$

$$\rightarrow \ldots \rightarrow \begin{cases} \text{T}_j \rightarrow \text{TS}_j \rightarrow \ldots \text{TS}_n \\ \emptyset \rightarrow \text{TS}_{i+2} \rightarrow \ldots \text{TS}_{n'} \end{cases}$$

where TS = tree structure

T_j = PASSIVE transformation

$\text{TS}_n = \text{E13(a)}$

$\text{TS}_{n'} = \text{E13(b)}$.

Thus, all trees in the derivation of TS_n and $\text{TS}_{n'}$ prior to the application of the PASSIVE transformation are identical both in terms of the set of semantic markers that they contain and in their structure; that is, the same terms occupy the same argument positions. All trees that are post-PASSIVE are different both structurally and in the set of English terms they contain.[4] The solution is, of course, to ensure that the projection rules operate on the trees prior to the application of the PASSIVE. This solution captures the

---

[3] The terms *underlying subject, deep subject*, and *logical subject* are usually used by transformationalists to refer to the NP argument that appears (or would appear) to the immediate left of the verb in Surface Structure if no permutation transformation has applied in the derivation of the Surface Structure. The term Surface Subject is used to refer to the nominal that appears to the immediate left of the verb in Surface Structure.

[4] This sentence is not strictly true, as the PASSIVE, for example, is formulated to introduce the Past Participle form or some equivalent marker that will cause that shape to occur in the final derived structure. The reasoning in the text is acceptable, as the transformations do not introduce meaning-bearing terms.

relation of paraphrase between the pair E10(b) and E11(b), as they also are transforms related by the PASSIVE transformation.

We return now to the problem of the ambiguity of sequences such as E2 (repeated here for convenience) :

The chicken is ready to eat.

Notice that we can paraphrase the two readings of E2 by E14(a) and (b).

E14. (?a)   The chicken is ready for someone to eat it.
 (?b)   The chicken is ready for it to eat something.

If it can be argued that there exist two sets of rules, rule 1 and rule 2, such that rule 1 accepts E14(a) as input and generates E2, and rule 2 accepts E14(b) as input and generates E2 as output. Then, given a set of projection rules defined on E14(a) and (b), we have given a precise formulation to the intuition that E2 is ambiguous and may be paraphrased by either E14(a) or (b). Speaking slightly more generally, we can characterize explicitly the intuition that some particular surface string S_i is n-ways ambiguous, just in case there exist n underlying structures and n derivations that result in a final derived tree with the form S_i. Such ambiguity is called Syntactic Ambiguity because it results from the fact that the syntax specifies an identical surface string as the final derived tree of more than one derivation from more than one underlying structure. The projection rules operate on the underlying structures where the logical relations such as argument position are represented. They perform this operation before the transformations introduce their specific distortions (as in the PASSIVE case, for example), thus capturing the obvious generalizations. Notice that this account does not explain the fact that E5 is ambiguous:

The suit is light.

The logical relations (for example, Argument Positions) seem to be accurately reflected by the present structure of the sequence E5. There seems to be no reason or set of reasons that would make us postulate some underlying structure for one or the other of the two readings of the sequence E5. As we pointed out earlier, the fact that E5 is ambiguous seems to be associated with no structural considerations but rather with the fact that the element *light* is itself ambiguous. The question is: Exactly how do the two components of the semantic theory under discussion handle this fact? Consider what we already know about the lexical entry for the word *light*:

F4. light   [phonological markings]; [+ Adj, . . .]; [R_1 v R_2]
 where $R_1 = SM_1, SM_2, \ldots, SM_n$;
 and $R_2 = SM_1, SM_2, \ldots, SM_n$.

The set of semantic markers R_1, say, characterizes the semantics of the term *light* when used to describe the property of weight; the R_2 set of semantic markers characterizes the semantics of the term *light* when used to describe the property of color. As we pointed out before, each such set of semantic markers contains a special set of distinguishers that specifies semantic environments in which they may not occur without deviance. Refer now to the tree representation of E5, that is, E7:

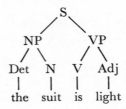

The schema E15 is intended to represent the result of the projection rules on E7:

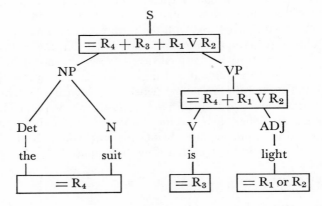

In effect, the final Amalgamated Path for E15 (the string of symbols at the level of the S-node) claims that the whole tree means whatever the constituents $(NP = R_4) + (V = R_3) +$ either $(ADJ = R_1)$ or $(ADJ = R_2)$ mean.

Since nothing in the semantic environment forbids the occurrence of either of the readings of the lexical item *light,* either one meaning or the other is possible. This type of ambiguity is called *lexical ambiguity*. The fact that the semantic environment in the E6(a) sequence (repeated here as E15) contains marker R_1, which refers to the property of weight (contained in the item *carry*), and the fact that the lexical entry for *light* in one of its readings (R_2) contains distinguishers that block its occurrence in such a semantic environment accounts for the fact that E16 is unambiguous.

E16. The suit is too light to wear on such a cold day.

The sequence E6(b) is unambiguous, similarly, as its semantic environment contains reference to color and one of the two entries for the lexical item *light* contains distinguishers blocking its occurrence in such an environment.

In this chapter we have presented the outline of the first semantic theory designed to be compatible with the model of grammar proposed by the early transformationalists. The system consisted of two subsystems: a lexicon and a set of projection rules. The objects for which the projection rules were defined were the semantic markers from the lexical items in the given tree structure plus some necessary structural information, such as argument position. The output of the operation of these projection rules was a set of Amalgamated Paths that specified what the meaning or meanings of the tree were.

It is important to remember that the projection rules were designed to operate on the tree structures *before* applying any transformations that would distort the structural information needed. For example, the PASSIVE transformation can be shown to interchange at least two of the argument positions in a given tree structure.

In Chapter 8 we will see how the principles of the Fodor and Katz theory, along with the results of the research of the early transformationalists, were synthesized into the first attempt at a coherent explicit transformational model of language intended to explicate the regularities of both Set A and Set B. This model was constructed by Noam Chomsky (1965a).

EXERCISES

1. Sentence (a) is an example of lexical ambiguity. Construct at least two sentences in which the same item occurs unambiguously. Then determine what property the item would have to possess in its lexical entry in order to distinguish the two.

    (a) George wants a plane for Christmas.

2. In Navajo the single sequence /naalnish/ can have all of the following meanings (as well as some others that are not relevant to this problem):

    He is working.
    She is working.
    They two are working (male or female, or both).
    It is working.

Would it be possible for a set of semantic markers to be used in order to distinguish these various meanings from one another?

3. It happens that in Navajo the situation described for /naalnish/ applies for every third-person verb form that does not contain the marker meaning "three or more." Let's assume that the Navajo language does use the system of gender and number marking that is described in the answer to the second question in Exercise 2. What would be the consequences for the grammar?

4. On the basis of the answer to Exercise 3, can you think of a better solution to the problem of a verb that is ambiguous as to gender and number?

ANSWERS

1. (a) George needs a plane to make that table.

(b) George needs a plane to go to Yreka.

Just as color and weight were the two properties that would serve to distinguish the two meanings of *light,* the lexical item *plane* would require that *means of transportation* be part of one entry and *tool* be part of the other.

2. Yes, of course. The verb form would simply need to have as many identical readings (sets of semantic markers) as there are possible interpretations, with those readings differing only in the markers + MASCULINE, + SINGULAR.

3. Every verb in the language would have to have at least six duplicate entries, differing only in gender and number markings. If a verb had several possible semantic readings, each of those readings would also have to have all six entries. The increase in complexity of the grammar would be enormous, and could be defended only if it were the best available solution to the disambiguation of the lexical item.

4. It seems clear that it would always be possible to disambiguate these verbs by context and that this would involve no complication of the grammar. Consider the following set of English sentences:

(a) He can sing.

(b) She can sing.

(c) They (two) can sing.

(d) They (eight hundred and three) can sing.

(e) It can sing.

The same situation obtains for the so-called *modal* verbs in English as obtains for the Navajo verb in the exercise; that is, there is no change in the verb to indicate gender or number. Nonetheless, it is possible to indicate these two factors unambiguously in many ways; for example, by the use of the personal pronouns of English, which *do* make gender and number distinctions. Note that *it can sing* remains ambiguous as to gender, as does *they can sing*. But there is nothing ambiguous about *the boys and girls can sing* or about *the mother bird can sing*. Since the other lexical items in a sentence will serve to make gender and number of a verb clear where clarity is *required,* there appears to be no reason to add such a complication to the markings of the verb.

Chapter 8

The First Complete Model—
Chomsky's Aspects
of the Theory of Syntax

In this chapter we present the outline of the model proposed by Chomsky (1965a). Until recently,[1] this model occupied a privileged position within the field of linguistics because it represented the only model that was complete, in that it attempted to account explicitly for the regularities in both the Set A (the set of well-formed sound sequences) and Set B (the set of well-formed semantic representations). This synthesis was only possible because of the work of Fodor and Katz in their development of the semantic theory (see Chapter 7), the work of early transformationalists such as Postal, Klima, and Lees, and more recently the work of Katz and Postal (1964). The contribution by Katz and Postal had as its objective the task of providing "an adequate means of incorporating the grammatical and the semantic descriptions of a language into one integrated description." The authors commented:

> The conception of a linguistic description proposed here combines the generative conception of grammar developed by Chomsky with the conception of semantics proposed by Katz and Fodor. . . . Among the questions for which definite answers are given are these: What are the syntactic structures that are semantically interpreted in describing the meaning of a sentence? Do transformations contribute anything to the meaning of sentences? What changes in the form of syntactic description must be made to accord with this integration of syntactic and semantic description? (Katz and Postal, 1964.)

[1] See G. Lakoff (1970) for one statement of the Generative Semantics model.

Katz and Postal began by pointing out that if one considers the set of transformations so far proposed, one finds that they divide up rather nicely into those that had been claimed to be obligatory (those whose application was necessary in every derivation where their Structural Index was met for the resultant surface structure to be well formed) and those that had been claimed to be optional. The (a) and (b) variants of E1 and E2 are related by transformations that had been argued to be obligatory, while those of E3 and E4 are related by so-called optional transformations.

E1. (a)   The girl kiss the boy.
    (b)   The girl kisses the boy.   NUMBER AGREEMENT *(obligatory)*

E2. (a)   He called up her.
    (b)   He called her up.   PARTICLE MOVEMENT *(obligatory)*

E3. (a)   Harry saw someone.
    (b)   Who did Harry see?   QUESTION FORMATION *(optional)*

E4. (a)   Harry saw someone.   NEGATIVE TRANSFORMATION
    (b)   Harry didn't see anyone.   *(optional)*

There was, of course, an interesting semantic correlate of this distinction between the set of obligatory and the set of optional transformations: The semantic effect of obligatory transformations was zero, while in the case of optional transformations, the transformed and the nontransformed versions differed radically in their meaning. Consider the pair of sequences E4(a) and (b), which had been initially claimed to be related by the NEGATIVE transformation. The sequences are related perfectly semantically; that is, they are contradictory in that the (a) version is true if and only if the (b) version is false, and vice versa. But we have already seen that the original proposal regarding the NEGATIVE transformation had been revised in the work done by Klima (1964b), who had argued convincingly for an abstract marker (NEG) in the underlying tree structure of sequences such as E4(b). Further, the structural index of the NEGATIVE transformation required the presence of the abstract element NEG in the sequence that was to undergo the NEGATIVE transformation. But if this is the case, then it is simply false to claim that E4(a) and (b) are related by the NEGATIVE transformation, since it is obvious that E4(a) contains no occurrence of the element NEG and is therefore not properly analyzeable with respect to the NEGATIVE transformation. Given Klima's analysis, it is clear that the pairs of trees represented by the sequences E5(a) and (b), and E5(a) and (c) are related by the NEG transformation.

E5. (a)   NEG Harry see someone.
    (b)   Harry didn't see anyone.   (NEGATIVE TRANSFORMATION)
    (c)   Harry saw no one.

Notice now that the transformation NEGATIVE is no longer optional under this new analysis. Correlated with this fact is the observation that if we were to ensure that the projection rules operated on structures of the form E5(a) and that if we were to make the projection rules sensitive to the abstract marker NEG, then we could determine the meaning of the tree E5(a) and allow the NEGATIVE transformation to apply, altering the tree E5(a) to either E5(b) or (c), but allowing the meaning to remain constant. The general hypothesis now becomes clear:

R1.   Transformations are meaning-preserving.

R1 claims that every two contiguous trees in a derivation must be semantically equivalent. No transformation has the effect of changing meaning. We may generalize, then, and say that every pair of contiguous trees in a derivation is related by some transformation. If the projection rules were to operate on the deepest underlying tree representation—the ones prior to the operation of any of the transformations—then by R1 we know that the meaning will remain constant in the derivation of that tree. The defense of the hypothesis R1 was the subject matter of the Katz and Postal monograph. Klima (1964b) had argued on purely formal grounds for the existence of an abstract marker NEG in the underlying tree representation of surface sentences that displayed negation in different forms, but with a strikingly parallel syntactic distribution. In the same way, the successful defense of R1 required that Katz and Postal argue for the existence of some marker in the underlying tree representation of every Surface Structure that had been previously thought to be related to some other Surface Structure by an optional transformation that obviously changed meaning. If their argument was successful, they then had to rewrite any transformation that had had a semantic effect in such a way that it would be sensitive to these underlying markers also, so that the semantics could be properly characterized. Under this system, the sequences E3(a) and (b) would not be transformationally related. The underlying structure for E3(a) would be E6(a) and that for E3(a) would be E6(b):

E6. (a)   (b)

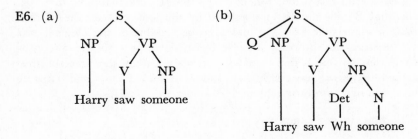

The semantic difference between E3(a) and (b) is now easily captured. The projection rules operating on these structures will use the presence of the abstract markers Q and Wh in the underlying tree E6(b) to derive an Amalgamated Path that characterizes the semantic difference between its surface interpretation and that of the similar but different Surface Structure E3(a) whose underlying tree representation contains no occurrence of the markers Q and Wh. Further, the transformation that derives the surface form of E6(b) requires for its operation the presence of the markers Q and Wh.

F1. QUESTION FORMATION

	X	Q	Y	Wh $+$ N	Z
Structural Index	1,	2,	3,	4,	5
Structural Change	1,	$2 + 4$	3,	$\emptyset$,	5

Katz and Postal's defense of the meaning-preserving hypothesis R1 was generally considered to be successful. We may turn now to a consideration of Chomsky's Aspects model.[2]

The Aspects grammar was organized into three major components: the syntactic, the phonological, and the semantic. The syntactic component had two subcomponents: One was called the *base* and the other the *transformational component*. This organization is outlined as:

F2.
- A. Syntactic Component
  - (i) The Base
    - (a) PSG rules
    - (b) Lexicon, with rules of lexical insertion
  - (ii) The Transformational Component
- B. Semantic component (Set B)
- C. Phonological component (Set A)

The syntactic component was said to be *generative,* in the sense that it was this component that enumerated the set of tree representations (Deep Structures) that served as input to the other two components. The semantic and phonological components were called *interpretive.* That is, they were said to interpret the output of the syntactic component, with the semantic component giving as its output the meanings and the phonological component giving as its output the sound sequences.

The function of the base was to specify fully developed tree structures whose terminal nodes were the set of words and abstract markers that the semantic component could interpret, to give the Amalgamated Path that specified the meaning of the tree. These fully specified trees were called the Deep Structures. The transformational component mapped trees into trees,

[2] See Chomsky (1965a:84) for a more formal statement.

beginning with the Deep Structures and terminating with the final derived tree, which was called the Surface Structure.

We can now proceed to consider each of the proposed components of the grammar in isolation.

The base contained the lexicon, which we have already discussed in detail in Chapter 7, with the lexical items entered in the way described. In addition to the lexicon, the base contained two general types of rules: first, the Phrase Structure Grammar rules whose function it was to specify the tree structure up to the point where lexical items were introduced; second, the lexical insertion rules whose function it was to map the entries in the lexicon onto the tree structures. The PSG rules were of two forms: Context Free (CF) and Context Sensitive (CS). An example of some CF-PSG rules in the Aspects model would be the following:

R2. $S \rightarrow NP\ VP$

$$VP \rightarrow \left\{ \begin{array}{l} \text{Copula Predicate} \\ V \left\{ \begin{array}{l} \text{(NP) (Prep Phrase) (Prep Phrase) (Manner)} \\ S' \\ \text{Predicate} \end{array} \right\} \end{array} \right\}$$

$$\text{Predicate} \rightarrow \left\{ \begin{array}{l} \text{Adjective} \\ \text{(like) Predicate Nominal} \end{array} \right\}$$

$$NP \rightarrow \text{(Det) N (S')}$$

$$\begin{array}{ll} \bullet & \bullet \\ \bullet & \bullet \\ \bullet & \bullet \end{array}$$

As can be seen from an inspection of the form of these rules, all are of the CF-PSG variety. The operation of these rules yielded structures such as E7:

E7.

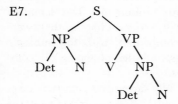

The next portion of the CF-PSG rules now applied. These rules functioned to specify features on certain nodes of the tree E7. R3 contains samples of such rules.

R3.   N → [+ N]
     [+ N] → [± Count]
     [+ Count] → [± Animate]
     [+ Animate] → [± Human]
       •   •
       •   •
       •   •

The object that resulted from the application of all these rules was called a Complex Symbol. The idea of the Complex Symbol was new to transformational grammar and was one of the significant additions to transformational theory made by the Aspects model. E8 is an example of a tree with Complex Symbols:

E8.

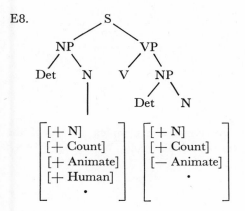

The Complex Symbol specified what kind of noun could occur under the node of any given tree. For example, in E8, the Noun *boy* could appear under the leftmost N-node but not under the rightmost. The lexical entry for the word *boy* is marked [+ Animate], which agrees with the marking in the Complex Symbol of the leftmost N, but conflicts with the marking in the Complex Symbol of the rightmost N.

As can be seen by examining E8, Aspects grammar rules of the type that developed features (as in R3) were restricted in their application. There were, for example, no feature-developing rules for the node V (Verb).

The mechanism that developed the Complex Symbol under such nodes as V was a Context-Sensitive PSG rule of the following form:

R4.   V → CS/ *a* _____ (Det *β*)
     where *a* and *β* are nouns

This rule has a formidable appearance, but all it says is that the node V is to be rewritten as a Complex Symbol by copying the markings of the Noun (α), which precedes it, and the markings of the Noun (β), which follows it. Schematically, the effect of such a rule operating on E9(a), is shown in E9(b):

E9. (a)

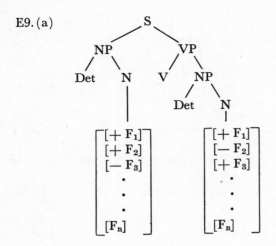

where F is some feature placed on the complex symbol of the N-node by one of the feature-developing rules,

(b)

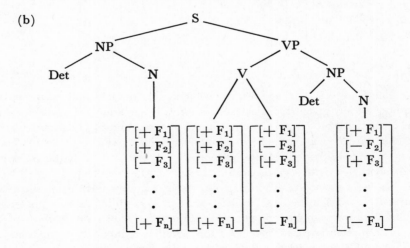

The CS-PSG rules captured the dependencies that existed between certain grammatical categories and positions. Consider the deviancy of the sequences of E10:

E10. (*a)   The man drank the rock.
      (*b)   The truth punched the wall.

The deviancies of the sequences of E10 were attributed to violation(s) of Selectional Restrictions. More specifically, it was claimed that the objects of the verb *drink* must be things that are fluid; the term *rock* is usually understood to refer to an object that is not fluid. The verb *punch* is usually said to require that the nouns which occur in its subject position refer to objects having size, weight, and similar physical characteristics. The term *truth* is usually understood to refer to an abstract concept possessing none of these characteristics. By using a C(ontext) S(ensitive) PSG rule to mark the Complex Symbol under the V-node, and by making that Complex Symbol simply a copy of the features on the subject and object N-nodes, the Aspects system ensured that the features relevant for preventing selectional restrictions violations are available; that is, it ensured that the markers present in the V Complex Symbol matched the markers in the N Complex Symbols.

Now we may see how the CS-PSG rule interacts with the next mechanism, the lexical insertion rule. Notice that the bottom line of the tree structure E11 now consists of a series of Complex Symbols. We saw in Chapter 7 that the typical lexical entry also contains a set of markers of the same type as found in the Complex Symbol. The lexical items from the lexicon may now be inserted into the tree structure if the markers in the lexicon for that item and the markers in the Complex Symbol under that particular node do not conflict. Let us continue with our previous example; E11 is the result of the application of R4 to E8:

E11.

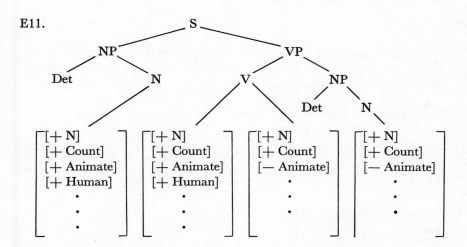

Given the E11 tree with its Complex Symbols and the following dictionary entries.[3]

E12. (a) *boy* [phonological markers]; [+N, . . . other syntactic markers]; [+ Count, + Animate, + Human, . . . other semantic markers]

    (b) *truth* [phonological markers]; [+ N, . . . other syntactic markers]; [+ Count, — Animate, . . . other semantic markers]

    (c) *like* [phonological markers]; [+ V, . . . other syntactic markers]; [+ N . . . , + Animate . . . other semantic markers]

we see that E12(a) may be inserted into the tree structure E11 under the subject-node Complex Symbol, since there is no conflict in markers, but E12(a) cannot be inserted into the tree under the object N-node Complex Symbol because the markers in the Complex Symbol under that N-node include the marker [— Animate] and the lexical entry E12(a) contains the marker [+ Animate]. Conversely, the markers in the Complex Symbol under the subject N-node demand a [+ Animate] item and the lexical entry E12(b) includes the marker [— Animate], and is therefore prevented from being inserted into that position. Similar considerations hold for the insertion of other lexical categories; verbs, for example, contain in their lexical entries information about what selectional restrictions their subjects

and object must meet. The marker
$$
\begin{bmatrix}
[+ \text{N}] \\
[+ \text{Animate}] \\
\cdot \\
\cdot \\
\cdot
\end{bmatrix}
[\underline{\qquad}]
$$

in the lexical entry for *like* captures the fact that the nouns that occur as its subject must be [+ Animate]. Thus, the fact that E13(a), but not E13(b), is possible is accounted for.

E13. (a) The boy likes the truth.
    (*b) Form likes the truth.

Notice that, in fact, E13(a) is a sequence resulting from the tree E11, the lexical entries in E12, and the rule of lexical insertion, which we have been discussing.

[3] In the E12 schema for the lexical entries, the reader will find blanks flanked by category symbols such as NP. The blanks are a notational device used simply to indicate that the lexical entry being described appears in that position; that is, it is flanked by the category symbols stated.

E14.

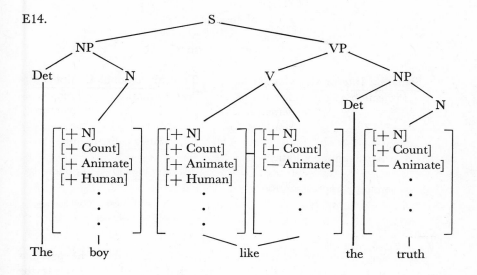

This object, E14, was a distinguished object in the Aspects model and was called the Deep Structure.

If we now return to a consideration of the schema of the Aspects model, F2, we see that the Deep Structure was the input to the Semantic Interpretive Component, which we discussed in Chapter 7; in addition, it was also the input to the Transformational Component. The function of the Semantic Interpretive Component was to match the Deep Structure with some Amalgamated Path that represented its meaning. The function of the Transformational Component was to map the Deep Structure onto the Surface Structures by means of transformations. The Surface Structures represent the input to the phonological component for their interpretation as sequences of sounds.

The Aspects model represents the first attempt to specify fully the form of a grammar that accepted as its legitimate task the statement in a principled way of the regularities that the native speaker can identify in both the set of well-formed semantic representations (the set of Amalgamated Paths, Set B) and the set of well-formed surface sequences (the output of the phonological component, Set A). F3 depicts the form of the grammar, considering the types of mechanisms and the types of formal objects over which these mechanisms were defined.

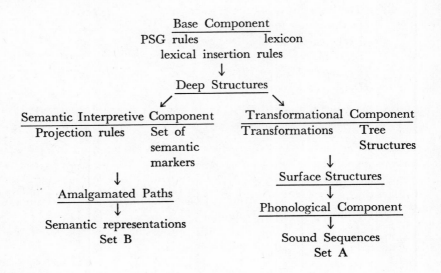

It is very important to note that this system maintains the previous insistence on the separation of levels. Notice that the only place where the syntax and the semantics come into contact is the Deep Structure. The syntactic and the semantic components are then independent. The addition or deletion, for example, of some or all of the mechanisms in the Semantic Interpretive Component would have no repercussions in the syntactic component. This assumption of the autonomy of syntax from semantics is presently the central point in a controversy in transformational linguistics, the controversy between the theory as described thus far (including its more recent developments) and the theory called Generative Semantics. In Chapter 10 we will return to this topic and discuss this controversy in some detail.

EXERCISES

1.   Consider the following sets of sentences. All contain exactly the same lexical items. On the basis of the framework developed in this chapter, decide whether or not all members of each set are transformationally related, and explain your answer.

   (a)   John flew away.
           Away John flew.
           Away flew John.
   (b)   The little girl sat in the corner.
           In the corner the little girl sat.
           In the corner sat the little girl.
   (c)   Mary liked refried beans.
           Refried beans Mary liked.
           Refried beans liked Mary.

2.   In the Aspects system, the sentence *Refried beans liked Mary* would presumably never be generated in any case. Why?

3.   Given the answers to Exercises 1 and 2, can we now conclude that the problem is solved and that the set of sentences in (c) of Exercise 1 is just like the others except that it contains some sort of semantic anomaly? Would the feature agreement required by the Aspects model take care of this adequately?

4.   In French, there is a rule that all adjectives must agree with their nouns in gender. Thus, we find the following:

   (a)   Pierre est grand.
           (Peter is tall.)
   (b)   Marie est grande.
           (Mary is tall.)

This rule holds even if the actual facts contradict the grammar. So, a woman professor, since "professeur" is masculine, will be described by the sequence

   (c)   Le professeur est grand.

Can this situation be handled by the Aspects system? If so, how?

ANSWERS

1.   Although the superficial patterns exhibited by these sets of sentences are the same, only sets (a) and (b) are transformationally related; the members of set (c) could not be. The reason this is clear is that *Refried beans Mary liked* does not mean the same thing as *Refried beans liked Mary,* and transformations must be meaning-preserving.

2.   The complex symbol would undoubtedly reflect the fact that only lexical items with the feature [+ Animate] can *like* anything. Therefore there would be no possible semantic interpretation of the string.

3.   No. Consider the following set of sentences, which would contain no string that has a conflict in feature markings.

(d)   Mary liked John.
       John Mary liked.
       John liked Mary.

4.   (a)   No. The formalism of Aspects grammar with its strict separation of levels would have difficulty here. The information that some particular professor was female would not be available to the syntactic component.

Chapter 9

The Cycle

In this chapter we assume the framework provided by the theory outlined in Chapter 8 for the Aspects model. We will consider in more detail the functioning of the transformational component. In particular, we will consider the question of the interaction of some of the transformations mentioned previously. We begin by stating some of the rules that are of interest for the discussion.

The PASSIVE Rule

We have already considered pairs of sequences such as E1(a) and (b):

E1. (a) The wombat bit the elephant.
    (b) The elephant was bitten by the wombat.

We have mentioned that the logical relations (the semantic effect of the argument position) remain constant in pairs of sequences such as these. Other arguments can be presented in support of the hypothesis that these pairs are transformationally related. Consider the fact that the members of each such pair are paraphrases; thus, in the Aspects model, if they were to be derived from the same Deep Structure, that fact would be automatically accounted for. Or consider the fact that the "subject" argument NP of the active sequence [the E1(a) version] and the NP argument that follows the preposition *by* in Surface Structure display the same set of selectional restrictions. For example, the verb *bite* requires a [+ Animate] subject NP in the active; predictably (if the pair is transformationally related), the NP argument that follows the preposition in the E1(b) version must be [+ Animate].

E2. (a) The $\left\{ \begin{matrix} \text{wombat} \\ \text{*rock.} \end{matrix} \right\}$ bit the elephant.
   (b) The elephant was bitten by the $\left\{ \begin{matrix} \text{wombat} \\ \text{*rock} \end{matrix} \right\}$.

Such correspondences are automatically accounted for if the pairs are related by R1:

R1. PASSIVE		X	[NP	V	NP	Y]	Z
			s			s	
Structural Index		1	2	3	4	5	6
Structural Change		1	4	$be + 3$	Ø	$5 + by + 2$	6

The rule, then, has the effect of interchanging the "subject" NP and the NP that *immediately* succeeds the verb within the same clause.

The INDIRECT OBJECT MOVEMENT Rule

Notice the relation between the (a) and (b) versions of E3:

E3. (a) Pete gave the pipe to George.
   (b) Pete gave George the pipe.

The usual considerations lead one to postulate the existence of a transformation that relates this pair. The transformation must map E4(a) into E5(b):

E4. (a)

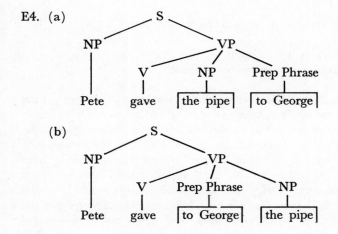

   (b)

A later rule of *To*-deletion will delete the *to* because it is contiguous to the Verb, V. Notice that the pair is judged by native speakers of English to be synonymous and that the set of selectional restrictions which exist for the object of the preposition *to* in the structures of the form E4(a) are identical to the set of selectional restrictions displayed by the NP that immediately succeeds the Verb in structures of the form E4(b). Such facts motivate the incorporation of the rule of INDIRECT OBJECT MOVEMENT into the grammar of English.[1]

R2. INDIRECT OBJECT MOVEMENT	X	[V	NP	NP	Y]	Z
		VP			VP	
Structural Index	1	2	3	4	5	6
Structural Change	1	2	4 + 3	Ø	5	6

The First Interaction

The fact that the two rules PASSIVE and INDIRECT OBJECT MOVEMENT (R1 and R2) exist in the grammar of English allows us to present the argument for the ordering of transformations. Notice that the PASSIVE creates new "subjects" by moving the NP that *immediately* succeeds the verb: The INDIRECT OBJECT MOVEMENT rule R2 has the effect of placing a new NP immediately contiguous to the Verb. Now consider the ordering possibilities. If the order were PASSIVE > INDIRECT OBJECT MOVEMENT, then —given the underlying tree structure suggested by the sequence E5(a) (tree structure E6(a))—we would predict the sequence E5(b) (the tree structure E6(b)).

E5. (a) Pete gave the pipe to George.
    (b) The pipe was given to George by Pete.

The prediction is accurate in that the sequence E5(b) is grammatical, a sequence of English synonymous with E5(a), and related to it by the PASSIVE rule.

---

[1] Notice that we blithely refer to phrases such as *to George* as an NP. Traditionally, and in earlier trees in this text, such phrases are referred to as Prepositional Phrases. The set of arguments needed to establish the claim that all cases of Prepositional Phrases are to be regarded as NP's is far beyond the scope of this text. See Rosenbaum (1967), Postal (1966), and Fillmore (1968) for some of the considerations that lead one to make such a claim.

E6. (a)

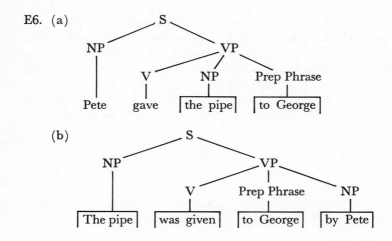

(b)

But now consider the order INDIRECT OBJECT MOVEMENT > PASSIVE. If this were the order and the transformation INDIRECT OBJECT MOVEMENT were optional [as it must be, given the fact that E3(a) is a grammatical sequence of English; that is, it is not necessary for the transformation to apply even if its Structural Index is met for the final derived tree in that derivation to be grammatical], then we would predict that, given the underlying structure E3(a), there are two corresponding Passive forms, E7(a) and (b):

E7. (a)   The pipe was given to George by Pete.
     (b)   George was given the pipe by Pete.

The only way that E7(b) could have been derived is if the transformation INDIRECT OBJECT MOVEMENT had applied prior to PASSIVE, moving the NP *George* contiguous to the Verb, the position from which the PASSIVE will move it into subject position. We see that the sequence E7(a) is the result of a derivation in which the optional transformation INDIRECT OBJECT MOVEMENT failed to apply; the sequence E7(b) is the result of a derivation in which the optional transformation INDIRECT OBJECT MOVEMENT did, in fact, apply. Note that, given the order PASSIVE > INDIRECT OBJECT MOVE-MENT, the perfectly grammatical sequence E7(b) could never be derived; thus, the argument demonstrates that the order must be

INDIRECT OBJECT MOVEMENT > PASSIVE

The REFLEXIVE Rule

In English, there is a set of *self* forms that we refer to as Reflexives. The set of Reflexives includes the forms listed in E8:

E8.
$$\left\{ \begin{array}{c} \text{myself} \\ \text{herself} \\ \text{yourself} \\ \text{themselves} \\ \cdot \\ \cdot \\ \cdot \end{array} \right\}$$

The distribution of Reflexive forms in English is rather highly restricted. Let's assume that a distinction is granted between emphatic Reflexives E9 and regular Reflexives E10.

E9.　(a)　Jake$_i$ himself$_i$ couldn't have done better.
　　　(b)　Jake$_i$ couldn't have done better himself$_i$.

E10.　(a)　Jake$_i$ hurt himself$_i$.
　　　(b)　Martha$_j$ shaved herself$_j$.

We can now state one of the essential characteristics of the distribution of regular Reflexives in English by saying that the Reflexive form must have a coreferential antecedent somewhere within the same clause; we will call this the Clause Mate restriction on Reflexives. The ill-formedness of the sequences of E11 can be attributed to a violation of this Clause Mate restriction.

E11.　(*a)　Jake$_i$ said that Martha$_j$ hurt himself$_i$.
　　　(*b)　Martha$_j$ hoped that Jake$_i$ would shave herself$_j$.

Indeed, the tree representations for E3(a) and (b) show that the reflexive and its coreferential antecedent are not dominated by the same S-node (that is, are not Clause Mates) :

E12.　(a)

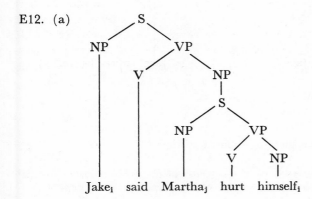

(b)

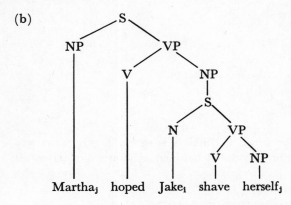

Martha$_j$ hoped Jake$_i$ shave herself$_j$

Notice that the only possible understanding of E10 is that the Reflexive is coreferential with the subject NP of its clause. Within the framework of the Aspects model (Chapter 8), it would be desirable to represent the Deep Structures of R3 as containing two occurrences of the item *Jake* in E10(a) and two occurrences of the item *Martha* in E10(b). Given such Deep Structures as the input to the semantic interpretive component, the correct readings or meanings of the sequences of E10 would be automatically derived. We need, then, the transformation R3:

R3. REFLEXIVIZATION   X   NP   Y   NP   Z
    Structural Index   1   2   3   4   5
    Structural Change   1   2   3   4   5
                                   [+ reflex]
        where 2 = 4

This rule will convert the tree E13(a) underlying E11(a) into E13(b):

E13. (a)   (b)

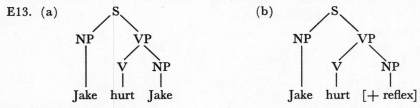

The configuration

    NP
  [+ reflex]

is spelled out in the phonological component as *himself*.[2]

---

[2] Notice that the information as to the gender of the item originally there is needed to determine the phonological shape of the pronoun; that is *he,* not *she.*

The RAISING Rule

The RAISING rule relates the (a) and (b) versions of E14 and E15.

E14. (a) Jake believed that Martha was an idiot.
     (b) Jake believed Martha to be an idiot.

E15. (a) It seems that Adolph has arrived.
     (b) Adolph seems to have arrived.

The transformation has as its function the raising of the subject NP of an embedded clause into the next highest dominating clause. The tree for E14 (namely, E16) shows the effect of this transformation.

E16. (a)

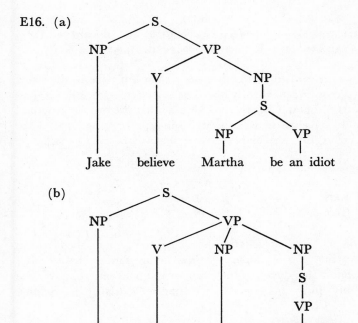

(b)

There are several ways in which one can argue to demonstrate the fact that the NP subject of the embedded clause has been raised into the object position of the next higher clause. One indication is the fact that the verbal form of the embedded clause is always nonfinite, usually taken to be an indication that the subject of that clause is missing. Perhaps a more satisfying argument is one making use of the Clause Mate property of Reflexives in English. Notice that the Reflexive (as predicted by the

Clause Mate restriction) is not possible in the case of a nonraised embedded subject NP, E17(b):

E17. (a) Sam$_j$ expected that he$_i$ would be able to see the Apocalypse.
      (*b) Sam$_i$ expected himself would be able to see the Apocalypse.

As we mentioned before, the RAISING rule (R4) raises the subject NP of the embedded sentence into the immediately dominating VP. Thus, the rule has the effect of creating new Clause Mates. If the rule is correctly stated, we should be able to raise an embedded subject NP into a higher clause that contains a coreferential NP in subject position in that higher clause; that is, to create the proper environment for the rule of REFLEXIVIZA-TION, R3.

E18. (a) Sam$_i$ expected that he would be able to see the Apocalypse.
      (b) Sam$_i$ expected himself$_i$ to be able to see the Apocalypse.

The prediction is thus verified by the presence of the Reflexive in the string E18(b). Since we know independently that the REFLEXIVIZATION rule requires Clause Mates in its Structural Index, the only way that the proper structural configuration could have arisen was through some process that moved the embedded subject NP into the higher clause; that is, the rule of RAISING:

R4. RAISING   X   V   [NP Y]   Z
                                     $_S$ $_S$

	X	V	[NP	Y]	Z
Structural Index	1	2	3	4	5
Structural Change	1	2 + 3	Ø	4	5

The existence of the rule of RAISING has been well established within transformational work. For example, we saw in an earlier chapter that under certain conditions there is the transformational insertion of the semantically empty form *there*—as, for instance, in E19(a)—yielding E19(b).

E19. (a) A boy is in the garden.
      (b) There is a boy in the garden.

Now consider the triplet E20(a), (b), (c).

E20. (a) Martha believed that a boy was in the garden.
      (b) Martha believed that there was a boy in the garden.
      (c) Martha believed there to be a boy in the garden.

The preceding examples make it obvious that either the rule of RAISING is to be included in the grammar of English or that we must specify a rule of THERE insertion for object position. But notice that the latter suggestion is not even coherent, since the rule would have to be constrained so that it would apply only in the case that there was a sentence of the form that was the normal environment for THERE insertion and which was embedded immediately below the clause into which the *there* must be inserted in object position. In addition, if such a solution is to be attempted, then one will also be required to accept a PSG rule, such as R5, in the base component.

R5. $S \rightarrow \emptyset \, VP$

A number of arguments[3] can be presented for the existence of RAISING, making use of peculiar restrictions displayed by certain lexical items in English. For example, notice the following restriction:

E21.   (a)   Anyone is able to do that.
      (*b)   Anyone is unable to do that.

The same restrictions appear in the case where we see that R4 has applied:

E22.   (a)   Anyone seems to be able to do that.
      (*b)   Anyone seems to be unable to do that.

If the grammar contains a rule of RAISING to derive the sequences E22(a) and (b) from the sequences E23(a) and (b), respectively, then the well-formedness of the (a) versions and the ill-formedness of the (b) versions is immediately explicable with reference to the same constraint as the one that marks E21(b) as ill-formed but allows E21(a).

E23.   (a)   It seems that anyone is able to do that.
      (*b)   It seems that anyone is unable to do that.

In any grammar of English that does not contain the rule of RAISING (or some equivalent mechanism), the constraint involving items such as *anyone* and *unable* must be stated at least twice: once for the simple case where they both appear in the clause (such as E21) and again for the complex sentences such as E22. In addition, of course, there exist surface sequences where the rule of RAISING has applied repeatedly; the triplet E24 shows the process.

---

[3] These arguments are taken from an unpublished paper by Postal in which he presents 40 distinct arguments for the transformation Raising.

E24. (a)   It appears that it is likely that anyone will be $\left\{ \begin{matrix} \text{able} \\ \text{*unable} \end{matrix} \right\}$ to do that.
  (b)   It appears that anyone is likely to be $\left\{ \begin{matrix} \text{able} \\ \text{*unable} \end{matrix} \right\}$ to do that.
  (c)   Anyone appears to be likely to be $\left\{ \begin{matrix} \text{able} \\ \text{*unable} \end{matrix} \right\}$ to do that.

The fact that the item *anyone* can be raised twice as in E24(c) and the fact that the result is still well formed if the item *able* occurs, but is ill formed if the item *unable* occurs, forces anyone attempting to specify a grammar of English without the rule of RAISING to state the *anyone–unable* constraint minimally three times. If additional cases can be found, say, where the item *anyone* is moved n times by the rule of RAISING, then in the grammar that does not include the rule, the constraint must be stated n times. Even if this solution were to prove coherent, it is nevertheless obvious that such a grammar, containing n statements of the constraint, would be highly redundant and would fail to capture the generalization about the relation between the items *anyone* and *unable* in those n cases. Notice that the domain of application for the two rules PASSIVE and RAISING is different (as can be seen by an inspection of their structural indices): The PASSIVE applies to terms within a simple clause, but the rule of RAISING has a structural index that requires that a minimum of two clauses be involved.

The Argument for the Cycle

We now have the information necessary to present the classic argument from syntax for the cyclic ordering of transformations. We begin by noticing that there are pairs such as the (a) and (b) versions of E25 where the PASSIVE has applied in the embedded clause.

E25. (a)   Jake believed that John irritated Martha.
  (b)   Jake believed that Martha was irritated by John.

The new subject of the embedded clause, the derived subject, is in the proper structural position to be lifted by RAISING. E25(c) shows us that this is correct.

E25. (c)   Jake believed Martha to have been irritated by John.

Thus far we have seen that the order must be PASSIVE $>$ RAISING to derive E25(c). To finish the argument, we need only point out that E25(d) is a well-formed sequence.

E25. (d)   Martha was believed by Jake to have been irritated by John.

We know independently that the PASSIVE applies, interchanging the subject and object NP within a clause; obviously E25(d) is derived from E25(c) by the PASSIVE. But for the PASSIVE to apply, moving the NP *Martha* into subject position in the highest clause, the NP *Martha* must first have been raised into object position in the highest clause by the rule of RAISING. Further, for the rule of RAISING to have applied to lift the NP *Martha* into the higher clause, the NP *Martha* had to be moved into subject position within the lower clause by the PASSIVE transformation. Thus, we can conclude that the order of application must have been PASSIVE > RAISING > PASSIVE. If the derivation of other sequences is examined [say, that of E26(b) with respect to E26(a)], it becomes obvious that a cyclic principle is required.[4]

E26. (a)   Maxine thought that Jake believed that John irritated Martha.
     (b)   Martha was thought by Maxine to have been believed by Jake
           to have been irritated by John.

A careful examination of E26(b) will reveal that the order of application of the two transformations in question must have been

PASSIVE > RAISING > PASSIVE > RAISING > PASSIVE

Arguments such as these have motivated the adoption of the cyclic application of transformations. Transformations[5] are ordered with respect to each other and are then applied as a set to the most deeply embedded clause(s) in the Deep Structure tree representation. When all transformations whose structural indices are met have applied, the cycle is complete for that portion of the tree. The set of linearly ordered rules is then applied to the next most deeply embedded clause in the tree representation. The process is iterative, terminating when the entire tree structure has been subjected to the set of transformations.

---

[4] Kimball (1971) has argued for a noncyclic grammar that attempts to handle the same set of data.

[5] It should be pointed out that not all transformations are cyclic. There has been argued to be a set of transformations that are postcyclic, that is, they apply on the last cycle after all the cyclic transformations have applied; see Postal (1971c) for a lucid discussion.

The set of cyclic transformations that obviously includes the PASSIVE and RAISING then applies to the most deeply embedded clause first; that is to S^3, using the tree structure E27 underlying E26 as an example:

E27. (a) Cycle 1 on S^3: RAISING not applicable; PASSIVE applies.

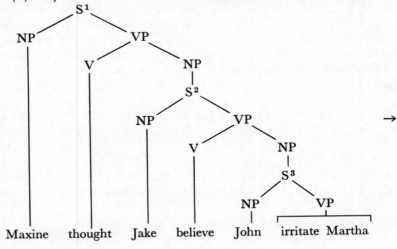

→

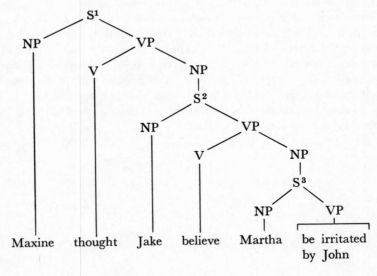

(b)   Cycle 2 on S² and cycle 3 on S¹: RAISING applies, PASSIVE applies.

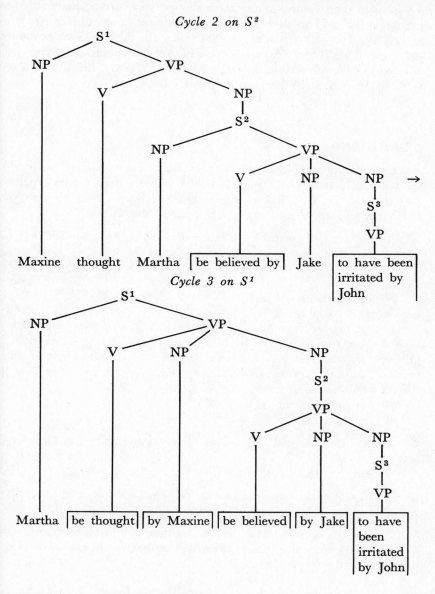

Cycle 2 on S²

Cycle 3 on S¹

The set of trees in E27 shows the effect of the cyclic application of the two rules of RAISING and PASSIVE as they combine to move the original Deep Structure object of the most deeply embedded clause into the subject position of the highest clause in Surface Structure.

In this chapter we have discussed the interrelationship of various rules. Their interaction demonstrates that a simple linear arrangement of transformations will not account for the set of relations in the surface structures of English. This fact provides the motivation for the cyclic application of transformations. The cyclic application of rules in the grammar has been claimed to be a universal of natural language (Chomsky, 1965b:29), a universal in the sense to be discussed in Chapter 13.

EXERCISES

One of the main issues discussed in this chapter was the question of the relations that can be argued to hold between different transformations in the grammar. The following exercises are intended to increase your familiarity with arguments for one such relation, that of ordering.

1. Assume that the correct formulation of the transformation which moves question words to the front of the sentence is (a):

(a)	X	Wh + Noun Phrase	Y	WH-Q MOVEMENT (obligatory)
Structural Index	1	2	3	
Structural Change	2 + 1	Ø	3	

Show what the ordering must be between Wh-Q Movement and each of the following transformations by presenting a set of strings that would be predicted by one order and comparing it with a set of strings that would be predicted by the other order. Thus, show that only one order produces the correct set of surface structures.

    A. PASSIVE (optional)
    B. REFLEXIVIZATION (obligatory)

2. Assume that the ordering between THERE INSERTION (in Chapter 6) and PASSIVE is

    THERE INSERTION > PASSIVE

Give a series of examples of ungrammatical sentences that would be derived with this order.

3. Assume the opposite order for the transformations of Exercise 2; give a series of examples of grammatical sentences that would not be derived if this were not the correct order.

ANSWERS

1. Assume that the ordering is as follows:

    WH-Q MOVEMENT > PASSIVE

Given an underlying structure such as the one indicated by

    (a)   Martha thought that Wh + someone kissed Elizabeth,

and the order indicated, the grammar includes derivations that result in the well-formed string

    (b)   Who did Martha think kissed Elizabeth?

Notice, however, that the well-formed string (c) will not be generated under this ordering assumption:

    (c)   Who did Martha think that Elizabeth was kissed by?

This is true because if the transformation WH-Q MOVEMENT (obligatory) applies prior to the transformation PASSIVE, it will remove the embedded subject NP (*Wh + someone*) and the resulting tree structure will not be properly analyzeable with respect to the structural index of PASSIVE. The other ordering,

    PASSIVE > WH-Q MOVEMENT

will yield both strings.

    Assume the following order:

    WH-Q MOVEMENT > REFLEXIVIZATION

Given the underlying structure represented by

    (d)   Martha thought that Wh + someone$_i$ liked someone$_i$, and the order specified, the grammar includes derivations that result in the ill-formed string

    (e)   *Who$_i$ did Martha think liked him$_i$?

Further, the grammar fails to include the well-formed string

    (f)   Who$_i$ did Martha think liked himself$_i$?

The reverse order will yield the correct results.

2.   Some examples of ungrammatical strings generated under this hypothesis are

    *A great noise was arose by there

from

    There arose a great noise.

    *A small boy was been in the garden by there.

from

    There was a small boy in the garden.

    *A unicorn eating cabbage was come by there.

from

    There came a unicorn eating cabbage.

3.   Some examples of grammatical strings that would not be generated if the correct order were not PASSIVE > THERE INSERTION are

    There was believed to be a dragon in the pipe.

    There was rumored to be joy in the kitchen.

    There was said to be an end to all this.

Chapter 10

Generative Semantics
versus
the Extended Standard Theory

In the period since the publication of the first complete transformational model for natural language (the Aspects model), there has been an explosion of research. The majority of this research has been reported in mimeographed papers circulated in the linguistics departments of an ever increasing number of universities. This research has uncovered a number of phenomena whose impact has been to challenge even some of the most basic assumptions about the organization of the grammar presented in the Aspects model. The present state of transformational linguistics is not the monolithic structure suggested by the Aspects model. Even the author of the Aspects model (Chomsky, 1965a) appears to have rejected important segments of the grammar. We may begin to explore these changes by reviewing some of the claims upon which the Aspects model was based and which have since been challenged.

As we discussed earlier, the task of Katz and Postal (1964) was to establish the following thesis:

T1. Transformations are meaning-preserving operations.

Such a thesis was necessary for the claim that the Deep Structure was the correct level of structure for the interpretation by the Semantic Interpretive Component, which establishes the meaning of the sequence. Another way of stating T1 is to say that the Deep Structure contains sufficient information to specify the meaning(s) of the tree structure, which is then mapped into the Surface Structure. This mapping by transformation, while radically altering the syntactic structure, preserved the meaning of the Deep Structure tree. With the publication of the Aspects model, T1 became axiomatic, assuming the character of a methodological assumption, perhaps more accurately stated as

A1. No transformation if properly formulated changes meaning.

The separation of levels of analysis insisted upon by the structuralists' school was respected in the Aspects model, since the semantic and syntactic components were independent, articulating only at the point of Deep Structure. Each component possessed its own set of mechanisms (projection rules and transformations), whose operation typically handled distinct sets of objects (sets of semantic markers and Phrase Markers) that resulted in different formal objects (Amalgamated Paths and final derived Phrase Markers, or Surface Structures).[1]

In order to understand the two major conflicting orientations present within transformational grammar at present, we may consider one of the phenomena that (as used by G. Lakoff, 1969) provoked the original split of transformational grammar into Generative Semantics and the Extended Standard Theory (the term used by Chomsky, 1969). Note that the following two points are beyond dispute: First, for the Aspects model to function properly, it was necessary to defend T1. Second, the transformation called PASSIVE was a transformation to be included within the English grammar. Given these two points, consider the meaning relationship between E1(a) and (b), two sequences that are obviously related by the PASSIVE.

E1. (a) Many people don't accept the present social structure.
    (b) The present social structure isn't accepted by many people.

A careful consideration of the sequences E1(a) and (b) will reveal that they are not, in fact, synonymous. The fact, for example, that E2(a), but not E2(b), is considered by most speakers of American English to be well formed shows that they are not semantically equivalent.

E2. (a) Many people don't accept the present social structure, but many people do accept it.
    (*b) The present social structure isn't accepted by many people, but many people do accept it.

[1] More correctly, the result of the syntactic derivation of a Phrase Marker is the input to the phonological component. The Surface Structure is a term usually reserved for the result of the phonological interpretation of the final derived Phrase Marker.

The sequences E1(b) and E2(b) are obviously counterexamples to T1 as it is presently formulated. The dilemma is clear. There is a set of cases (all previous examples of PASSIVE) in which application of the transformation PASSIVE has no semantic effect (that is, is consistent with T1), but in another set of cases (E1, for example) its application causes a change in meaning. In such cases, the resultant Surface Structures have different interpretations, depending on whether the PASSIVE has applied in the derivation.

On the one hand, the alternative of rejecting the PASSIVE as a transformation in English grammar is unacceptable; yet if the transformation is accepted, the problem of capturing the meaning difference arises.

Notice that the set of cases in which the meaning difference appears can be characterized quite easily. Individuals studying the system of language, whether natural languages or artificial ones, have distinguished a special set of terms, sometimes referring to them as Logical Predicates. This set includes what are called the Quantifiers (*all, every, some, . . .*) and the Negation Predicate *not* (or more accurately, in the linguistic framework, the Abstract Predicate NEG). The set of cases in which the PASSIVE will cause a meaning shift, if allowed to apply, can now be identified as just those cases where its application would cause two logical predicates to cross (to reverse their linear order). Schematically, using the sequences E1 as an example,

E3. (a)   many, . . . , not, . . . $= E1(a)$
    (b)   not, . . . many, . . . $= E1(b)$

Support for this claim (that is, that the Logical Predicate crossing, not the PASSIVE itself, is the relevant feature in the meaning difference) comes from a consideration of other pairs of sequences related by Permutation transformations other than the PASSIVE, whose application has reversed the order of logical predicates. If the claim that the relevant factor in the meaning difference between the sequences such as E1(a) and (b) is the fact that one logical predicate has crossed another, then the meaning difference should occur whenever two logical predicates are permuted, no matter which transformation causes the shift.

It has been claimed that there is a transformation in English grammar that relates pairs like[2]

E4. (a)   Jack thought that Bob wasn't quite right.
    (b)   Jack didn't think that Bob was quite right.

Notice that the transformation called NEG Transportation apparently raises the logical operator NEG from the lower clause into the one immediately

[2] See R. Lakoff (1969) and Lindholm (1969).

dominating. In doing so, it appears to cause the NEG to cross the subject NP position of the embedded clause.[3] By placing a quantifier in the subject position of the embedded clause, we may test the claim.

E5. (a) Jack thought that many people weren't quite right.
     (b) Jack didn't think that many people were quite right.

Once again the meaning difference can be made to emerge by appending an additional clause, as in E6(a) and (b).

E6. (a) Jack thought that many people weren't quite right, but he thought that many were.
     (*b) Jack didn't think that many people were quite right, but he thought that many were.

Both positions agree that the generalization to be captured is one that is to be stated with respect to the crossing of logical predicates, not the PASSIVE or any other particular Permutation transformation. More specifically, advocates of the two positions agree that the problem is one of scope. The logical operator *not* is said to be within the scope of the logical predicate *many* in E3(a); the converse is true of E3(b). The meaning difference associated with the different scopes is illustrated by the pairs E2 and E6.[4]

The response to this dilemma by the transformational linguists divides them into factions favoring two different approaches, known as Generative Semantics and the Extended Standard Theory. We consider the Extended Standard Theory first.

[3] Within the theoretical framework where this transformation is usually accepted, the Logical Predicate NEG would have a Deep Structure representation in which it appears outside the clause in which it actually appears in Surface Structure; thus, the statement that the transformation NEG TRANSPORTATION raises the NEG element out of the clause that also contains the MANY predicate. The example works and is relevant, as within the framework involved the predicate MANY is itself a higher predicate; thus the effect of the NEG TRANSPORTATION is, in fact, to cause a crossing of the two logical predicates. We return to the question of higher predicates shortly in the text.

[4] The meaning difference within the pairs E2 and E6 is an illustration of the typical difference in the scope of Logical Predicates. One additional example may assist the reader. Compare the following pair:
   (i)   Everyone loves someone.
   (ii) Someone is loved by everyone.
The sequence (i) describes a situation where, for any arbitrary person you meet, it's true that that person loves some other individual. On the other hand, (ii) describes a situation where there is at least one person whom everybody else loves. Hence, in the world described by (i), there may be no single individual such that everyone else loves him.

The linguists who support the Extended Standard Theory (hereafter EST) typically respond to this dilemma by

1. giving up the hypothesis that transformations are meaning-preserving operations;
2. proposing an additional set of projection rules (often called rules of Surface Interpretation).

These new projection rules are, of course, defined on derived structure, that is, on the tree structures that exist post-transformationally. We will call these type P_2, to distinguish them from the set of projection rules that applies to Deep Structure trees, type P_1. This interpretive solution is not yet explicit, as the linguists who are developing it have not yet presented an actual rule of interpretation for derived trees. In the absence of such an example, there cannot be any discussion of the formal nature of these rules. There are a number of questions that would have to be answered with regard to these interpretive rules. For example, what constraints (if any) apply to them? Do they represent a totally new kind of rule or are they (as their name suggests) formally related to the projection rules defined on Deep Structures (type P_1) in the Aspects system? Are they obligatory or optional? Are they contingent on the presence of some semantic element or syntactic element or do they simply apply each time a particular transformation or set of transformations applies? These questions must of course be deferred until the position is made more clear by the linguists proposing the rules. Although no formal mechanisms have been proposed, it is clear from the discussions reported that the notion of scope is regarded as the crucial notion with respect to Logical Predicate crossing.

Linguists who support the Generative Semantics (GS) position have responded to the dilemma by extending the assumption regarding the meaning-preserving hypothesis to derivations. This response is quite natural, considering the chronological development of the concept of Deep Structure within the transformational theory. As we noted previously, if the meaning-preserving hypothesis with respect to transformations is correct, then (by implication) the meaning of any particular tree structure is constant across the set of structures in the entire derivation. It is important to see why this is so. For any particular tree structure S_i, its meaning can either be read directly off the Deep Structure or off any other arbitrary tree structure S_j that appears in the derivation of S_i, provided there exists some transformation T_i that accepts S_i as input (that is, S_i is properly analyzeable with respect to the Structural Index of T_i) and produces S_j as output; the meaning is constant. Since T_i, being a transformation, is subject to A1, we may safely conclude that S_i and S_j mean the same thing. But now notice that for any two contiguous trees in a derivation, S_i and S_j are related by a transformation. Being so related, then, by A1, they mean the same thing. Thus, we see that derivations preserve meanings.

Specifically, the response by Generative Semantics (hereafter GS) to the meaning differences between pairs of sequences involving Logical Predicates and apparently related by some particular Permutation transformation is to point out that the two sequences in question must be derived from distinct Deep Structures because they mean different things; in particular, consider the pair E1(a) and (b). The semantic representations for these two strings would be E7(a) and (b) respectively.[5]

E7. (a) Many { people, [NEG, < accept { people, present social structure } >] }

  (b) NEG { Many, [people < accept { people, present social structure } >] }

The important point about the representations in E7 is that the difference in meaning corresponds to the different order of logical predicates. In the case of E7(a), NEG is in the scope of *many,* while in E7(b) *many* occurs within the scope of NEG. Independent of this phenomenon, the generative semanticist would propose that Logical Predicates be represented by clauses higher in underlying tree structures. Thus, the Deep Structures for E1(a) and (b) would be E8(a) and (b):

E8. (a)

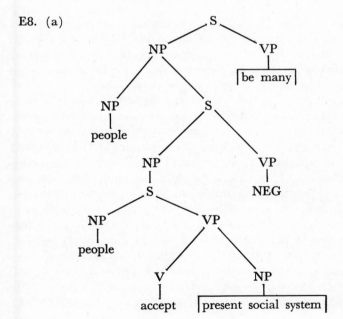

---

[5] It is quite easy to develop an algorithm or mechanical procedure for converting bracketed structure such as E7 to tree structures of the type used for the representation of linguistic objects.

(b)

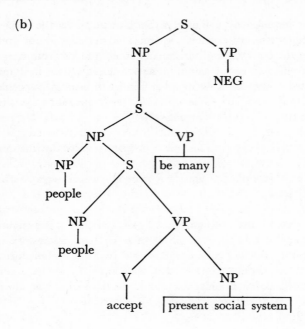

Given the existence of these distinct Deep Structures, GS will make the general statement that the relative height of Logical Predicates in Deep Structure must correspond to their left-to-right order in their various Surface Structures.[6] In particular, in this case, given two logical predicates L_i and L_j and a Deep Structure in which L_i appears in a clause that dominates the clause in which L_j appears, L_i must appear to the left of L_j in Surface Structure. Notice that in this formulation no transformations are mentioned; rather, the generalization is about the relative scopes of logical predicates in Deep Structures and Surface Structures. The constraint regarding logical predicates may then be viewed as a constraint that determines the well-formedness of derivations. Thus, the transformations apply freely to any tree structure that is properly analyzeable with respect to the Structural Index of that transformation. Any derivation that terminates in a Surface Structure where the order of logical predicates does not conform to the configurations specified by the constraint is ill formed. Constraints like the Logical Predicate Constraint are referred to as Derivational Constraints.

The Deep Structure trees proposed by GS for E1(a) and (b) and the Deep Structure trees proposed by EST tend to be quite different. Here lies one of the major conceptual differences between the two approaches.

[6] A more accurate version of this constraint would be complicated by additional factors such as the dominance relations that hold in Surface Structure. See G. Lakoff (1970b) for a full discussion.

The EST has a base component not unlike that contained in the Aspects base. This base component enumerates the set of Deep Structure trees, which are then subjected to semantic interpretation by the projection rules (type P_1) in the Interpretive Semantic Component, resulting in Amalgamated Paths that give the meaning of that Deep Structure (or possibly a partial meaning, which will be completed by the projection rules that operate on derived structure). The GS model, on the other hand, attempts a simplification of the theoretical apparatus. Claiming that trees constitute an adequate notation for the semantic relations involved in the meaning of the sequences of natural language, GS proposes to do away entirely with projection rules and identify Deep Structure by semantic representation. The semantic representation of any tree *is* the Deep Structure of that tree.

EST maintains, then, the position that the syntactic and semantic levels of natural language must not be mixed in analysis, the position held over from the structuralist school. The GS denies the necessity of such a separation, maintaining that there is no difference in the set of formal objects that represent semantic and syntactic structures (namely, trees). We can represent the two positions by means of the schema F1:

F1. (a) Extended Standard Theory

$AP_i, AP_{i+1}, \ldots, AP_j \qquad PM_i, PM_{i+1}, \ldots, PM_{i+k}$

$\begin{bmatrix} \text{produced by} \\ \text{projection rules } (P_1) \end{bmatrix}$ $\qquad$ $\begin{bmatrix} \text{produced by transformations and, in some} \\ \text{cases, with semantic structures produced} \\ \text{by projection rules (type 2)} \end{bmatrix}$

where AP $\quad$ = Amalgamated Path

PM $\quad$ = phrase marker

PM_i $\quad$ = deep structure

PM_{i+k} = surface structure

(b) Generative Semantics

$PM_i, PM_{i+1}, \ldots, PM_{i+k}$

$\begin{bmatrix} \text{produced by} \\ \text{transformations} \end{bmatrix}$

where PM $\quad$ = phrase marker

PM_i $\quad$ = deep structure (the semantic representation)

PM_{i+k} = surface structure.

Of more interest than schema F1 (or any comparative list of mechanisms employed by the two theories) are the differences that they possess in their ability to explain natural language phenomena. For the remainder of this chapter, we will consider some of these differences.

In particular, we will focus on those arguments that have been claimed to distinguish between the two theories.

The REMIND Argument

In a recent article, Postal (1970a) presented a particularly interesting argument for the GS model. He began by pointing out that sentences such as E9 and E10 are near-paraphrases.

E9.   (a)   John strikes me as being similar to Harry.
      (b)   It strikes me that John and Harry are similar.

E10. John reminds me of Harry.

If this is so, reasons Postal, the Deep Structures of E9 and E10 will be similar if not identical. Remember that in the GS model the Deep Structure of a sentence is its semantic representation. Suppose that we agree to represent meanings by English words in capital letters: The meaning that the word in capital letters represents will be quite close to the meaning of that word. For example, we will use the symbol SIMILAR to represent the meaning of the word *similar*. Postal postulated the structure E11 as the Deep Structure for E9 and E10.[7]

E11.

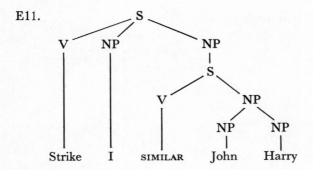

[7] The reader will notice that there has been a shift from underlying trees that show the V-node occurring to the right of the nominal node that is considered the underlying subject to a system of representation in which the leftmost node under the S is the V-node. The claim made by such a representation is that English is a Verb-Initial language in Deep Structure. The fact that many English sentences such as questions begin with a verb is a result that follows from this claim without any special statement. The fact that other sentences of English require a surface subject preceding the verb in Surface Structure is accounted for by a transformation that moves the first nominal node after the verb to a position immediately preceding the verb at a specified point in the derivation. The claim that English is a Verb-Subject-Object language was first presented by McCawley (1970a). The arguments for this claim are, without exception, methodological in nature. For example, the formulation of PASSIVE is significantly simplified.

McCawley presented a series of such simplification arguments that motivate the Verb-Initial formulation for English. We adopt the representation for the remainder of this chapter.

Postal argued at length for the derivation of E9 and E10 from the Deep Structure E11. For our purposes, we may consider only a fragment of one such argument. Note that the sentences in E12 and E13 are unacceptable.

E12. (*a) John$_i$ strikes me as being similar to himself$_i$.
      (*b) It strikes me that John$_i$ is similar to himself$_i$.

E13. *John$_i$ reminds me of himself$_i$.

We can immediately argue that E12(a) and (b) are to be excluded by a very general constraint to the effect that conjunctions of coreferential NP are ill formed. Thus, such a constraint is needed independently in the grammar because of sequences such as E14, and is therefore well motivated.

E14. (*a) John$_i$ and $\begin{bmatrix} \text{he}_i \\ \text{him}_i \end{bmatrix}$ are similar.
      (*b) John$_i$ and himself$_i$ are similar.
      (*c) $\begin{bmatrix} \text{he}_i \\ \text{him}_i \end{bmatrix}$ and John$_i$ are similar.
      (*d) Himself$_i$ and John$_i$ are similar.

Since both E12(a) and (b) are derived from the ill-formed Deep Structure E15, they are both excluded by the constraint.

E15.

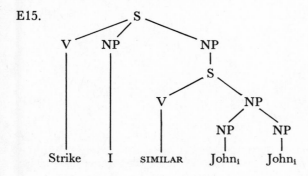

The explanation of the deviancy of E13 distinguishes nicely between the two theories. The GS model claims that the Deep Structure of E13 is the ill-formed Deep Structure E15; thus the deviancy of E13 is automatically explained in terms of an independently justified constraint. The EST, on the other hand, will point to the same constraint in accounting for the deviancy of E12 and E14, but since the Deep Structure of E13 is not E15 in that theory, some different constraint will have to be proposed. Presumably, the constraint will be highly specific—something to the effect that the surface subject of the verb *remind* may not be an NP that is coreferential with the object of the preposition *of* in the structure *NP remind NP of*

NP. Thus, what in the GS approach is a unified phenomenon appears to require two constraints in the EST.

The Notion of Possible Lexical Item

An examination of the schema F1(a) and (b), which list the mechanisms and objects to be found in the two approaches, indicates that the only mechanism included in the GS model is the transformation.[8] Such a claim is coherent only in a theory in which semantic representations are identified with the objects over which transformations are defined; namely, tree structures. In addition to simplifying the theory, the fact that the transformation is the only mechanism that operates on semantic representations relating one to another, combined with the constraint T2 on Lexicalization (the conversion of semantic material into a set of phonological and syntactic markers—in general, a word), gives an explicit characterization to the notion of possible lexical item.[9]

T2. Lexicalization is restricted to constituents.

Considering the abstract tree E16, lexicalization could replace the subtree *ab* or the subtree *ef* or the subtree *def* but not *abc, bc, cd, de,* or any other subtree of S.

E16.

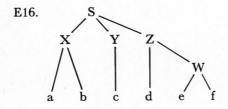

McCawley proposed that the semantic representation for a sequence such as E17,

E17. Sam killed Pete.

would be:

---

[8] This is not entirely accurate, as the operation that substitutes actual lexical items for constituents of the tree structure is obviously a necessary component of the GS model. A similar mechanism will be required by the EST.

[9] This condition was first proposed by McCawley (1968a).

E18.

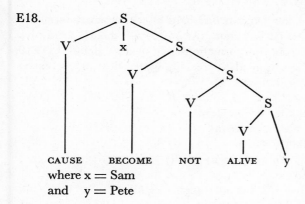

where x = Sam
and   y = Pete

In addition, McCawley proposed the transformation PREDICATE RAISING, which lifts a lower predicate into the next higher clause, adjoining it to the predicate of that clause. Successive applications of PREDICATE RAISING will produce the following structures, given E18 as input:

E19. (a)

(b)

(c)

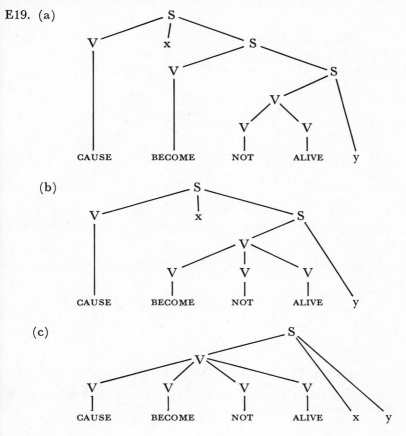

The transformation PREDICATE RAISING has as its effect the creation of new constituents. Thus, because T2 is a constraint in the GS model, there must be a direct relation between transformations and lexical items. In E19, since the transformation has applied to create new constituents, we expect and have the following lexicalizations:

E20. (a) Sam caused Bill to become dead.
          (E19)a) : NOT ALIVE = dead)
     (b) Sam caused Bill to die.
          (E19(b) : BECOME NOT ALIVE) = die
     (c) Sam killed Bill.
          (E19(c) : CAUSE BECOME NOT ALIVE) = kill

The fact that there is this indirect relation between transformations and lexicalizations, and the fact that there exist a number of constraints defined over the set of transformations, allow us to make the distinction in question. Consider the Deep Structure E21.[10]

E21.

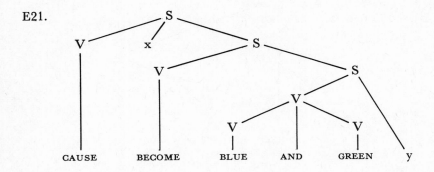

Given the transformation PREDICATE RAISING and E21, we expect the following derived trees:

[10] The elements in the tree structure in capital letters are intended to represent bundles of semantic features.

E22. (a)

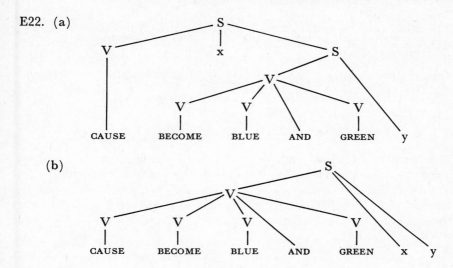

(b)

The claim, then, within the GS model is that the tree structures E22(a) and (b) represent possible, although not actually occurring, lexical items. E22(a) and (b) are to be sharply distinguished from E23(a) and (b).

E23. (a)

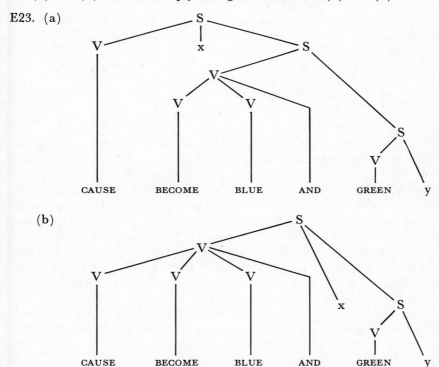

(b)

The claim by the GS model is that E23(a) and (b) do not represent a possible lexical item in any language. E24 shows how these two trees would have to be used:

E24. (a)   Sam caused Bill to phond green.
            (*phond* = BECOME BLUE AND)
     (b)   Sam phondened Bill green.
            (*phonden* = CAUSE BECOME BLUE AND)

The reason that *phond* and *phonden* do not represent possible, but not occurring, lexical items is that there exists a well-motivated constraint defined over transformations called the C(onjoined) S(tructure) C(onstraint), Ross (1967b); the CSC says, in effect, that no transformation may move a portion of a Conjoined Structure. The term Conjoined Structure is illustrated by the schema E25:

E25.

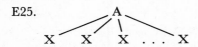

Notice that the lowest predicate in the Deep Structure E25 meets the criterion for Conjoined Structure:

E26.

The argument now becomes clear. A lexical item may exist only in the case where there exists some constituent that it may replace; the only way the subtrees BECOME BLUE AND and CAUSE BECOME BLUE AND could have arisen is for the transformation PREDICATE RAISING to have raised the predicate BLUE AND out of the Conjoined Structure E26; therefore, the constituents BECOME BLUE AND and CAUSE BECOME BLUE AND can never arise, and there are no lexical items with the meaning of the nonoccurring constituents.

Notice that the argument depends crucially on the fact that the mechanism that creates constituents is a transformation and is therefore subject to the CSC, a constraint well defined for tree structures only. As yet, there has been no discussion of the counterparts of constraints such as the CSC in the Interpretive Semantic Component. Such constraints would presumably be defined over the set of possible projection rules. Thus far, then, there is no characterization of the notion of possible lexical item within the EST.

The SCOPE AMBIGUITY Argument

Morgan (1969) pointed out that the sequence E27 is ambiguous:

E27. Sam almost killed Pete.

The ambiguities of E27 may be paraphrased by E28:

E28. (a) Sam caused Bill to become almost dead.
    (b). Sam caused Bill to almost become dead.
    (c) Sam almost caused Bill to become dead.

In the GS model, the scope ambiguity is accounted for by the fact that the word *almost*[11] could be attached to any of the S-nodes of E18; within the EST, it is not clear how the scope ambiguity is to be accounted for.

The DERIVED NOMINALS Argument

Consider the meaning relations between the three sequences of E29:

E29. (a) That John criticized the book surprised no one.
    (b) John's criticizing the book surprised no one.
    (c) John's criticism of the book surprised no one.

For most speakers of English, the (a) and (b) variants of E29 are paraphrases. On the other hand, while there are obvious phonological, syntactic, and semantic similarities between the (a) and (b) variants (as a unit) and the (c) version, it is very difficult for most speakers to accept (c) as a paraphrase of (a) and (b). The difficulty is that one surely wants to maintain a transformational relation between the (a) and (b) sequences, but how are the similarities that exist between the (c) sequence and the other two to be captured? Within the GS framework, since the only mechanism available to capture such relations is the transformation, one must provide motivated, distinct Deep Structures. Chomsky (1968a) cataloged the differential syntactic and semantic behavior displayed by so-called gerundive nominals E29(b) and the derived nominals E29(c). For example, he pointed out that while the structure of the (a) versions of E30 and E31 would seem to be close, if not identical, and that both have associated gerundive nominals [the (b) versions], the derived nominal is possible in only one of the cases.

[11] Logically, there is a missing scope ambiguity, the one where the scope of *almost* is the lowest predicate in tree structure E18 alone.

E30. (a)   John is easy to please.
      (b)   John's being easy to please. . . .
     (*c)   John's easiness to please. . . .

E31. (a)   John is eager to please.
      (b)   John's being eager to please. . . .
      (c)   John's eagerness to please. . . .

Or, once again, it would appear that derived nominals, but not gerundive nominals, have internal structure as the differences in the (b) versions of the following sequences suggest:

E32. (a)   The proof of the theorem. . . .
     (*b)   The proving of the theorem. . . .

E33. (a)   John's unmotivated criticism of the book. . . .
     (*b)   John's unmotivated criticizing of the book. . . .

The EST approach to the explanation of the (b) differences takes the following form: The lexicon may include an entry for the item *criticism,* say, separate from the lexical entry for the item *criticize.* The fact that one, but not the other (or more accurately, the derived nominals like the item *criticism* but not the gerundive nominals derived transformationally from the other entry *criticize*), of the forms involved may occur in certain syntactic environments would be registered in the lexical entry for those items. The portions of the two items that are identical would be handled by relating the two forms within the lexicon itself by means of lexical rules. There has, as yet, been no successful attempt to treat this subject within the GS approach.

In this chapter we have indicated briefly what we feel are the major developments since the publication of the Aspects model. We have presented an outline of the positions that now serve as the research frameworks within which work is presently being done and reported. The last portion of the chapter concerned itself with some of the arguments that have been presented, to show the desirability of one system over the other.

EXERCISES

1. In the Aspects model and in the research that immediately succeeded it, there was a general constraint to the effect that transformations could not act either singly or in combination to change the node label that

dominated a lexical item. Thus, once a lexical item was substituted under a labeled node *n,* it was necessarily true that that lexical item would be dominated in surface structure by the node labeled *n.* In all formulations of the transformation EQUI-NP DELETION, the transformation has been written so that the relation of coreference, which must hold between the two nodes involved, holds between two nominal nodes. What is the point of the following examples with respect to the two claims presented above?

(a)   (i)   That America attempted to withdraw surprised Max.
       (ii)   The American attempt to withdraw surprised Max.

(b)   (i)   That Russia desired to sign the treaty was obvious to all.
       (ii)   The Russian desire to sign the treaty was obvious to all.

2.   Find an additional example of scope ambiguity and describe the ambiguity.

3.   Using the sequence given as your answer to Exercise 2, demonstrate how application of the same transformation would make clear the problem of scope. That is, is there more than one possible surface string that can result from the application of some transformation in this case, and if so, are the two (or more) strings synonymous?

4.   In the system proposed by Generative Semantics, how would the results of Exercise 3 be accounted for?

5.   In the system proposed by the interpretivists, what would be the most probable way of accounting for results of Exercise 3?

ANSWERS

1.   If the claim that transformations cannot change node labels is to be maintained, then EQUI-NP DELETION will have to be rewritten to allow the transformation to apply when the controlling element is an adjective as well as when it is an NP, since "American" and "Russian" in the (ii) versions of (a) and (b) are adjectives.

2.   Mary remembered the policeman at the rock festival.

In this sentence it is not possible to determine unambiguously from the surface string whether the sequence *at the rock festival* is attached to the same node as *remembered* or to the same node as *policeman.*

3.   Use PASSIVE:
The policeman was remembered by Mary at the rock festival.
The policeman at the rock festival was remembered by Mary.

4. Generative Semantics would claim that the Deep Structures for these two sentences were the results of two different Deep Structure trees, one in which the sequence *at the rock festival* was attached to the verb, and one in which it was attached to the noun *policeman*.

5. It would be assumed that the two sentences in Exercise 3 came from the same underlying Deep Structure but that there was a rule of surface interpretation that would assign scope to these sequences.

Chapter 11

The Application
of Transformational Grammar
to Literary Analysis

In this chapter we discuss a special area of language, which we will refer to as *literary language,* an area often discussed in the literature under the terms *poetics* and *stylistics*. As we use the term here, it should be understood to refer to the body of linguistic material left over when one has excluded gibberish on the one hand and ordinary discourse on the other. This description hardly constitutes a definition and would, of course, be of little value in assisting someone to determine whether a particular piece of linguistic material is or is not literary language.

We will not attempt to describe any decision procedure that might allow the automation of the process of deciding when a given linguistic object is literary language; rather, we will make an overt appeal to the reader's intuitions regarding the identification of such material. The aim of this chapter is thus somewhat more modest than many of those that have preceded it. We wish to argue for an extension of the principles of analysis which have been used thus far in the book to this body of language known as literary language. We wish to claim that literary language, like all other language, is within the proper domain of linguistics, and that the grammar which generates literary language and that which generates ordinary discourse are one and the same in the sense that one includes the other.

While it may at first seem obvious that one would use the same system of analysis for both literary and nonliterary language, there has been much resistance to the incorporation of literary language in the set of material to be subjected to explicit analysis. It seems clear that the resistance of opponents to such incorporation is based on two facts: They do not believe that literary language constitutes a systematic body of linguistic material, and they do not believe that literary and nonliterary language are systematically related.

Since it appears that it is the strikingly different surface structure characteristics displayed by literary language versus nonliterary language that people feel most acutely represent the difference between the two types of language, and since it is in poetry that one finds the most extreme surface differences (with respect to normal discourse), we will confine the discussion in this chapter to poetry. It should be understood, however, that much of what we have to say with regard to poetry is intended to apply to the entire range of literary language.

If you are a native speaker of English, you will probably say that you know what a poem is; that is, you know one when you see one. But, if someone asks you to *tell* him, specifically or even generally, what one is, you are likely to find yourself in difficulty. That difficulty, the inability to specifically define a poem as such, has never yet been resolved, and transformational grammar is no closer to such a definition than any other sort of grammar is.

If, then, we are forced to rely upon the intuition that we recognize a poem when we are confronted with it, can we make some sort of specific statement about the reasons for that recognition?

First of all, we recognize a poem as such because of the recognition conventions that we have been taught. Some of these conventions will be culture-specific; in English literature they include things like the following:

1. A small block of language is arranged in isolation on a page, surrounded by a broad margin of white.

2. Instead of the type running from side to side of the page in uniform strips that fill it margin to margin, the right-hand side of the text is chopped off, either in varying lengths or some patterned length that does not extend all the way across the page.

3. At the top of the block of type there is a *title,* a few words in length and centered a space or two above the balance of the text.

4. The language used shows patternings of sound and rhythm, such as rhyme, assonance, alliteration, and meter.

Also in English literature, poetry may exhibit the phenomenon of special line-patterning to produce specific forms, such as the sonnet.

Having identified some linguistic object as a poem, we have learned to expect certain things of it. We expect to find a surface difference from ordinary discourse. We expect to find surface strings that we would not accept as well-formed in ordinary discourse, but that we will accept within the poem. This characteristic, this difference, is referred to in transformational grammar as *deviance.*

The deviance may be very slight indeed. In much traditional poetry it is confined entirely to the presence of rhyme and metric pattern. If, on the other hand, you examine some of the more experimental poets, you may be tempted to conclude that a line of poetry is a completely unrestricted thing. *Poetic license* appears to some to be a license to throw down any random selection of words, slap a title at the top, and call the result a poem. This impression is misleading, but it is exceedingly common and vastly seductive.

Another characteristic we can expect to find is that many things will matter to us about this chunk of language that do not matter at all in ordinary conversation. Assume, for example, that we are at the dinner table and someone says, "Pass the peas, please." The result should be only that we pass the requested vegetable. On the other hand, if we find that same surface string in a poem, we are going to notice that the line is made up of four monosyllables, that three of them begin with the same sound, that the last two rhyme, and so on. The number of such things we notice will vary with the amount of interest and training that we have in the interpretation of poetry, but at least some of them will be noticed by any native speaker. Moreover, those characteristics that are overlooked at first will be readily understood by any native speaker once they have been pointed out to him. Thus, it would seem that the intuitional experience of an individual carefully examining a section of poetry is not unlike the experience of an individual discovering a previously overlooked ambiguity in ordinary discourse. If we consider the "pass the peas, please" example, it is clear that the fact that such sound patterning is overlooked in ordinary discourse but is important in literary language suggests one major difference between the two types of language. Namely, when dealing with literary language, every feature of the linguistic object—phonological, semantic, orthographic, or any other(s)—must be carefully considered and assumed to be relevant.

This in itself would be enough to distinguish poetic language from ordinary discourse, since it would be highly inefficient to have to consider all features of stretches of language in ordinary communication. Buildings would burn down while firemen pondered the significance of the phonological sequences and imagery of the call for help. Conversation would be impossible; business transactions would come to a halt. In other words, while the function of the phonological sequences "selected" by the speaker in ordinary discourse is simply to allow the listener to recover the Deep Structure (meaning) of that sequence, the sequence of phonological units occurring in a line of poetry serves a double function. It allows the listener or reader to recover the Deep Structure, and at the same time it affords him a kind of sensual and esthetic pleasure.

It is clear that stylistic recognitions are going to vary greatly from person to person, just as is the case with judgments of grammaticality. Intensive training in the interpretation of literary language will cause an individual to see a great deal more of the total content of a piece of literary language as relevant than he would have done otherwise. Classes in the appreciation and analysis of literature are based upon this fact. But even the infant human, who presumably has had no such training, will react instinctively to such stylistic factors as rhythm and repetition.

Another characteristic of poetic language marks it off irrevocably from ordinary discourse: It cannot be paraphrased or tampered with without being destroyed in the process. This is not true of ordinary speech. Consider the following sentences:

E1. (a)   I'd like you to build me a house.
    (b)   I want you to build a house for me.
    (c)   What I want you to do is build me some place to live in.
    (d)   I need a house built and I'd like you to do it for me—I plan to live in it myself.

You could expand this list for a long time, and still there would be no change in the items of information involved. You want a house, you want the person you are speaking to to build it, and you intend the house as a dwelling for yourself. No one of the sentences is particularly better than another. It is difficult to imagine anyone fighting about whether he had actually said "I'd like you to build me a house," or "I want you to build a house for me," because the differences are of little importance. But consider the following sequence:

E2. Build thee more stately mansions, O my soul.

This is, of course, a line from a poem by Oliver Wendell Holmes. It is addressed to the soul of the poet (wherever and whatever that may be) and it conveys the message that the poet wishes the soul to construct for itself dwellings that are more stately. Now consider the following:

E3. (a)   Build thee more stately houses, O my soul.
    (b)   Construct thee statelier mansions, O my soul.
    (c)   Build bigger and better houses for yourself, O my soul.

The information content of the sentences in E3 is the same as that of E2, but not one of the three sequences of E3 is substitutable for the original line. This characteristic, the fact that paraphrase is not possible, is one of the most important ways we have of distinguishing poetic language from ordinary language. Once a poem has been written, a sort of web of relevance relations is established for it. The set of phonological items becomes entangled with the semantic ones, the syntactic arrangements are not separable from the typographic ones, and the entire balance of the web is destroyed if any part of it is tampered with.

Now we have established the fact that poetry appears to be different from ordinary language and that, for various reasons, we are able to recognize it as poetry and deal with it on that basis. At this point we come to the question that is an issue of dispute in transformational grammar today, namely, just *how* this "deviant" body of language is to be dealt with.

Notice that the word *deviant* itself is a relational word. That is, something must be deviant with respect to some standard, not in isolation. In the case of poetry, it is probably the nonliterary language that serves as that standard. However, nonliterary language is not characterized by transformational grammarians in some statistical manner, but rather by a set of explicit rules—a grammar. Thus, we arrive at a more interesting characterization of the *deviancy* of poetic language; namely, poetry is seen as a result of the extension, omission, or alteration of members of the set of transformations applied to the set of Deep Structures (meanings). The interesting question is, what sort of alterations in the set of transformations are possible? We will argue that the alterations are systematic and can be systematically described.

There have been a number of traditional ways of dealing with the problem. There is the approach that appeals to "divine inspiration" (states flatly that since we cannot understand, we can only admire) and treats poetry as completely outside the rest of language and therefore no part of linguistics in any way. If you happen to belong to this group, there is no point in your reading any farther. There is the idea of fiddling around with the surface differences and doing research based upon them, which leads to things like counting the number of times Tennyson used the letter "l" in any given body of text. There is the painful *explication de texte* that is the systematic destruction of a poem or literary work. All these things have their place, but they are the periphery, the *symptoms* of literature. They are a way of going around and around the issue without touching it.

The transformational linguist hopes to go considerably beyond this respectful skirting of the issues. He hopes to take up the question of literary language, not in isolation from the rest of the language but as a living and vital part of it. This involves his assuming that poetry is generated by a grammar, just as ordinary discourse is, and this involves a problem. Consider the following:

E4. (a)   He danced his dance.
     (b)   He danced his did.
     (c)   He danced his paper bag.

E4(a) is ordinary language, E4(b) is a line from a poem by e. e. cummings (*Poems 1923–1954,* Harcourt Brace Jovanovich, Inc.), and E4(c), unless some evidence can be found to the contrary, is nonsense. (It should be noted that there is nothing about E4(b), in isolation, to indicate that it is a line of poetry or to distinguish it from E4(c); this is a case of special knowledge.)

But, if you are going to allow a grammar to generate a line of poetry like *He danced his did,* and you are going to treat that as acceptable, how are you going to prevent a sequence like *He danced his paper bag?* On the surface it appears that *he danced his paper bag* should be a lot less deviant than *He danced his did,* since it is at least structurally identifiable as a proper expansion of an English sentence. No Phrase Structure Grammar of English, however, offers as a possible expansion the following sequence of rules:

R1. (a) S → NP VP
     (b) VP → Verb Determiner Verb

It is precisely these two rules that would be required to generate *He danced his did.*

One solution to this problem that has been proposed is that each poem should be set up as a dialect of the language being used, with its own grammar. Thus, just as the sequence *He ain't* is marked as deviant in our grammar, but is certainly acceptable in several American dialects, *He danced his did* is assumed to be an acceptable sequence in the dialect of the poem, which presumably contains rule R1(b).

This solution effectively isolates the dangerous linguistic object and makes it impossible for it to contaminate the grammar of ordinary discourse. It also allows a grammarian to take a straightforward, old-fashioned English sentence like *e.e. cummings in this line has used a verb where in ordinary discourse a noun would be used* and write it out in symbols that certainly look more impressive than the sentence did. Moreover, it handily makes it unnecessary for the grammarian to do anything more, since every poem becomes a wild card in its private, observationally adequate box.

But if we take this proposal, that each poem is to be treated as a separate dialect, seriously, let's stop and consider what this is going to force us to do.

We must remember that no one has as yet found any really satisfactory way of defining, in any formal manner, just what constitutes literary language, or poetic language, or a poem. Our judgments in this regard will not be uniform from speaker to speaker. It should therefore be clear that there is no way to draw a line that will restrain the scope of the proposed "separate dialect" system. Without a formal definition of the poem, which would allow us to make principled decisions as to what is to be excluded or included, we cannot proceed in any useful way. For example, if a chunk of language set off in the middle of a page is to be called a poem, what do you do about such things as advertisements that may have a similar characteristic? (And in fact much advertising copy not only cannot be excluded from literary language but constitutes one of the most effective bodies of nonordinary language in contemporary society.)

Consider also what sort of language mechanism would be required in order to make the dialect system operate. We would have to assume that each time a poetic stretch of language turned up in a body of otherwise nonliterary language, the individual who had been previously using the ordinary grammar of English would suddenly switch to a new dialect, only to switch back to ordinary English at the end. There would have to be a continual flip from normal grammar to these multitudinous dialects and vice versa.

These criticisms, however justified, are not in themselves sufficient reason to support the claim that the grammar which generates literary language is the same that generates ordinary language. They constitute negative reasons; what is needed is a set of positive ones. We will next consider some of these.

First of all there is the obvious fact that both types of language, literary and ordinary, use the same phonology, the phonology of the given native language. The first letter of the word *peas* is a voiceless bilabial stop in English poetry, just as it is in ordinary English discourse. And just as in ordinary discourse the sequence 'mbiq' is not interpretable as an English word, so in literary language the same holds true.[1]

A second fact is that both ordinary and poetic language use the same lexicon. Consider the following lines from Shakespeare (Sonnet 44):

E5. When I have seen the hungry ocean gain
    Advantage on the kingdom of the shore. . . .

The word *ocean,* which occurs in the first line of this pair, has exactly the same lexical reading as it does in the following sentence:

E6. I can see the ocean from here.

Certainly it is not likely that in ordinary discourse one would say, "I can see the hungry ocean from here." Nonetheless, this use of the word *hungry* is understood as a metaphorical extension of the same word in ordinary discourse and not as some new and unique word having some other lexical reading.

---

[1] This is not to imply that a poet might not use a device such as a sequence of sounds that violates the phonological rules of English; he certainly might. But the fact that such a sequence was a violation would remain true for the poem, just as it would for an ordinary sentence. The rule that everything must be considered relevant will cause the reader to note these deviant sound sequences and assume that there is a reason for their being present. It will *not* cause him to accept them as members of Set A for English.

It is also the case that poetry follows the same syntactic rules, in exactly the same way, as does ordinary discourse. If a poet wishes to form within the boundaries of a poem a command, a question, a relative clause, a comparative, or any other structure of English, he has open to him only those syntactic processes that he would have if he were using ordinary discourse. It is not possible even to imagine some new way of asking a question within the boundaries of a poem that would not be one of the mechanisms for forming a question in ordinary discourse, for example.[2]

We propose, then, that a poem (or any other piece of literary language) begins, just like any other piece of language, as a tree structure. This tree structure contains all semantic elements of the total content of the poem. This Deep Structure is then related to its Surface Structure by a derivational process—the series of transformations of the English language— just as is any other Deep Structure. The resulting Surface Structure, however, is then subject to a series of optional transformations that are forbidden for ordinary language. We will return to this point and discuss these supplementary transformations later in this chapter.

If we establish that the Deep Structure of a poem undergoes the same basic transformational operations as does any ordinary Deep Structure, and if we establish that the most immediately obvious "deviancies" are due to a very late set of optional processes, the problem that remains is that of deciding just where the essential difference between poetry and ordinary discourse lies.[3] The word *essential* must be carefully stressed, since the majority of the differences noticed are not essential. An example of a purely stylistic, and therefore superficial, difference would be the following:

E7. (a)   Three little girls came through the woods.
    (b)   Through the woods came three little girls.

This is certainly not an essential difference. Even if it is pushed further, as in the following example, it remains stylistic:

E8. Little girls three through came the woods.

There are reasons for such stylistic changes. They are not random, but have significance for the poet and are intended to be noticed, but they are surface phenomena. We must look elsewhere for the basic difference we are seeking.

The question to ask is this: Ignoring the surface manifestations that

---

[2] To claim that the structures of literary language are not the result of operation of rules of ordinary syntax would cause us to have within the grammar duplicates of every rule. That is, we would have to postulate a literary and a nonliterary PASSIVE rule, a literary and nonliterary EQUI-NP DELETION rule, and so on.

[3] At this point we are referring specifically to poetry and not to all literary language.

make poetry different, and keeping in mind the characteristics (such as resistance to paraphrase and relevancy of all factors present) that we have already established as differences, can we select some single most important factor that sets off poetry from ordinary discourse? The most satisfactory answer seems to be: the characteristic of saying a great deal very well in a very small space. Let us call this characteristic *compression.*[4] All the things that happen to language in a poem and that do not happen to language in ordinary discourse are motivated by the attempt to establish and maintain this elusive compression without losing the Deep Structure (meaning) in the process. Since we know that the total semantic content of the poem is present in the Deep Structure, we must assume that those elements that have been affected to achieve the highly compressed Surface Structure have been affected transformationally by systematic processes such as deletion, permutation, insertion, and substitution.

We will now return to the discussion of these transformations that apply only to poetic language. It is important at this point to state that although the transformations we are about to discuss are extremely rare outside of poetry, it is not possible to exclude them entirely from the language of prose. For example, we would not be surprised to find them operating in the novels of James Joyce or Gertrude Stein. The question then becomes a venerable one; that is, are we to say that such works are prose, making extensive use of poetic techniques, or that they are really poetry, making use of prose techniques? We will not attempt to settle this question here.

The following schema represents the grammar as it deals with poetic language, whether in poetry or in other literary contexts:

F1.   *Deep Structure (Semantic Representation)*

Transformational Component 1 | Successive stages in the syntactic derivation linked by transformations $t_1 \ldots t_n$

↓

Surface Structure

Phonological Component | Successive stages in the phonological derivation linked by phonological rules

↓

Phonologically Interpreted Surface Structures

Transformational Component 2 | Successive stages in the literary derivation linked by transformations $t'_1 \ldots t'_n$, all of which are optional

↓

Literary Language

[4] Notice that, having isolated this characteristic, we are no nearer a definition of poetry, since compression might also be the defining characteristic of telegrams and headlines.

The transformations listed in schema F1 as $t_1 \ldots t_n$ include those that have already been discussed in this text. Now we want to consider those transformations that are shown above as $t'_1 \ldots t'_n$.

We will confine our discussion to two transformations (OVERLAP and TECHNIQUE DELETION), which appear to be well motivated for the grammar of English and which can be demonstrated to be extensions of transformational processes already needed independently by the grammar.

Overlap Deletion

OVERLAP DELETION is a transformation that applies within a body of poetic language when two phonologically identical sequences occur immediately contiguous to one another under specific conditions, and which operates to delete one of the pair of identical items. Consider the following pair of sentences from ordinary discourse:

E9. (a)   I will jump in the lake, and then Bill will jump in the lake.
     (b)   I will jump in the lake, and then Bill will.

E9(b) is derived transformationally from E9(a) by deletion of the identical sequence *jump in the lake*. This transformation is called VERB PHRASE DELETION.

The constraint on this sort of deletion is very rigid, as is necessary for ordinary communication. Ordinary discourse does not present itself for review and interpretation as literary language does; it is transient and can rely upon no special consideration. This is not true for poetry, since it is expected that the reader or listener will have the time and make the effort to take into account all factors that enter into the interpretation of the poem. It is therefore reasonable to expect that constraints upon deletion in poetry will be less rigid than those upon ordinary discourse.

The following lines (by e. e. cummings, "There is a here and," *Poems 1923–1954,* Harcourt Brace Jovanovich, Inc.) demonstrate the extension of this process of deletion under identity to poetic language:

E10. . . . the ocean
        wanders the streets are so
        ancient. . . .

In E10 the two Deep Structures are the following:

E11. (a)   The ocean wanders the streets.
      (b)   The streets are so ancient.

The transformation OVERLAP DELETION has applied to delete one instance of *the streets* under identity with the other.[5]

The condition of phonological identity of the immediately contiguous items is very rigid, as shown by E12.

E12. (a)   I will touch you/you will touch me →
            I will touch you will touch me.
      (b)   I will touch him/he will touch me →
            *I will touch him will touch me.

It is clear that identity of syntactic function is not required, since in the examples we find one of the twin sequences functioning as the object of a preceding verb or preposition, and the second functioning as the subject of the upcoming verb, and the transformation still applies. For English, however, it appears to be necessary that the two items have the same lexical reading.[6] To show that this is true, consider the following examples:

E13. (a)   Never tell a lie.
      (b)   Lie in my bed →
    (*c)   Never tell a lie in my bed.

Although application of OVERLAP DELETION to E13(a) and (b) certainly yields a comprehensive and grammatical English sentence and a perfectly possible line of English poetry, it is at once obvious that the resulting sequence E13(c) cannot be understood as containing the original pair of Deep Structures. Since the whole point of OVERLAP DELETION is to achieve compression by allowing the possibility of the single combined sequence yielding the meanings of both original sequences, the transformation cannot apply; this result is perfectly consistent with the basic concept that transformations may not change meaning.

There is still an additional constraint upon this transformation in English. Consider the following line by T. S. Eliot ("Burnt Norton," *Four Quartets,* Harcourt Brace Jovanovich, Inc.) :

E14. Only through time time is conquered.

[5] Since it is not possible to tell from the resulting surface string which of the twin items has been deleted, we will arbitrarily decide that it is the second.

[6] This constraint does not necessarily hold for other languages. For example, in Japanese it is possible for OVERLAP DELETION to apply not only to individual items with different lexical readings but also to portions of those items. The analogous procedure for English would allow us to apply OVERLAP DELETION to the sequence *friendship/shipmates* and delete only the identical segment *ship*. The result for English would be the clearly unsuccessful *friendshipmates.*

The item *time* in this line would appear to satisfy all the conditions previously specified for the transformation; nonetheless, it cannot be reduced to *Only through time is conquered* without destroying the deep structure. If we examine the Deep Structure of the Eliot line, we will be able to see the essential difference here. The Eliot line has a Deep Structure something like the following:

E15. Someone conquers time only through time.
       [+ PRO]

This sequence would be dominated by a single S-node at the time application of OVERLAP DELETION took place, which is not true of any of the preceding examples. We can therefore add the additional constraint for English that the transformation can apply only if the two identical items originate in separate underlying strings.

OVERLAP DELETION may then be formulated for English as follows:

R2.   Within the context of poetic language, if a given sequence s_i is followed immediately by another sequence s'_i, delete s'_i, where
   (i) s_i and s'_i are phonologically identical.
   (ii) s_i and s'_i share the same lexical reading.
   (iii) s_i and s'_i are dominated by separate S-nodes at the time OVERLAP DELETION applies.

You will notice at once that this transformation is formally rather different from the transformations we discussed before. For example. the effect of this transformation would be to reduce a structure like E16:

E16.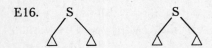

to a structure[7] like E17:

E17.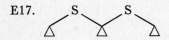

Nonetheless, although this transformation is formally unusual—to such an extent that a new formalism would be required to allow us to write the Structural Index and description of the rule—there is nothing whatever

---

[7] This structure was suggested to us by Professor Yuki Kuroda.

about it that is not already a part of the grammar of ordinary English discourse.[8]

Technique Deletion

We have seen that OVERLAP DELETION is the logical extension of the transformations that effect deletion under identity in ordinary discourse, such as VERB PHRASE DELETION. The second transformation we will consider, TECHNIQUE DELETION, is the logical extension of the transformation in ordinary discourse known as UNSPECIFIED AGENT DELETION.

Consider the following:

E18. (a)   John wants to leave.
      (b)   The door opened.

The deleted item in E18(a) is uniquely recoverable; it can be only *John*. This is an example of EQUI-NP DELETION. But the sentence of E18(b) is a different matter. Here there is no single lexical item that can be specified as having served as the Deep Subject of the verb *open*. It is, instead, the case that there is a small set of such items and, as native speakers of English, we know what items may or may not be members of this set. We know that the item must be *someone* or *something*, and we know roughly what characteristics the someone or something must have. We know it cannot be the case that the original structure was *the diagonalized matrix opened the door* or *the newborn baby opened the door*.

The same process is operative in poetic language, but operative in a less rigid manner. Consider the following:[9]

---

[8] The reader may be familiar with the device known as *double syntax*, which was used extensively by Shakespeare and has a long and respectable history in English literature. Double syntax appears to be equivalent to OVERLAP DELETION plus one additional constraint. Consider the following example:

For the victims of war we offer nothing
but the best.

In this example the reader or listener has the possibility of stopping either at the end of the first line given or at the end of the second, with resulting complete strings in both cases. The difference between double syntax and OVERLAP DELETION is, however, that for double syntax the resulting *combined* sequence must be grammatical in the traditional sense of the word. Thus, *for the victims of war we offer nothing but the best* is just as grammatical as *for the victims of war we offer nothing*. However, although *the ocean wanders the streets* is grammatical, *the ocean wanders the streets are so ancient* is not. It would appear, then, that for English, the constraint that the combined sequences be grammatical has been dropped from the grammar, in just the same way that a phonological or syntactic rule might be so dropped.

[9] A very similar sequence appears in the work of e. e. cummings.

E19. this small horse newly
      he is fresh from his mother's flanks

If the poet intended this sequence to mean *this small horse newly purchased,* he is in much the same situation as the speaker who intends *the door opened* to mean *the diagonalized matrix opened the door,* or who intends *John wants to leave* to mean *John wants Mary to leave.* Instead, we can safely assume that there is a small set of possible items that could have occurred after *newly* and that, because of the overt items, we can specify that set fairly closely. The set of eligible items is probably the following:

E20. born, dropped, foaled, nursed

We can determine this because of the semantics of the material present and because we are provided by the poet with the following phonological sets:

F2. (a) /n/ . . . newly
     (b) /r/ . . . horse, fresh, mother
     (c) /f/ . . . fresh, from, flanks
     (d) /l/ . . . small, newly, flanks

Given these phonological sets, we can safely eliminate *dropped* from the set of candidates E20, leaving us with the other three. This is a degree of ambiguity that is tolerable in poetic language, and is in fact desirable, since the several possibilities for the deleted item allow a high degree of compression.

To apply this transformation, the poet relies upon the stylistic devices at his command, such as rhyme, meter, and parallelism. If the transformation is misapplied, he will have changed the meaning of the underlying string or produced a degree of ambiguity that is not tolerable, in the sense that he has made even approximate recovery of the deleted item(s) impossible. Since this process is less constrained than deletion in ordinary discourse, it is likely that it will be more often misapplied than is UNSPECIFIED AGENT DELETION. This does not mean that it is unsystematic, but rather that the performance factor figures very highly in the application of this transformation.

Now consider the following example:

E21. snowflakes round and round through air

The missing item here is the verb. The degree of ambiguity is relatively high, but given the phrase *round and round* we know that it is restricted to a verb of motion and that the motion must fall within the category *circular*. If the poet meant the verb to be *explode,* then he should have told us so; he has misapplied the transformation.

It is more likely that we will be given additional information, as in E22.

E22. snowflakes round and round through air like ballerinas

The set of possible lexical items is now specified more completely.[10] To the original circular-motion idea of *round and round,* we have now added the idea of "dance," and we can safely claim that the set of items contains at least the following:

E23. whirl, twirl, spin, dance

Let us further restrict this set of items, as follows:

E24. two snowflakes round and round through air like twin ballerinas

We now have the lexical item *twirl* reinforced by its phonological similarity to the word *twin* and by its orthographic similarity to the word *two.* We also have the item *spin* reinforced by the fact that it rhymes with the word *twin.* We can now say that the set of possible deleted items contains the two members *twirl, spin,* and is no more ambiguous than a set containing the two category items *someone* and *something.*

A tentative formulation of the transformation TECHNIQUE DELETION for English might be the following:

R3. Where a lexical item (i) is one of a small finite set of possible items, and (ii) can be reinforced in the Surface Structure by such technical devices as rhyme, assonance and alliteration, and meter, that lexical item may be deleted from the surface string of poetic language.

It should at once be clear that it would be even more difficult to write the formal Structural Index and description of structural change for this transformation than it was to do so for OVERLAP DELETION. This is a difficulty caused by the limitations of our formalism; it should not be allowed to obscure the fact that this is a transformational process of English, that it is systematic rather than random, and that it is an extension of similar

[10] There are a number of formal mechanisms for describing this process. For example, we could borrow from the work of Weinreich (1966) the mechanism called a Transfer Feature, which would operate to extend feature markings from one morpheme to another under specific conditions.

processes already present in the grammar of the ordinary discourse of English.

It is obvious that the process of deletion is far more complex in poetry than in ordinary language and that it is based upon more intricate conditions. As we have said before, this is possible because the language of poetry is available for extended consideration and examination.

Notice that in giving a formulation to the transformations involved in the enumeration of possible strings of literary language, we have employed the same vocabulary and the same notation that has been used throughout this text. That is, while the set of transformations we are discussing in this chapter differs from those considered in previous chapters in that they are defined on the output of the phonological component and are always optional, they appear to be otherwise indistinguishable.

Other Techniques

It must be pointed out that it appears that some techniques are employed in literary language which cannot be readily accounted for by means of transformations, either of the type proposed in this chapter or of the type associated with the enumeration of strings of nonliterary language. We will illustrate by example.

Ross (1967b) studied extensively the set of restrictions that are usually referred to as Universal Constraints on transformations. It is characteristic of these constraints that they are of the form shown in R4:

R4.   Given some string s_i and some transformation t_i such that s_i is properly analyzable with respect to the Structural Index of t_i, t_i may not be applied to s_i if such and such a condition obtains.

Consider a specific example of such a universal constraint on transformations, that constraint known as the *Conjoined Structure Constraint,* or CSC. We will use the strings of E25 as an example, along with the transformation PASSIVE.

E25.   (a)   Sam kissed Sue.
       (b)   Sam kissed Sue and her sister.

The CSC can be stated now in the format suggested by R4:

R5.   Given some arbitrary string s_i and some arbitrary movement transformation t_i, t_i may not apply to s_i if the application of t_i to s_i would split a conjunction.

The transformation PASSIVE is an example of a movement rule, and is thus relevant. The arbitrary string E25(a) contains no conjunction; however, the string E25(b) does, namely, the sequence *Sue and her sister*. Now consider the effect of the application of PASSIVE to the two strings.

E26.   (a)   Sue was kissed by Sam.
        (*b)   Sue was kissed and her sister by Sam.

It is clear from the linear sequence of elements E25(b) that PASSIVE has applied to a conjunction in such a way as to split it. The effect of the transformation is the production of a deviant string, since the transformation has applied in spite of a constraint to the contrary. The CSC is not limited in its application to the movement transformations contained within the grammar of English, but is proposed as a constraint on movement transformations in all human languages. This is a claim of importance, and one that we will discuss in detail in Chapter 13.

Consider, however, the following lines from Milton: [11]

E27. . . . Is not the earth
        With various living creatures and the air
        replenished. . . .

Clearly, the lines from Milton violate the CSC. It is equally clear that we can be sure that random violations of the CSC do not occur in Milton or in any other literary work. As we mentioned earlier in this chapter, the traditional characterization of literary language as being deviant seems to us to be interpretable only in the sense of deviancy with respect to the set of well-formed strings enumerated by the nonliterary grammar. We have been attempting to show that the transformations that enumerate the set of well-formed literary strings are defined over the output of the phonologically interpreted strings of the nonliterary portion of the grammar. In the case of the example from Milton, we can give an explicit characterization of what has happened.

Without becoming involved in disputes regarding the consciousness with which the poet does what he does, we can say that Milton's example makes it clear that high-level constraints defined over the set of nonliterary transformations may be relaxed in certain instances to achieve a particular literary effect. The determination of the set of circumstances where such

[11] This example, for which we are indebted to Ann Banfield, is from *Paradise Lost*, VIII:369–371.

constraints may be relaxed would contribute much to the understanding of the limits of literary language.[12]

Thus we return to the point of this chapter. We have explained a number of literary language phenomena. We have proposed two transformations that operate only in poetic language, but which are extensions of transformational processes within ordinary discourse. We have done this in an attempt to support the claim that the conceptual schema and mechanisms developed by transformational syntax provide an insightful approach to the explicit analysis of literary language. We assume that by making an explicit analysis of literary language we are giving serious content to the traditional claim that it is the poet who is master of his language.

EXERCISES

1. In this chapter examples were given of recognition conventions that apply to English literary language. Consider the literature of a culture that does not have a written language and relies upon oral presentation. What would be probable recognition conventions for such a literature? List as many as you can.

2. The following sequences are lines from various poems that show "deviancy" with regard to the syntax of ordinary discourse. See if you can systematically characterize these deviancies in each case. If there are problems, state them.

   (a)   And I will do a funniest thing. . . .
        (Gavin Bantock, "Buddha," *Poetry Review* 61:3, Fall, 1970.)
   (b)   This is the TV parlor
        in the best ward in Bedlam.
        The night nurse is passing
        out the evening pills.
        (Anne Sexton, *To Bedlam and Part Way Back,* Houghton Mifflin Company, 1960)
   (c)   There thou, great Anna, whom three realms obey,
        Dost sometimes council take, and sometimes tea.
        (Alexander Pope, *Rape of the Lock*)

---

[12] It seems reasonably certain that even literary language will have to exhibit some form of the constraint first formulated by Perlmutter (1968a) to the effect that an otherwise permissible transformation will be blocked if it results in a surface string that is identical to one resulting from a totally different derivation. We might then propose that the Milton example is possible, precisely because there can be no derivation resulting in a sequence that would have the earth *replenished* with the conjoined NP *living creatures and the air.* However, much more research will be necessary before any such claim can be made precise.

3. Try to find some other transformations from the literary set. Give examples if you can.

ANSWERS

1. (a) Presentation of literature in some oral traditions is restricted to some specific person, such as a shaman or medicine man, for use on specific occasions such as religious rituals. The fact that such a ritual was taking place and that the shaman was speaking would constitute a recognition convention.

(b) An oral formula made up of particular syllables, either with or without meaning, may serve to indicate that the language immediately following or preceding is literary. (Notice that the word *Amen* serves a similar function in English.)

(c) In some oral literature, the actual phonological shape or the words may differ from that of ordinary discourse, or the language may employ words that are otherwise taboo, archaic, or for some other reason extremely rare in ordinary discourse. This would function as a recognition convention.

2. (a) In English, the superlative (-est) form of an adjective is not normally preceded by an indefinite article.

(b) This sequence appears to be an example of OVERLAP DELETION as described in this chapter. The two possible strings are *The night nurse is passing* and *The night nurse is passing out the evening pills*. But the problem here is that the verb *pass* in the sequence *pass out* NP does not have the same lexical reading as the verb *pass* in a sequence like *The mailman is passing the house*. The poet, in fact, must be very careful not to put the word *out* on the wrong line, since she does not want the nurse *passing out* in the sense of becoming unconscious. Since there is also the possibility of the patients *passing out* after taking their pills, a striking degree of compression has been achieved here. It is difficult to see, therefore, how OVERLAP DELETION could be formulated to allow the rule to describe what has been done in these two lines.

(c) This is the result of applying a transformation called CONJUNCTION REDUCTION to the following two sequences: *Anna sometimes takes council* and *Anna sometimes takes tea*. If you will consider the effect in ordinary discourse of combining the following two sequences in the same way, you will see what has been done here.

This afternoon Benjamin took offense at Kathleen's remarks.
This afternoon Benjamin took a walk.
*This afternoon Benjamin took a walk and offense at Kathleen's remarks.

3.   An example of a literary transformation that might be proposed would be a process analogous to TECHNIQUE DELETION and that might be called TECHNIQUE SUBSTITUTION. This process is probably that responsible for puns, both humorous and serious, and that responsible for parody. The parody line that turns *Isle of Capri* into *pile of debris* and gives us the line *Twas on a pile of debris that I found her* is an excellent example of this transformation.

Chapter 12

Generative Phonology

Recall the statement of the task of the linguist as it is conceived by transformationalists: the construction of an explicit statement that will specify which sound sequences are associated with which meanings; that is, the pairing of members of Set A with their corresponding members in Set B.

Phonology deals most directly with Set A. It is the phonology of a language that tells us which sound sequences are acceptable as part of that language and which are not, and which accounts for the varying forms that those sequences may take in terms of sounds.

The native speaker of a language does not need to know anything about the formal discipline of phonology to be competent in this respect. His own intuitions will tell him what constitutes a member of Set A for his own language, even if he has never heard the word *phonology*.

In order to understand what this means, consider the situation of an English speaker suddenly faced with a linguistic object that is being presented to him as an English word and which he has never encountered before. If this putative word happens to be 'bik' the English speaker will say that he hasn't heard it before, but that it sounds like a perfectly fine English word. An attempt to present /mbik/ as English, however, will provoke an entirely different response—that no such word exists, and if it did, it certainly couldn't be English.

The whole point of phonology is to characterize this particular ability of the native speaker that allows him unhesitatingly to accept or reject sound sequences as members of Set A for his own language. Traditional phonology has approached this problem in a number of ways; generative phonology has formulated what seems to be a more interesting, more useful, and more effective way. But before we can discuss the generative approach, we need to look briefly at the traditional one.

The first task in dealing with the phonology of a language is to isolate its sounds and characterize them effectively. This is no problem for your native language because you know how to produce the sounds and you know which ones matter. But what if it were not your own language? What if you were suddenly faced with a language totally new to you and given the same task?

You can be sure that it would be discouraging. If you listened to a native speaker of this new language, you would have the feeling that you were listening to a rush of incomprehensible gibberish. There is a very good chance that some of the sounds you heard would be sounds that you could not even produce. Almost without exception you would find it difficult or impossible to decide where breaks, such as breaks between words, were occurring. You might well feel that the task of sorting out the sounds and making an analysis of them was simply not possible—but this is a panic reaction. If you stopped to consider calmly the flow of sounds you were hearing, you would find that there were many things you could say that would be useful.

For example, you would be able to note that the native speaker was making some particular sound by touching both lips together, that another sound required his mouth to be opened wide, and that still a third required his lower lip to touch his upper teeth. Such a classification of sounds, in terms of the places they are made and the physiological areas that make them, was customary with the traditional phonologists. Table 12.1 is based upon one such classification of the consonant sounds of English.

Table 12.1

Bilabial	Labio-dental	Dental	Alveo-palatal	Velar	Glottal
p	f	θ t	sh	k	h
b	v	δ d	zh	g	
m		s	ch	η	
w		z	j		
		n	y		
		l			
		r			

The terms that head the columns in Table 12.1 are defined as follows:

1. *Bilabial:* a sound produced by touching both lips together.
2. *Labio-dental:* a sound that requires that one of the lips touch the teeth; so far as is known, this will always involve the lower lip and the upper teeth, although the converse is perfectly possible.
3. *Dental:* a sound produced by touching the tip or front of the tongue to

the upper teeth or to the area immediately behind the upper teeth (called the *alveolar ridge*).

4. *Alveo-palatal:* a sound that requires contact between a portion of the body of the tongue (and often the tip as well) and roughly the upper central portion of the mouth, from back of the alveolar ridge to and including the palate.

5. *Velar:* a sound articulated in the area of the velum (that part of the back of the mouth that ends in the uvula, the small appendage that you can see hanging down if you open your mouth very wide and look in a mirror).

6. *Glottal:* a sound made in the area of the glottis, at the very back of the mouth and throat.

Another kind of fact that you would be able to determine rapidly would be that certain sounds made by the speaker were more "hissing" than others, that some appeared to be very smooth and liquid while others were rough and harsh, that some sounds had a buzzing quality that others lacked, and so on. If we add this new information to Table 12.1, we have a traditional chart of the consonant sounds of English described in these terms, as in Table 12.2.

Table 12.2

	Bilabial	Labio-dental	Dental	Alveo-palatal	Velar	Glottal
Stops						
voiceless	p		t		k	
voiced	b		d		g	
Fricatives						
voiceless		f	θ s	sh		h
voiced		v	δ z	zh		
Affricates						
voiceless				ch		
voiced				j		
Nasals						
	m		n	η		
Liquids						
			l r			
Glides						
	w			y		

The terms that appear at the left-hand side of Table 12.2 are defined as follows:

1. *Stops:* a sound produced when the flow of air is completely cut off; stops involve the raising of the velum so that the nose is also closed off completely. You will find it dramatically easy to understand what a stop is if you try to hum one.

2. *Fricatives:* sounds produced by friction of the flow of air in the mouth; these sounds can be made continuous, as in hissing.
3. *Affricates:* sounds that begin like a stop and end like a fricative.
4. *Nasals:* sounds produced with the oral cavity completely closed as for stops, but with the velum lowered so that air can flow through the nasal cavity.
5. *Liquids:* sounds for which, as in the production of consonants, there is a shutting off of the flow of air, but in which some of the air is allowed to escape by a lowering of one or both sides of the tongue.
6. *Glides (or semivowels):* sounds made very much as vowels are, but with the oral cavity much less open than in the production of vowels.
7. *Voiced/voiceless:* a sound is voiced if its production requires that the vocal cords be vibrating.

This way of setting up sounds and describing them has many things to recommend it, but is has one major disadvantage. A new chart has to be made for each language, and new descriptive terms have to be found for each sound that has not yet appeared on some previous chart.

To improve upon this system, linguists conceived the idea of setting up a classification system based on *features*.[1] The hope was that some single set of features could be found that would apply to all human languages in a uniform and interesting way. A sound segment of any given language could then be marked as plus or minus any feature.

Let's first consider this problem by examining a more familiar situation in the same way. We might think of people as having features such as tallness, fatness, and intelligence. We can see at once that if we have both "tall" and "short," we need choose only one of them, and then we have the tall man marked as "plus tall" and the short one as "minus tall."

Figure 12.1 shows 12 consonants of English displayed on a diagram known as a Feature Matrix.

This matrix includes some of the features proposed by Jakobson, one of the linguists who was an important figure in the developing of the concepts of features, as well as some more recently proposed ones. There have been many more features proposed than are shown here.[2] The turnover in

---

[1] You will remember from previous chapters the application of the concept of feature marking.

[2] Three sorts of criteria are used for choosing phonological features, as follows: *articulatory,* where the sound is produced and the parts of the vocal tract involved in its production (for example, the feature *coronal*); *acoustic,* a criterion that relies on such things as evidence from spectrograms (for example, the feature *strident*); *perceptual,* a criterion based upon evidence provided by the senses (for example, although it is not possible to demonstrate the presence of *stress* by either articulatory or acoustic measurements, there is no question as to its reality, since it can be clearly heard by the ear).

CONSONANTS

	p	t	k	b	d	g	m	n	s	z	l	r
Consonantal	+	+	+	+	+	+	+	+	+	+	+	+
Vocalic	−	−	−	−	−	−	−	−	−	−	+	+
Sonorant	−	−	−	−	−	−	+	+	−	−	+	+
Continuant	−	−	−	−	−	−	−	−	+	+	−	−
Strident	−	−	−	−	−	−	−	−	+	+	−	−
Nasal	−	−	−	−	−	−	+	+	−	−	−	−
Voiced	−	−	−	+	+	+	+	+	−	+	+	+
Front	+	+	−	+	+	−	+	+	+	+	+	−
Coronal (articulated with front portion of tongue)	−	+	−	−	+	−	−	−	+	+	+	+

Fig. 12.1. Feature matrix of English consonants

proposed feature sets is so rapid in generative phonology that almost any set that might be suggested would probably be obsolete by the time it appeared in print. This does not happen because generative phonologists are unable to make up their minds as to what features they want. Instead, it is the unavoidable result of the facts that only a very few of the world's languages have been studied as yet, and that as linguists acquire new data they find that the features already proposed are simply not adequate.

When and if a set of features is developed which actually proves adequate to describe all known human languages, linguists will have said something valuable about language as a whole. Since every new proposed feature is in a sense a proposed claim about all human languages, generative phonologists make an effort not to suggest new features without adequate motivation.

Now look at the English feature matrix (Fig. 12.1) with the idea of seeing exactly what it is that the features are telling you. You will see at once that there are large blocks of pluses and minuses that seem to form clusters. Such blocks are used by the linguist to define Natural Classes of sound segments for human languages. For example, on the English chart you will see that there are six segments (p, t, k, b, d, g) that share the following feature specification:

+ consonantal
— vocalic
— sonorant
— continuant
— strident
— nasal

This subset of features defines the natural class of English stops. In English the stops will appear in roughly the same places in words and will behave in roughly the same way throughout the language; it will therefore be possible to write rules that need mention only the class and not its individual members.

You will also see that the two English segments /s/ and /m/ have almost no features in common and that they in turn have very little in common with the segment /l/. You would not expect, then, to find any sort of phonological rule for English that dealt with these three segments (/s/, /m/, and /l/) as a group. They do not form a natural class.[3]

Figure 12.1 is what is known as a Fully Specified Matrix. This means that every segment is specified as plus or minus every feature. Look at the English matrix carefully. You will see that in no case is there any such thing as a segment marked [+ NASAL] which lacks the feature [+ VOICE]. Therefore, since a voiceless nasal simply cannot exist in English, it is not at all necessary to specify voicing for nasals. In the literature of generative phonology, you will often find that feature matrices are not fully specified and that only necessary information is given. This extracting of redundant information is one of the most important ways of showing how a native speaker's phonological competence works.

In addition to the features we have been discussing, which apply to individual segments, phonologists are concerned with what are referred to as Suprasegmental, or Prosodic, features. These are features such as stress, accent, and pitch, which give to a language its characteristic intonation contour. These features extend over larger stretches of sound than single segments, and may often make a marked difference in meaning. Consider the following pair of sentences, which is a classic example of such a difference:

E1. (a)   What are we having for dinner, Mother?
    (b)   What are we having for dinner—*Mother?*

The suprasegmental features will not ordinarily appear on feature matrices, since such matrices are confined to specification of individual segments, and therefore we will not discuss them further in this introductory text. They are, however, a fascinating subject for study.

Let's go back now to our native speaker who is confronting us with the stream of unfamiliar sounds.

There are two terms we need for dealing with this problem. One is the concept of the Phoneme and the other is the Allophone. The history of the phoneme throughout phonology has been a very stormy one. A few

---

[3] This does not mean that the linguist can be sure he will *never* encounter such a rule, but it is very unlikely.

examples of definitions of the term proposed by linguists should suffice, as follows:

D1. Hockett (1958): The phonemes of a language, then, are the elements that stand in contrast with each other in the phonological system of the language.

D2. Schane (in press): Segments whose function is to contrast forms are called Phonemes.

D3. Harms (1968): One of the set of segments that contains only distinctively specified features—and from which no distinctive feature specifications have been deleted by virtue of environmental (sequential-constraint) redundancies—and that underlies the segments actually used to designate morphemes.

None of the above definitions will tell you what a phoneme is, but you can easily demonstrate to yourself the nature of this linguistic animal.

Consider for a moment the two English words *pin* and *bin*. If you are an English speaker, you know that these are two different words, and you have no problem telling them apart. You also know that they contain three sound segments each and that only the first such segment in each word allows you to differentiate between the two words. That is, it is the difference between /b/ and /p/ that allows you to do so.

The two words *pin* and *bin* constitute what is known in linguistics as a Minimal Pair. This means that they are two words, readily identified by the native speaker as being different, and differing in only one segment. Such a pair is taken by the linguist as evidence that the two segments which act to differentiate them are phonemes of the language. He would say that /p/ is one English phoneme and that /b/ is another, and he would not be surprised to find many more examples of such pairs, /pat—bat/, /pet—bet/, and so on.

Each language, then, will have an inventory of these elements, the phonemes, and it will be that inventory that will function in the phonology. It is customary to write phonemic data between slashes, as /p/, /b/. (Note that phonetic symbols are written in brackets.)

Now let's consider another pair of English words, *pin* and *spin*. The English native speaker will tell you that one of these words contains three sound segments and the other four, and that they differ only in the segment *s*, which is initial in the word *spin*. He will be telling you, in other words, that the group of segments *pin* in the word *pin* and the group of segments *pin* in the word *spin* are the same. To find out whether his judgment is accurate, try the following: Put your hand close to your mouth and say aloud the word *pin*. Now do the same thing with the word *spin*. Notice the puff of air that you feel on your hand with *pin* but not with *spin*.

You can see that in fact the English speaker is not quite accurate in his statement. There is a difference between *pin* and *spin* minus *s*. That difference is in the puff of breath you felt when you pronounced one word and did not feel when you pronounced the other—the phenomenon known linguistically as Aspiration.

The difference between the sound *p* with aspiration (indicated phonetically as [pʰ]) and the sound *p* without it is not important to the native speaker of English. There exists no minimal pair like [pin]/[pʰin], which must be differentiated on the basis of the presence or absence of aspiration. In a language like Korean, where aspiration is important to differentiation, there are minimal pairs differing only in the presence or absence of aspiration, and it would be necessary in the phoneme invertory to set up two phonemes, /p/ and /pʰ/.

The situation as it is in English, where there is never a context in which the aspirate/nonaspirate distinction can create confusion, is described by use of the other term mentioned at the beginning of this discussion, the Allophone. In English we say that there is a phoneme /p/, and that it has two allophones—two possible phonetic realizations—one of which is aspirated and one of which is not. These two allophones are written [p] and [pʰ]. This allows us to make a phonetic distinction and at the same time to continue to capture the generalization that these two phonetic segments constitute only one phonemic one, and that to an English speaker a *p* is a *p* is a *p*.

Just as [p] and [pʰ] differ only in the presence or absence of aspiration, [p] and [b] differ only in the presence or absence of voicing. In Korean, the phoneme /p/ becomes voiced when it occurs between two vowels, and is therefore phonetically [b], but this only means that, for Korean, [b] is an allophone of the phoneme /p/; it does not necessitate setting up a separate phoneme /b/ as is needed for English.

The situation we have been describing—that of being faced with a totally or almost totally unknown language and the task of analyzing it— is the normal situation dealt with by the linguist doing field work with a language that has not yet been studied or described. The linguist's first step in such field work is to establish an inventory of phonemes and allophones for the language, using the strategies discussed above.

It is sometimes the case that a segment will be pronounced in varying ways in a language and that this variation will not be a process that can be specified by rule. In English, for example, although word-final voiceless stops are not aspirated normally, some speakers routinely aspirate them in very formal speech (as in a lecture), saying [tipʰ] for [tip], [bitʰ] for [bit], and so on. This type of variation is stylistic; in other cases it may not be possible to determine the reasons for the variation even as firmly as this. When the linguist has to describe segments of this kind, he says that they are in Free Variation.

The Combining of Segments

It should now be clear how a linguist goes about dividing the flow of sound from a native speaker into meaningful segments (that is, phonemes with their allophones) that can be described systematically. The next step is to attempt to find out how these meaningful segments may or may not be combined into sequences.

You will remember that at the beginning of this chapter it was pointed out that no English speaker would accept as a word of English the sequence 'mbik' because he knows, as a native speaker, that English phonology will not accept as a word-initial sequence an *m* followed by *b*. He also knows, although he may not know that he knows, that this information can be further generalized and that English phonology will not accept *any* initial sequence of nasal consonant followed immediately by a stop[4] Thus, he would rule out any such sequence as /ndik/ or /ngap/ or /mtod/ as being an impossible sequence in English.

The important thing to note here is that it is not necessary for the native speaker to have an individual rule forbidding each of these nonwords. He has a single rule, generalizable for the entire body of English, that will automatically rule out any such sequence.

It is important also to notice that such rules must be sensitive to the position of the forbidden sequence if that is relevant. Certainly the sequence of nasal followed by stop is not intrinsically forbidden in English. It occurs frequently, in words like *number, mumble,* or *frequent.* It is the sequence in word-initial position that is not allowed, and therefore, just as in syntax, boundaries will have to be a part of phonological rules. The rule for English might look like the following:

R1. * # C C
  [+ NASAL] [
  — SONORANT
  — CONTINUANT
  — STRIDENT
  — NASAL
  ]

This rule simply says that it is forbidden to have a word-initial nasal consonant followed immediately by a stop. It happens, in fact, that in English a nasal consonant may be followed initially only by a vowel, and therefore R1 might be further simplified as follows:

R1A. * # C C
  [+ NASAL]

[4] In Swahili, a Bantu language, such sequences are extremely common.

Such rules make it unnecessary for the information contained in them to be restated redundantly each time a nonpermissible sequence occurs. For example, the vowel that appears before the letter *s* in the formation of many English plurals (as in *bushes, birches, tresses*) is a vowel that is inserted to avoid the formation of a forbidden final-consonant cluster of two consecutive strident phonemes. Such a vowel is called an Epenthetic vowel.

The Derivation in Phonology

The assumption of generative phonology is that the processes that go into the production of the final set of sound sequences of any human language can be systematically described by the grammar. The concept of an abstract underlying form that undergoes a transformational derivation to produce the final surface "pronounced" form is the same in generative phonology as it is in generative syntax.

Consider, for example, the fact that the word *electric* has a related word *electricity* in the English language. It is obvious to the native speaker that the sequence /elektrik/ is present in both, even though one contains the phoneme /s/ and the other the phoneme /k/. The phonologist captures this relationship by pointing out that there is a rule in English called Velar Softening, which causes a velar consonant occurring in a word immediately before the suffix "-ity" to change systematically. In both cases, it is assumed that the underlying form contains "electric," but in the derivation of the word "electricity" the velar softening rule has applied.

Thus, a single phoneme may appear with different surface phonological shapes as a result of the application of rules; this does not in any way invalidate the generalization about the underlying phonological shapes. Notice that the underlying form "electric" remains constant in such surface forms as "electrical." One of the most basic problems a phonologist has is that of making principled decisions as to which of the various shapes that a phoneme or morpheme (a meaningful sequence of phonemes) appears in does indeed constitute the basic form from which all others are derived.

In previous chapters you became accustomed to the concept of a derivation as it is applied to the syntax and the semantics of language. This same concept is used in generative phonology. Let's consider an example of a phonological derivation from Navajo.[5]

The singular of the Navajo verb *to work* in the continuative imperfective has the following surface forms:

naashnish   I work
nanilnish   you work
naalnish   he, she, it works

[5] This example is taken from an unpublished paper by Ken Hale of M.I.T., who has very kindly allowed us to use the material.

The relevant morphemes are the following:

F1.

na- (or naa-)	adverbial prefix
-sh-	1st person singular subject marker
-ni-	2d person singular subject marker
-l-	classifier
-nish	stem

Examination of the partial paradigm for the verb shows some interesting differences and apparent irregularities. For example, the adverbial prefix contains a short vowel in the second person singular, but has a long vowel in the other two persons. The classifier that appears in the second and third person is not present in the first person form. In addition, there is no marker at all for subject in the third person form, since the third person subject pronoun has no phonological realization (that is, no surface form.)

One way to handle this situation would be to simply memorize the forms, noting that they are irregular. Before doing that, however, let's look at the underlying forms, as follows:

	Prefix	Person Marker	Classifier	Stem
1.	na	sh	1	nish
2.	na	ni	1	nish
3.	na	Ø	1	nish

These underlying forms are perfectly regular and systematic, showing none of the differences that appear in the surface forms.

Navajo has a rule, however, that says:

R2. If there is no other vowel present between the prefix /na-/ and the verb stem, the vowel of /na-/ must become long, changing /na-/ to /naa-/.

If this rule is applied to the first or third persons in the schema F1, it will lengthen the vowel in both cases, since neither of these forms has any other vowel between the prefix and the stem. (It should be obvious that this "rule" as described is only descriptively adequate and that it is completely unsatisfactory as an explanation for the phenomenon. However, for our purposes, the statement made does describe the effect of the process, whatever the formal rule may turn out to look like after further research.)

The second rule of Navajo (R3) says:

R3. The segment /l/ is deleted whenever it occurs between two consonants, and acts to prevent the formation of unpronounceable consonant clusters.

When this rule is applied to the first person singular form in the schema F1, it will delete the /-l-/ segment, the classifier.

We see, then, that of these three forms, which were completely regular in their underlying forms, only the second person singular 'nanilnish' reaches the surface unchanged.

There are at least two possible ways of writing a rule like R3 (the /l/ deletion rule) in generative phonology, as in R4:

R4. (a) $/l/ \rightarrow \emptyset$ $/C\_\_\_\_C$
  (b)   C /l/ C
       1, 2, 3 $\rightarrow$ 1, $\emptyset$, 3

You will find examples of both types of rule writing in the literature, depending on the individual phonologist and the situation with which he is dealing. The choice between the two is ordinarily made on methodological grounds alone, since both rules say the same thing and will have the same effect in a derivation.

The two rules that operate in the Navajo derivation (R_2 and R_3') are unordered with respect to one another. However, there are ordered rules in phonology just as there are in syntax, and in many cases the decision as to relative ordering is a major problem for the phonologist.

The problem with the ordering of rules in phonology is, of course, the same as in syntax; that is, one rule may create or destroy the environment for the next. It is necessary for the phonologist to order rules in such a way that all the correct surface forms and no incorrect ones will be generated.

Consider the following example, from Luiseño, a Uto-Aztecan language spoken in California:[6]

E2. The stem form for the word *pet* in Luiseño is /-'aach/. (The line under the vowel indicates that it is stressed.) The first person singular possessive prefix *my* is /no-/. The accusative ending is /-i/ and the plural is /-um/. There are three rules involved in the derivation of the accusative plural form *my pets*.

R5. $V \rightarrow \emptyset$ /   V   C____CV
                [+ STRESS]

That is, any vowel that is preceded by the sequence of a stressed vowel followed by a consonant, and which is followed by the sequence of consonant and then vowel, is deleted.

---

[6] This example (the derivation of which has been somewhat simplified) was furnished to us by Pamela Munro of U.C.S.D.

R6. V → [-long] / _____CC

This rule says that long vowels become short when they occur before a sequence of two consonants.

R7. /ch/ → /sh/ / _____ $\begin{bmatrix} C \\ \# \end{bmatrix}$

R7 indicates that the consonant /ch/ becomes /sh/ when it occurs before a consonant or word-finally.

The correct surface form of the accusative plural, *my pets,* is /no'ashmi/. What ordering of the R5, R6, and R7 will give us this correct form?

We begin with the underlying abstract form:

	POSSESSIVE	STEM	PLURAL	ACCUSATIVE	
#	no	'aach	um	i	#

If we examine this sequence we find that we have a stressed vowel followed by a consonant, followed by another vowel /u/ and the consonant /m/. This is the correct environment for R5. If we apply R5, it will yield the following intermediate form:

	POSSESSIVE	STEM	PLURAL	ACCUSATIVE	
#	no	'aach	Øm	i	#

We now have a long stressed vowel followed immediately by two consonants. This is the correct environment for R6, which we now apply, yielding the intermediate form below:

	POSSESSIVE	STEM	PLURAL	ACCUSATIVE	
#	no	'Øach	Øm	i	#

We now have the consonant /ch/ immediately preceding another consonant, the environment for R7. We apply the rule and obtain the following:

	POSSESSIVE	STEM	PLURAL	ACCUSATIVE	
#	no	'Øash	Øm	i	#

As in syntax, there is a convention that removes boundary symbols and null symbols, yielding the final surface form /no'ashmi/. This is the correct output.

Now we will try a different ordering of the rules, beginning again with the underlying form /no-'aach-um-i/. This time we will assume that R6 is ordered first.

	POSSESSIVE	STEM	PLURAL	ACCUSATIVE	
#	no	'aach	um	i	#

R6 applies to long vowels occurring immediately before a sequence of two consonants. Since the underlying form contains no such sequence, the rule cannot apply. Now we assume that R7 is next:

	POSSESSIVE	STEM	PLURAL	ACCUSATIVE	
#	no	'aach	um	i	#

Since R7 applies to the segment /ch/ only when it is followed by another, consonant, it cannot apply here, and there is no change.

The last rule will be R5. This rule will find, since the vowel /u/ is preceded by the correct sequence, yielding the following form:

	POSSESSIVE	STEM	PLURAL	ACCUSATIVE	
#	no	'aach	Øm	i	#

When boundary symbols and nulls are removed, the final output will be the incorrect form /*no'aachmi/.

If we attempt the ordering R7, R6, R5, we will have exactly the same result, since neither R7 nor R6 can apply. This leaves us only the ordering R5, R7, R6, as follows:

	POSSESSIVE	STEM	PLURAL	ACCUSATIVE		
#	no	'aach	um	i	#	(Apply R5)
#	no	'aach	Øm	i	#	(Apply R7)
#	no	'aash	Øm	i	#	(Apply R6)
#	no	'Øash	Øm	i	#	

This ordering yields the correct surface form /no'ashmi/, *my pets*.

We have therefore established the proper ordering sequence for R5, R6, R7. R5 must precede both R6 and R7 in order to obtain the correct output, but R6 and R7 are unordered with respect to one another.

Note: Another area in which the concept of derivation and the principles we have been discussing is extremely useful is in historical linguistics. All the material in this chapter deals with phonology on a *synchronic basis*—that is, for a single given period of time. It is also possible to consider a derivation that is diachronic— that is, shows the development of a particular from over an extended period of time. There is not a great deal of literature available on historical linguistics dealt with from the transformational point of view because it is a relatively new idea, and the books and articles that do exist on the subject are extremely difficult to follow if you have not had extensive previous instruction in phonology. It can safely be assumed, however, that there will be a rapid development in this field in the next few years and that much work will be done.

Markedness

Another concept common to both phonology and syntax is that of Markedness. Essentially the marked/unmarked distinction serves to indicate what is unusual or unexpected. For example, it appears to be universally true that the first sounds children make in their acquisition of language are those that are physiologically easiest to produce. Thus, in language after language we find that the infant's word for *mother,* usually the first word a child produces, is a combination of the bilabial nasal *m* and a vowel like broad *a.* The American child, whose language is from the Indo-European language family, says *mama;* the little Navajo child, speaking an Athabaskan language, says *-ma.* The Ki-Hungan child speaks a Bantu language, but he says *maam.* These are the unmarked cases. If we were to come upon a language in which the infant's first word was a sequence like /tl'eezh/, we would be surprised because the sequence is complicated and requires a number of sophisticated movements of the vocal apparatus. Such an instance would be called a marked case.

In Chapter 13 we will take up the concept of language universals, and this marked/unmarked distinction will be discussed further. For the moment it will be sufficient to state that examination of many human languages allows the making of a number of generalizations. For example, no known human language has only nasal vowels and no oral vowels. If we were to discover such a language, it would, again, be an example of a highly marked case. However, it would not make it any less valuable to know the fact that for the vast majority of human languages the rule holds true.

In this chapter we have attempted to set out clearly the parallel between the application of generative theory to syntax and its application to phonology.[7] In syntax, we postulate deep structures, which are subsequently modified by application of ordered rules. In phonology, the deep structures are the abstract underlying forms that serve as input to the phonological component of the grammar, undergo modification by the phonological rules, and ultimately are spelled out in their final surface forms as the morphemes of the language. By this method, generative phonologists are able to substitute for a chaotic listing of all possible forms an orderly and systematic strategy for deriving all surface forms by rule from related underlying forms. The methods of generative phonology allow the linguist to

---

[7] Perhaps the clearest beginning text on generative phonology, if you are interested in reading further on this topic, is the text by Schane (in press).

produce a more economical grammar, using fewer and simpler rules, than could be produced by traditional methods.[8]

EXERCISES

1. Divide the class into groups and compare the way that various members of your group pronounce the vowels in the following words:

bath   leg
horse   pig
boat   house

You will probably notice a number of significant differences. Try to describe these differences.

Having done this first exercise, you should now be aware of two important facts: first, the pronunciation of English vowels varies amazingly from dialect to dialect; and second, the description of these differences is extraordinarily difficult. One proposed analysis of the vowels of English is the following:

	Front *Unrounded*	*Central*	*Back* *Rounded*
High	i (machine)	i (pig)	u (loose)
Mid	e (bed)	ʌ (but)	o (know)
Low	(cat)	a (father)	ɔ (ball)

2. The following data are not from a real language, but are constructed for this problem alone. Assume that these words are from a language and examine them carefully. What sort of statement can you make about formation of the plural in this language? Try to write a traditional statement and a generative one.

Singular	*Plural*
taha	tahas
bedani	bedanis
murel	murels
lan	lan
daam	daam
fli	flis
abesansa	abesansa

[8] In order to avoid confusion, it should perhaps be pointed out that transformational phonology is usually referred to by the term Generative. We have therefore deferred to the phonologists' preference and followed their usage in this chapter.

3. It is possible that the situation in a language like the one in Exercise 2 would not really be a statement about the plural at all. What is a possible alternative?

4. It is obvious that data constructed specifically for a phonology problem is not likely to be much like that from real languages. The following data are from a real language—Diegueño, an Amerindian language of the Yuman family. You are to find the rule or rules for forming plurals of Dieguño, verbs. Don't try to write them in formal notation; just state what happens. Since stress may be relevant for your rules, you should know that the final vowel of the verb is always stressed. The data are taken from Walker (1970).

	Singular	*Plural*	
1.	Lʸap	Lʸaap	*(burn)*
2.	muL	muuL	*(gather)*
3.	chuupul	chuupuul	*(boil)*
4.	saaw	saw	*(eat)*
5.	shuupit	shuupiit	*(close)*
6.	sii	sich	*(drink)*
7.	maa	maach	*(eat soft things)*
8.	tuuñaa	tuuñaach	*(pound)*
9.	iimaa	iimaach	*(dance)*
10.	kʷaa	kʷaach	*(crochet)*
11.	məwas	məwaas	*(be soft)*
12.	wir	wiir	*(be hard)*

5. How would a situation such as that described in Exercise 4—that is, some verbs, which apparently cannot be distinguished as any sort of semantic or phonological class, undergo some specific phonological process—be handled by the phonological component of a grammar?

6. Divide into groups and play Native Speaker.
Rules:
(a) One person is the Native Speaker.
(b) He must give the players (any number) an inventory of 15 phonemes, 10 consonants, and 5 vowels.
(c) He must tell the players if there are one, two, or three rules, three being the maximum.
(d) Each player in turn presents a "word" made up of members of the phoneme inventory, and the word is either accepted or rejected by the Native Speaker.
(e) The player's procedure is to attempt to determine what is the rule or rules that the Native Speaker is using to decide which forms are acceptable and which are starred; first one to work out the rule(s) wins.

Example:
Phoneme Inventory:
    a, e, i, ɨ, u   p, t, k, m, n, ng, l, s, z, sh
Rules:
(a)   Stop clusters are forbidden.
(b)   *Unmarked* vowel to break up such clusters is /i/.
(c)   If there is a preceding vowel, the epenthetic vowel must be identical to it.

Correct Forms	Incorrect Forms
ipita	*ipta
ipita	*apita
apata	*ipata
pipit	*pipt

ANSWERS

1.   Depends on individual student.

2.   The plural in this language is usually formed by simply adding /s/ to the singular. However, if the singular ends in a nasal consonant, the plural form will be identical to the singular. (TRADITIONAL)

The underlying form of the plural is /s/. The following rule applies:

$$-s \rightarrow \varnothing \quad / \quad \begin{matrix} C \\ [+ \text{NASAL}] \end{matrix} \underline{\quad\quad} \# \quad (\text{GENERATIVE})$$

3.   The sequence of nasal consonant followed by the segment /s/ is forbidden word-finally in the language.

$$* \quad \begin{matrix} C \\ [+ \text{NASAL}] \end{matrix} \quad s\#$$

Note: It is probable that the rules written above would not use the actual segment /s/ but would instead characterize it by its set of identifying features. However, the data given in the problem do not allow us to establish what those features might be.

4.   The data show us that we have at least three classes of plurals. The rules needed to generate all three classes are the following:

(a)   If the stressed vowel is long in the singular form, it becomes short in the plural, and vice versa.
(b)   If a singular verb ends in a vowel, the plural adds /ch/.
(c)   Some verbs follow both (a) and (b) rules, apparently idiosyncratically.

The forms that would be accounted for by each rule are the following:
Rule (a):   1, 2, 3, 4, 5, 11, 12
Rule (b):   8, 9, 10
Rule (c):   6, 7

5.   These verbs would have to be marked specifically in the lexicon for their idiosyncratic features.

Chapter 13

Universal Grammar

There is a claim that science is the human response to man's desire to understand himself. If this claim is paid more than the usual lip service, it at once becomes apparent that if linguistics is "about" anything, it is about man's head. And since this chapter has to do with the way linguistics relates to man's head, the material dealt with in this chapter is the justification for the entire endeavor that is called linguistics. We assume it is clear that Thales's "Know thyself" will have to provoke a more profound response from linguistics than the simple information that while "Know thyself" is well formed, "Know himself" is not. This chapter is devoted to an attempt to indicate what that more profound response ought to be like. We begin by repeating an argument that is familiar to transformational grammarians, whatever their theoretical orientation may be.

Suppose that, in accord with the most basic principles of science, we assume that when the child learns his native language he employs only the least complex of learning mechanisms. Let's agree to refer to this mechanism as a Language Acquisition Device (LAD). We will assume that this device has only the most basic of principles, perhaps those of association, contiguity, and reinforcement. The principle of association says that, given two events a and b, the more frequently these events occur simultaneously, the stronger the associative bond between them will be. If a and b occur one after another without some third event intervening, they are said to be contiguous, and the principle of contiguity states that the closer together temporally they occur, the stronger the bond will be. Finally, the principle of reinforcement states that things we associate with rewards—including the suspension of punishment—will be learned more readily than those that are not so marked. The interaction of these three learning principles with the organism's environment accounts for the knowledge and skills possessed by fully developed human beings, including the use of language. We will assume that the LAD has just this much to work with.

Now let's suppose that we may accurately describe the operation of the LAD by saying that whenever it receives as input some sequence of a natural language, that sequence is stored complete with its meaning, pronunciation values, its syntactic structure, and conditions specifying when its use is appropriate. This basic learning mechanism can be represented as a Markov process. The Finite State Grammar, discussed briefly in Chapter 4, is an example of one such Markov process. Suppose we limit the task arbitrarily and require that the machine "learn" all the grammatical strings of English that have the length of 20 words or less. We quote from Miller, Galanter, and Pribam's book, *The Plans and Structure of Behavior*.[1]

Information theorists tell us that English sentences carry about five bits per word on the average, so we can guess that there must be about 2^{100} different strings twenty words long that we should learn how to cope with. It seems reasonable to assume that each of these 2^{100} different sequences would leave the system in a different internal state. In order to incorporate the ability to generate a particular one of these strings of words into our planner—to create one of the 2^{100} different internal states that would be required—the planner would have to hear the string at least once. That is to say, our left-to-right generator has no grammatical rules other than the ones that say, "Having produced the words X up to this point, you must choose your continuation from the set Y." In order for a child to learn all of the rules of this left-to-right variety that would be required for the generation of perfectly acceptable sentences of twenty words or less, he would have to hear the rule, or hear instances of it from which the rule would be derived. Thus there seems no alternative but to insist that a child must hear 2^{100} sentences before he can speak and understand English. That is about 10^{30} sentences. In order to appreciate how ridiculous this condition is, recall the fact that there are only about 3.15×10^9 seconds per century. In short, the child would have to hear about 3×10^{20} sentences per second in order to be exposed to all the information necessary for the planner to produce sentences according to these left-to-right rules of grammar, and that is on the assumption of a child-

---

[1] Miller based his estimates on five bits per word in the average English sentence. This is a conservative estimate based on Shannon's data for letters. See C. E. Shannon, "Prediction and Entropy of Printed English," *Bell System Technical Journal*, (30:50–64) 1951. Repeated by N. G. Burton and J. C. R. Licklider, "Long Range Constraints in the Statistical Structure of Printed English," *American Journal of Psychology*, (68:650–653) 1955.

hood 100 years long with no interruptions for sleeping, eating, etc., and perfect retention of every string of twenty words after one presentation! (Miller et al., 1960:146, Holt, Rinehart and Winston, Inc.)

Would such a LAD, as we have now described it, be adequate to account for what a child actually does when he learns his native language?

If we remember the fact (established in an earlier chapter) that the set of well-formed sentences in any particular language is infinite, and add to it the fact that native speakers of languages produce and understand sequences of sounds to which they have never before been exposed, it is easy to understand why no transformational grammarian will accept the LAD, as described above, as an interesting proposal.

The stimulus-response (S-R) model of psychology (remember Jack and Jill and that apple, back in Chapter Three) is said to have been perfectly willing to accept the LAD described here. It should be obvious, however, that although it is possible (in laboratory psychology experiments, for instance) to impose on a human being a set of restrictions rigorous enough to produce behavior explicable in terms of an S-R model, such a model will fail totally to describe the language ability of human beings.

We cannot just brush away this fact by going along with the popular idea that the learning and use of one's native language represents one of man's higher cognitive skills and that the analysis of such skills must await the completion of the analysis of the less complex ones. While it is obvious at this point that the typical natural language system of man is indeed a rich, powerful, and complex system, and although no animal except man is known to possess such a system,[2] no one can seriously maintain that it represents one of man's higher cognitive skills. It seems, on the contrary, that anyone with a minimum of intelligence, if exposed to a natural language in the usual way, will become a competent speaker of that language (the estimated IQ requirement is about 50).[3]

It seems incredible that the S-R model could have ever been considered a viable model for the human language-learning mechanism, except if its advocates forgot just what it was to be a model of. The point is precisely that almost all children learn their language in a short time, without the help of any professional teacher, and that no other animal does. And the relevance of this for linguistics—and everything else—is that a grammar has

[2] The most interesting case concerning nonhumans and language systems that we are aware of is the case of Washoe, a chimpanzee who has been raised by two psychologists of the University of Nevada. The chimpanzee has been exposed to sign language on an exclusive and regular basis, and apparently is able to use appropriately several dozen signs and to respond appropriately to well over a hundred.

[3] This is the estimate made by Lenneberg (1967).

to be a formal description of principles that must be represented neurologically in the human head.

There are strong and weak versions of this claim. For example, the strong claim can be expressed as follows: The mechanism, the transformation as such, much itself have some direct neurological representation. It is difficult to know just what this claim would mean, or what possible form such representations could take. The weaker claim, which is that the formal properties of the grammar such as recursion must have some direct neurological representation, is more interpretable. Now, given this weaker claim, what can we say is the appropriate direction for linguistic investigation to take?

Let's consider a few facts that are relevant to answering this question. First of all, any child—no matter what language his parents speak, and therefore no matter what his linguistic "heredity"—will learn the language spoken in the culture that is his childhood environment. That is, the child of Chinese parents who grows up in a Samoan home will speak Samoan, not Chinese. Second, all languages studied so far have shown evidence of obeying a set—as yet only vaguely understood—of formal constraints such as the Conjoined Structure Constraint, which will be discussed later in this chapter. Navajo, (an Athabaskan language) obeys the CSC just as does English (an Indo-European language) or just as does Basque, which doesn't seem to be related to any other language at all. Third, even if one were to impose some artificial limit, such as restricting all sentences to a maximum length of 20 words, consider what the enormous task of learning to use a language would have to be if it were not in some way already "there" in the child's head. Fourth, it is just these kinds of things, things that appear to hold true no matter what language is involved, that would have to be innate in the human mind. It seems obvious, therefore, that the proper thing for linguists to do is to search for just those things, and the name that they have been given is "linguistic universals."

If we consider now the contribution that linguistics can make to the settling of this age-old dispute (that is, whether language ability is or is not innate), we find first of all that two basic areas in linguistic analysis must be distinguished:

1. The explicit description of the formal properties that are required in order to make explicable some particular phenomenon in some particular natural language.

2. The explicit description of the set of general constraints over the entire set of phenomena that form the subject of linguistic analysis.

An example of type 1 would be the fact that natural languages have pairs (at least pairs) of sequences that are equivalent semantically and which use the same set of morphemes, but which are distinct in that the linear word order in the two sequences is different. From this we might conclude that Permutation constitutes a formal property of human language and that this property can be explicitly described by the grammar. The set of properties discovered in particular natural languages will, of course, affect the structure of the general theory of language.

After the set of language phenomena to be described has been isolated by analysis, it is then necessary to move on to the second area and attempt to discover the constraints that hold over the entire set. The general theory, with respect to these phenomena, is nothing more than the inventory of possible relations that can occur between elements in natural languages—and this is not enough. The general theory must do more: It must establish a characterization of the notion of possible transformation. Consider the following linguistic frame, where X and Y are variables:

F1. X NP V _____ Y

If a grammar must choose between inserting *himself* or *herself* in the blank in this frame, the basis for that choice should be dependent on the structural and semantic relations between that term and some other term in the deep structure of the sequence, and not on whether the number of terms in the sequence is or is not a prime number. Yet nothing in the formal nature of transformations as such, as defined by the general theory, would prevent us from stating the rule of selection of *himself* or *herself* as a function of the number of words in the sequence. This is a serious inadequacy, for surely we should expect the theory to distinguish between possible and impossible transformational relations. It is felt that this problem will be solved by placing stronger and stronger constraints on the set of transformations until it will be impossible within the general theory to entertain a transformation contingent upon things like the number of words in a sequence but possible to state transformations for genuine linguistic phenomena.

Within the generative framework, there have been three general uses of the term "universal" itself, as follows:

D1. *Statistical universals.* This term refers to the surface structure patterns of various language groups.[4]

As an example of a statistical universal, data from many languages lead linguists to believe that if the Surface Structure of a language has as its typical surface-word order Verb followed by Subject followed by Object, then modifiers in that language will be typically found to the right of the term they modify.

[4] This is the type of universal reported by Greenberg (1966).

D2. *Substantive universals.* These universals are the terms of the vocabulary in which the general theory is stated.

Presumably the names of the set of grammatical categories necessary for tree-node labeling, names like Noun and Verb, are examples of substantive universals. Another example of this type of universal is the set of terms necessary for the characterization of the phonetic qualities possessed by the element of the sound systems of languages throughout the world.[5]

D3. *Formal universals.* This term refers to the statement of the abstract properties displayed by all human languages.

An example of a formal universal would be any member of the set of properties that distinguishes human languages from artificial ones. We must expect of the combination of substantive and formal universals that it will yield the explicit description of a class of grammars, a class that would be rich enough to allow the statement of the grammar of any particular natural language, yet restricted enough to distinguish such languages from artificial language systems. Such a description would be supremely important because it would be a definition of human language.

More crucial for the present is the fact that this resultant description would be a prime candidate for determining what it is that is present in a child's head when he arrives; in effect, it would constitute a portion of the definition of a human being.

For the rest of this chapter we are going to consider an example of a proposed universal that involves both the formal universal and the substantive universal categories. This universal was proposed by John Ross (1967b) and is called the Conjoined Structure Constraint (CSC). (We have referred briefly to this constraint elsewhere in the text.)

Consider the following set of sequences:

E1. (*a)   Maria was given and Toby a prize by Sam.
    (*b)   Robbie sent George a letter and Tricia.
    (*c)   I believe Sam George and $\left\{ \begin{array}{l} \text{to be fools} \\ \text{are fools} \end{array} \right\}$.

In each of the E1 sequences something has gone completely awry. The transformations that produced these sequences and the well-formed input structures are listed in E2.

[5] See Jakobson et al. (1967), Ladefoged (1968), and Chomsky and Halle (1968).

E2. (a) Sam gave Maria and Toby a prize. (PASSIVE transformation.)
- (b) Robbie sent a letter to George and Tricia. (INDIRECT OBJECT Movement.)
- (c) I believe [George and Sam are fools]. (RAISING transformation.)

The sequences listed in E3 are the results of the correct application of the indicated transformation to the input structures E2.

E3. (a) Maria and Toby were given a prize by Sam.
- (b) Robbie sent George and Tricia a letter.
- (c) I believe George and Sam to be fools.

Consider a representative of this first group E1 with respect to its transformation and input structure in order to discover what it is that has happened.

E4. (a)

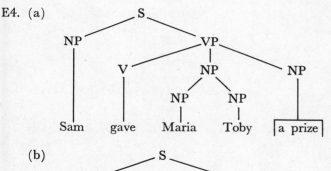

(b)

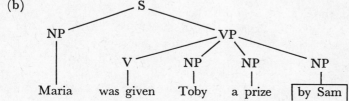

Now consider the structural index for PASSIVE:

R1. PASSIVE	X	[NP	V	NP	Y]	Z
		$\underset{\text{s}}{}$			$\underset{\text{s}}{}$	
Structural Index	1	2	3	4	5	6
Structural Change	1	4	$be + 3$	$\emptyset$	$5 + by + 2$	6

The analysis of E4(a) is ambiguous with respect to R1:

E5. (a)

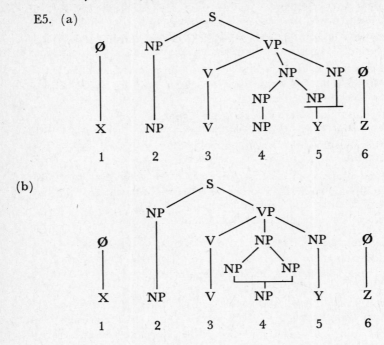

(b)

The analysis of E4(a) may be either E5(a) or (b); notice that if it is E5(a), then the result of the structural change will be E1(a); if, on the other hand, the analysis E5(b) is chosen, the result will be E2(a). A consideration of the other examples listed in E1 with their associated transformations and input structures shows this same property; namely, that the Structural Index may partition the terminal string in two ways. There is, of course, another property that the E1, E2, E4, and E5 sequences share; in each of them a Conjoined Structure is involved. We may for the moment define the term Conjoined Structure by the schema E6:

E6.

Now, putting these last two facts together, we can point out that in each of the sequences mentioned above, the Structural Index may partition the input sequence so that the entire Conjoined Structure is moved by the transformation, or so that only a fragment of the Conjoined Structure is so moved. Further, there is a perfect correlation between the partition selected and the resulting well-formedness. If the entire Conjoined Structure moves, the result is the well-formed E3; if only the E3(a) portion is moved, the result is bad. Thus, only the partition that maintains the integrity of the Conjoined Structure is to be allowed. The other case, where the partition of the input structure by the Structural Index splits the conjunction, is invariably ill formed. Thus, we might consider adopting R2 as a constraint:

R2. No Structural Index may partition a sequence in such a way as to split a Conjoined Structure.

The constraint R2 correctly prevents the sequences of E1 while allowing the sequences of E3. However, R2 itself will not be acceptable, as can be seen when pairs such as E7 and E8 are considered.

E7. (a) The man talked to my brother and my sister.
       (LEFT DISLOCATION transformation.)
     (b) My brother$_i$, the man talked to him$_i$ and my sister.

E8. (a) The man$_i$ said that the man$_i$ and the woman were leaving.
       (PRONOMINALIZATION.)
     (b) The man$_i$ said that he$_i$ and the woman were leaving.

For the transformations LEFT DISLOCATION and PRONOMINALIZATION to have converted E7(a) and E8(a) into E7(b) and E8(b), it is necessary that their Structural Indices partition the Conjoined Structures in such a way as to split them:

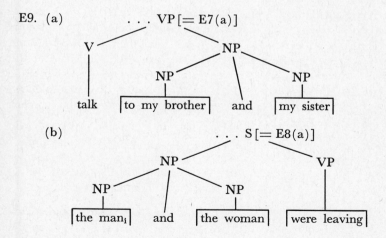

E9. (a) . . . VP [= E7(a)]

(b) . . . S [= E8(a)]

Thus, we see that R2 is incorrect. Ross (1967b) noticed, however, that E9(a) and E9(b) transformations can be distinguished formally from E2(a), (b), and (c). First, in the versions of E2, the transformation actually moves an element from one position in the sequence into some other position in the sequence. This property (that the E2 versions are MOVEMENT transformations) immediately distinguishes them from the PRONOMINALIZATION transformation. It remains only to distinguish the same set from the LEFT DISLOCATION transformation. The distinction is that in the LEFT DISLOCATION (but not in the others), a copy of the moved element is left in the original position. This is the distinction between chopping rules (no copy left) and copying rules (a copy must remain).[6] Thus, we arrive at the proper formulation of the CSC:

R3. No chopping transformation may move an element of a conjoined structure.

If it were the case that R3 were applicable to English only, it would be of limited interest. However, it appears that R3 has a larger range of application. There is no indication as yet that the CSC can be ignored in any natural language. The claim, then, is that the CSC is a universal. More specifically, the CSC says that no natural language may include a movement transformation of the chopping family which may split conjoined structures.[7] In many languages Question Formation is a movement transformation. In both E10(a) and (b), for example, the CSC has been violated and the result, as we predicted, is ill formed.

E10. (*a)   Wen hat Hans Lilo und gesehen (German)
            who did John Lilo and see
            'who did John see Lilo and'
      (b)   Chi ha visto Giovanni Maria e (Italian)
            who did see John Mary and
            'who did John see Mary and'

Thus, apparently, the CSC has a good chance of being maintained as a universal. Notice that its formulation requires reference to both formal and substantive universals. It requires, for example, the definition of Conjoined Structure E6, clearly a substantive universal. It makes reference to a certain class of transformations movement, that is, chopping transformations. Finally, it says that having identified the domain for the constraint, a certain set of relations may not occur in natural language; the CSC is a

---

[6] This terminology is due to Ross (1967c).

[7] There seems to be a similar constraint on deletion transformations. Using the Equi-NP Deletion transformation as an example, we would expect (b) to be well formed, which it is not.

  (a) John$_i$ hoped that John$_i$ and Mary would go to town.
  (*b) John$_i$ hoped (that) and Mary would go to town.

constraint on possible transformational relations. The constraint, then, is a constraint over the set of chopping movement rules, not the PASSIVE in English or the QUESTION FORMATION transformation in German. Based on our former discussion with respect to language acquisition, we would propose that the CSC be included in the general theory of language, that it be contained in a definition of what natural language is, or (equivalently) that it be included in the innate structure of the human mind.

We have attempted to indicate in this chapter why (besides the fact that it is fun) we do linguistics. In other words, we have tried to say what we think linguistics will eventually contribute to an understanding of ourselves. It seems clear to us that if we are to move to control our own lives and shape the kind of future we want, we must understand as well as we are able what we are now.

EXERCISES

Although the title of this chapter is *Universal* Grammar, we will restrict ourselves to English phenomena, as we cannot presuppose the readers' familiarity with other languages.

1.   We present a set of pairs of strings that involve the application of some transformation, all of which involve coreferential NP. Find the most general statement possible that is consistent with the data presented here, as well as other data that you may think are relevant, that prevent ungrammatical strings from being produced.

   (a)   (i) $John_i$ hurt $himself_i$.
           (*ii) $John_i$ was hurt by $himself_i$.
   (b)   (i) $John_i$ hurt $himself_i$.
           (*ii) $Himself_i$ was hurt by $John_i$.
   (c)   (i) $John_i$ hurt Wh + $someone_i$.
           (*ii) Who_i did $John_i$ hurt?
   (d)   (i)   I know the man_i [the man_i hurt Wh + $someone_i$].
           (*ii) I know the man_i who_i the man_i hurt.
   (e)   (i)   It was easy for $John_i$ to hurt $John_i$.
           (*ii) $John_i$ was easy for $himself_i$ to hurt.
   (f)   (i)   It was easy for $John_i$ to hurt $John_i$.
           (*ii) $Himself_i$ was easy for $John_i$ to hurt.
   (g)   (i)   It was easy for $John_i$ to hurt $John_i$.
           (*ii) $John_i$ was easy for him_i to hurt.

2.   All of the strings listed below have a common structural characteristic. Determine what that characteristic is and write the most general possible statement that will prevent the ungrammatical strings from being produced.

   (*a)   Who that talked to Mary disturbed Jack?
   (*b)   Who Sam talked to disturbed Jack?
   (*c)   I know the man who that talked to Mary disturbed Jack.
   (*d)   I know the man who Sam talked to disturbed Jack.

3.   All of the strings listed below have a structural property in common. Determine what that property is and write the most general statement that will prevent the ungrammatical strings from being generated.

   (*a)   Who did Max talk to the girl who kissed?
   (*b)   I know the person who Max talked to the girl who kissed.
   (*c)   Who was Sam surprised by the fact that Tom liked?
   (*d)   Who did the woman make the claim that saw Martha?

ANSWERS

The general point of these exercises is to show that there are rather general constraints on natural language processes, just as we showed in outline in the text that there are general statements that exclude ungrammatical strings which cannot be attached to any particular transformation but are statements that are general across the set of transformations (or some subset of the set of transformations).

1.   The "answer" to the first question is contained in Postal (1971a). Basically, the constraint says that no transformation may move an NP in such a way as to cause that NP to cross the position occupied by another NP that is coreferential with the first. For example, consider the pair a(i) and a(ii). This pair assumes that Reflexivization occurs after Passive. Reflexivization marks the rightmost of two coreferential NP for the reflexive form if those two NP are in the same clause. This is what has occurred in the first pair. The second pair, b(i) and b(ii) assumes that the order is

REFLEXIVE > PASSIVE

In both pairs, the result is clearly ill formed, showing that the constraint is independent of the ordering assumptions. An examination of the succeeding pairs will reveal that in each case a transformation has applied to move an NP over a position occupied by a coreferential NP; thus the deviancy.

2.   In each of the strings of this problem a transformation has applied to move an NP out of the structural configuration A:

(A)

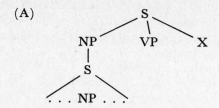

The constraint that prevents this was developed by Ross (1967b), and was called the Sentential Subject Constraint. It may be stated informally as: *No transformation may move an element out of the configuration* A.
3. In each of the strings of this problem, a transformation has applied to move an NP out of the structural configuration B:

(B)

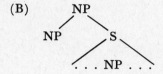

The constraint that prevents this was also developed by Ross (1967b), and was called the Complex NP Constraint. It states (informally): *No transformation may move an element out of the structural configuration* shown by configuration B.

Bibliography

Akmajian, A. (1968). "An Interpretive Principle for Certain Anaphoric Expressions." Cambridge, Mass.: M.I.T. Mimeographed.

‡ Bach, E. (1964). *An Introduction to Transformational Grammar*. New York: Holt, Rinehart and Winston, Inc.

Bach, E. (1968a). "A Note on Pronominalization." Austin: University of Texas. Mimeographed.

Bach, E. (1968b). "Nouns and Noun Phrases," in E. Bach and R. Harms (eds.), *Universals in Linguistic Theory*. New York: Holt, Rinehart and Winston, Inc.

‡ Bach, E., and R. Harms (eds.) (1968). *Universals in Linguistic Theory*. New York: Holt, Rinehart and Winston, Inc.

Baker, C. L. (1970a). "Double Negatives," *Linguistic Inquiry,* (1;2:169–186).

Baker, C. L. (1970b). "Notes on the Description of English Questions: The Role of an Abstract Question Morpheme." *Foundations of Language* (6;2:197–219).

Bar-Hillel, Y. (1967). "Do Natural Languages Contain Paradoxes?" San Diego: University of California. Mimeographed.

Bar-Hillel, Y. (1968). A review of J. A. Fodor and J. J. Katz (eds.) *The Structure of a Language*. San Diego: University of California. Mimeographed.

Bellugi, U., and R. Brown (1964). "Acquisition of Language," Society for Research in Child Development, *Monograph Series on Language and Linguistics No. 1,* Vol. 29, Washington, D.C.

‡Bever, T. G. (1970). "The Cognitive Basis of Linguistic Structure," in J. Hayes

‡ This symbol indicates references that tend to point in a particularly interesting and intelligible way toward new methods of approaching the analysis of human language systems.

(ed.), *Cognition and the Development of Language*. New York: John Wiley & Sons.

Bierwisch, M. (1967). "Some Semantic Universals of German Adjectivals," *Foundations of Language* (3:1–36).

Bierwisch, M. (1969). "On Certain Problems of Semantic Representations," *Foundations of Language* (5;2:153–184).

‡Bierwisch, M. (1970). "Poetics and Linguistics," in D. C. Freeman (ed.), *Linguistics and Literary Style*. New York: Holt, Rinehart and Winston, Inc., pp. 74–96.

Bloch, B., and G. Trager (1942). *An Outline of Linguistic Analysis*. Baltimore: Waverly Press.

Bloomfield, L. (1926). "A Set of Postulates for the Science of Language," *Language* (2:153–164).

Bloomfield, L. (1933). *Language*. New York: Holt, Rinehart and Winston, Inc.

Bolinger, D. L. (1950). "Rime, Assonance and Morpheme Analysis," *Word* (6:117–136).

Bolinger D. L. (1968). *Aspects of Language*. New York: Harcourt Brace Jovanovich, Inc.

Bresnan, J. (1970). "On Complementizers: Toward a Syntactic Theory of Complement Type," *Foundations of Language* (6;3:297–321).

Carnap, R. (1947). *Meaning and Necessity*. Chicago: The University of Chicago Press.

Carnap, R. (1959). *The Logical Syntax of Language*. Totowa, N.J.: Littlefield, Adams & Company.

Chapin, P. (1970). A review of T. G. Bever's "A Survey of Some Recent Work in Psycholinguistics," in *Linguistic Notes from La Jolla,* no. 4. San Diego: University of California.

Chatman, S. (1957). "Linguistics, Poetics, and Interpretation: The Phonemic Dimension," *Quarterly Journal of Speech* (43:248–256).

Chomsky, N. (1955). *The Logical Structure of Linguistic Theory*. Unpublished doctoral dissertation. Philadelphia: University of Pennsylvania.

‡Chomsky, N. (1957). *Syntactic Structures*. The Hague: Mouton & Co.

Çhomsky, N. (1962). "Explanatory Models in Linguistics," in Suppes, Nagel, and Tarski (eds.), *Logic Methodology and Philosophy of Science*. Palo Alto, Calif.: Stanford University Press.

Chomsky, N. (1964). A review of B. F. Skinner's "Verbal Behavior," in J. A. Fodor and J. J. Katz (eds.), *The Structure of Language*. Englewood Cliffs, N.J.: Prentice-Hall, Inc.

‡Chomsky, N. (1965a). *Aspects of the Theory of Syntax*. Cambridge, Mass.: M.I.T. Press.

Chomsky, N. (1965b). "On Certain Formal Properties of Grammar," in Luce, Bush, and Galanter (eds.), *Readings in Mathematical Psychology,* vol. II. New York: John Wiley & Sons.

Chomsky, N. (1966). *Cartesian Linguistics*. New York: Harper & Row.

Chomsky, N. (1968a). "Remarks on Nomalization," in R. A. Jacobs and P. S. Rosenbaum (eds.), *Readings in English Transformational Grammar*. Waltham, Mass.: Ginn/Blaisdell.

Chomsky, N. (1968b). "Deep Structure, Surface Structure and Semantic Interpretation." Cambridge, Mass.: M.I.T. Mimeographed.

‡Chomsky, N. (1968c). *Language and Mind.* New York: Harcourt Brace Jovanovich, Inc.

Chomsky, N., and M. Halle (1968). *The Sound Pattern of English.* New York: Harper & Row.

Chomsky, N., and M. Halle (1969). "Some Empirical Issues in the Theory of Transformational Grammar." Cambridge, Mass.: M.I.T. Mimeographed.

Davis, M. (1958). *Computability and Unsolvability.* New York: McGraw-Hill Book Company.

Dean, J. (1966). "Determiners and Relative Clauses." Cambridge, Mass.: M.I.T. Mimeographed.

Dinneen, F. (1964). *An Introduction to General Linguistics.* New York: Holt, Rinehart and Winston, Inc.

Dougherty, R. (1969). "An Interpretive Theory of Pronominal Reference," *Foundations of Language* (5:488–519).

Edes, E. (1968). "Output Conditions on Anaphoric Expressions with Split Antecedents." Cambridge, Mass.: Harvard University. Mimeographed.

Elgin, S. (1971). "Constraints on Deletion in Poetic Language." San Diego: University of California. Mimeographed.

Fillmore, C. (1963). "The Position of Embedding Transformations in a Grammar." Columbus: Ohio State University. Mimeographed.

Fillmore, C. (1965). "Entailment Rules in Semantic Theory." Columbus: Ohio State University. Mimeographed.

Fillmore, C. (1966). "The Grammar of 'Hitting' and 'Breaking.'" Columbus: Ohio State University. Mimeographed.

‡Fillmore, C. (1968). "The Case for Case," in E. Bach and R. Harms (eds.), *Universals in Linguistic Theory.* New York: Holt, Rinehart and Winston, Inc.

Fillmore, C. (1969). "Verbs of Judging: An Exercise in Semantic Description." Columbus: Ohio State University. Mimeographed.

Fodor, J. (1965). "Could meaning be an rm?" *Journal of Verbal Learning and Verbal Behavior,* 4:73–81.

‡Fodor, J. A., and J. J. Katz (eds.) (1964). *The Structure of Language.* Englewood Cliffs, N.J.: Prentice-Hall, Inc.

Fraser, J. B. (1965). "An Examination of the Verb-Particle Construction in English." Doctoral dissertation. Cambridge, Mass.: M.I.T.

‡Freeman, D. C. (ed.) (1970). *Linguistics and Literary Style.* New York: Holt, Rinehart and Winston, Inc.

Garvin, P. L. (ed.) (1964). *A Prague School Reader on Esthetics, Literary Structure, and Style.* Washington, D.C.: Georgetown University Press.

‡Gleason, H. A. (1961). *An Introduction to Descriptive Linguistics.* New York: Holt, Rinehart and Winston, Inc.

‡Greenberg, J. (ed.) (1966). *Universals of Language.* Cambridge, Mass.: M.I.T. Press.

Greene, G. (1968). "On *too* and *either* and not just *too* and *either,* either," in Papers from the 6th Regional Meeting of the Chicago Linguistic Society, Chicago, Ill.

Grinder, J. (1970). "Super Equi-NP Deletion," in Papers from the 6th Regional Meeting of the Chicago Linguistics Society, Chicago, Ill.

Grinder, J. (1971a). "Chains of Coreference," *Linguistic Inquiry* (2;2:183–202).

Grinder, J. (1971b). "On Deletion Phenomena in English." Unpublished doctoral dissertation. San Diego: University of California.

Grinder, J., and P. Postal (1971). "Missing Antecedents," *Linguistic Inquiry*, vol. II, no. 3.

Grinder, J., and P. Postal (1971). "A Reply to Super Equi as Dative Deletion," in Papers from the 7th Regional Meeting of the Chicago Linguistics Society, Chicago, Ill.

Grinder, J., and P. Postal. *Syntax and Semantics*. San Francisco: Academic Press, in press.

Gross, M., and A. Lentin (1970). *Introduction to Formal Grammars*. Berlin: Springer-Verlag.

Gruber, J. (1965). *Studies in Lexical Relations*. Unpublished doctoral dissertation. Cambridge, Mass.: M.I.T.

Hale, A. (1964). "Quantification and the English Comparative." Urbana: University of Illinois. Mimeographed.

Hall Partee, B. (1970). "Negation, Conjunction and Quantifiers: Syntax vs. Semantics," *Foundations of Language* (6;2:153–165).

Halle, M. (1964a). "On the Bases of Phonology," in J. A. Fodor and J. J. Katz (eds.), *The Structure of Language*. Englewood Cliffs, N.J.: Prentice-Hall, Inc.

Halle, M. (1964b). "Phonology in Generative Grammar," in J. A. Fodor and J. J. Katz (eds.), *The Structure of Language,* Englewood Cliffs, N.J.: Prentice-Hall, Inc.

Harman, G. (1963). "Generative Grammars without Transformational Rules: A Defense of Phrase Structure," *Language* (39;4:597–616).

Harms, R. (1968). *Introduction to Phonological Theory*. Englewood Cliffs, N.J.: Prentice-Hall, Inc.

Harris Z. (1946). "From Morpheme to Utterance," *Language* (22;3:161–183).

Harris, Z. (1957). "Co-occurrence and Transformation in Linguistic Structure," *Language* (33;3:283–340).

Harris, Z. (1968). *Mathematical Structures of Language*. New York: Interscience Publishers.

Hasegawa, K. (1968). "The Passive Construction in English," *Language* (44;2: 230–243).

Hayes, J. (ed.) (1970). *Cognition and the Development of Language*. New York: John Wiley & Sons.

Hempel, C. (1965). "The Theoretician's Dilemma," in *Aspects of Scientific Theory*. New York: The MacMillan Company.

Hockett, C. (1942). "A System of Prescriptive Phonology," *Language* (18:3–21).

Hockett, C. (1958). *A Course in Modern Linguistics*. New York: The Macmillan Company.

Hopcroft, J., and J. Ullman (1969). *Formal Languages and Their Relation to Automata*. Reading, Mass.: Addison-Wesley Publishing Co.

Horn, L. (1969). "A Presuppositional Analysis of *Only* and *Even,*" in Papers from the 5th Regional Meeting of the Chicago Linguistic Society, Chicago, Ill.

Jackendoff, R. (1969). *Some Rules of Semantic Interpretation in English.* Unpublished doctoral dissertation. Cambridge, Mass.: M.I.T.

Jackendoff, R. (1970). *Gapping and Related Rules.* Santa Monica, Calif.: The RAND Corporation.

Jacobs, R. A. and P. S. Rosenbaum (1968). *English Transformational Grammar.* Waltham, Mass.: Ginn/Blaisdell.

‡Jacobs, R. A., and P. S. Rosenbaum (1970). *Readings in English Transformational Grammar.* Waltham, Mass.: Ginn/Blaisdell.

‡Jakobovits, L., and D. Steinberg (eds.) (1969). *Semantics: An Interdisciplinary Reader in Philosophy, Linguistics, Anthropology and Psychology.* Cambridge, England: Cambridge University Press.

Jakobson, R., and M. Halle (1956). *Fundamentals of Language.* The Hague: Mouton & Co.

Jakobson, R., C. Fant, and M. Halle (1967). *Preliminaries to Speech Analysis: The Distinctive Features and Their Correlates.* Cambridge, Mass.: M.I.T. Press.

‡Jespersen, O. (1965). *The Philosophy of Grammar.* New York: W. W. Norton & Company, Inc.

‡Joos, M. (ed.) (1963). *Readings in Linguistics.* New York: American Council of Learned Societies.

Karttunen, L. (1969). "Problems of Reference in Syntax." Unpublished manuscript. Austin: University of Texas.

Katz, J. J. (1967). *The Philosophy of Language.* New York: Harper & Row.

Katz, J. J. *Semantic Theory.* New York: Harper & Row, in press.

Katz, J. J., and J. A. Fodor (1963). "The Structure of a Semantic Theory," *Language* (39;2:170–210).

Katz, J. J., and P. M. Postal (1964). *An Integrated Theory of Linguistic Description.* Cambridge, Mass.: M.I.T. Press.

Kimball, J. (1971). "Super Equi-NP Deletion as Dative Deletion," in Papers from the 7th Regional Meeting of the Chicago Linguistic Society, Chicago, Ill.

Kimball, J. *Cyclic and Non-Cyclic Grammars.* San Francisco: Academic Press, in press.

King, H. (1970). "On Blocking the Rule for Contraction in English," *Linguistic Inquiry* (1;1:134).

Kiparsky, P. (1968a). "Linguistic Universals and Linguistic Change," in E. Bach and R. Harms (eds.), *Universals in Linguistic Theory.* New York: Holt, Rinehart and Winston, Inc.

Kiparsky, P. (1968b). "How Abstract Is Phonology?" Cambridge, Mass.: M.I.T. Mimeographed.

Kiparsky, C., and P. Kiparsky (1968). "Fact," in M. Bierwisch and K. Heidolph (eds.), *Recent Advances in Linguistics.* The Hague: Mouton & Co.

Kisseberth, C. (1969), "On the Abstractness of Phonology: The Evidence from Yawelmani." Urbana: University of Illinois. Mimeographed.

Kisseberth, C. (1970). "A Global Rule in Klamath Phonology." Urbana: University of Illinois. Mimeographed.

Kisseberth, C. (1971). "Cyclical Rules in Klamath Phonology," Urbana: University of Illinois. Mimeographed.

Klima, E. S. (1964a). "Relatedness between Grammatical Systems," *Language* (40;1:1–20).

Klima, E. S. (1964b). "Negation in English," in J. J. Katz and J. A. Fodor (eds.), *The Structure of Language*. Englewood Cliffs, N.J.: Prentice-Hall, Inc.

Kuhn, T. (1962). *The Structure of Scientific Revolutions*. Chicago: University of Chicago Press.

Kuroda, S-Y (1967a), "Notes on English Relativization and Certain Related Problems." San Diego: University of California. Mimeographed.

Kuroda, S-Y (1967b). *Yawelmani Phonology*. Cambridge: M.I.T. Press.

Kuroda, S-Y (1968). "A Topological Study of Context-Free Languages." San Diego: University of California. Mimeographed.

Labov, W., P. Cohen, and C. Robins (1965). *A Preliminary Study of the Structure of English Used by Negro and Puerto Rican Speakers in New York City*. New York: Columbia University.

Ladefoged, Peter (1968). *Elements of Acoustic Phonetics*. Chicago: University of Chicago Press.

Lakoff, G. (1966b). "Stative Adjectives and Verbs in English," National Science Foundation, 17–I.

Lakoff, G. (1968a). "Instrumental Adverbs and the Concept of Deep Structure," *Foundations of Language* (4;1:4–29).

Lakoff, G. (1968b). "Pronouns and Reference." Cambridge, Mass.: Harvard University. Mimeographed.

Lakoff, G. (1970). "On Generative Semantics." Ann Arbor: University of Michigan. Mimeographed.

Lakoff, G. (1970a). "Global Rules," *Language* (46;3:627–639).

Lakoff, G. (1970b). *Linguistics and Natural Logic*. Ann Arbor: University of Michigan.

Lakoff, G. (1970c). *Irregularity in Syntax*. New York: Holt, Rinehart and Winston, Inc.

Lakoff, G. (1970d). "Repartee," *Foundations of Language* (6;3:389–422).

Lakoff, G., and J. R. Ross (1966a). "A Criterion for Verb Phrase Constituency," National Science Foundation, 17–II.

Lakoff, G., and J. R. Ross (1966b). "Deep and Surface Grammar." Cambridge, Mass.: Harvard University. Mimeographed.

Lakoff, G., and S. Peters (1966), "Phrasal Conjunction and Symmetrical Predicates," National Science Foundation, 17–VI.

Lakoff, R. (1969). "A Syntactic Argument for Negative Transportation," in Papers from the 5th Regional Meeting of the Chicago Linguistics Society, Chicago, Ill.

Lakoff, R. (1971). "Passive Resistance," in Papers from the 7th Regional Meeting of the Chicago Linguistics Society, Chicago, Ill.

Langacker, R. (1966). "On Pronominalization and the Chain of Command," in D. A. Reibel and S. A. Schane (eds.), *Modern Studies in English*. Englewood Cliffs, N.J.: Prentice-Hall, Inc.

Langacker, R. (1967a). *Language and Its Structure: Some Fundamental Linguistic Concepts*. New York: Harcourt Brace Jovanovich, Inc.

Langacker, R. (1967b). "A Note on Double-Crosses in Linguistics." San Diego: University of California. Mimeographed.

Langacker, R. (1968). "Mirror Image Rules in Natural Languages." San Diego: University of California. Mimeographed.

Langacker, R. (1970). "Predicate Raising: Some Uto-Aztecan Evidence." San Diego: University of California. Mimeographed.

Lees, R., and E. S. Klima (1963). "Rules for English Pronominalization," *Language* (39;17–28).

Lees, R., and E. S. Klima (1966). *The Grammar of English Nominalizations.* The Hague: Mouton & Co.

Lenneberg, E. 1967). *The Biological Foundations of Language.* New York: John Wiley & Sons.

Levin, S. R. (1964). "Poetry and Grammaticalness," in H. G. Lunt (ed.), *Proceedings of the 9th International Congress of Linguists.* The Hague: Mouton & Company.

Levin, S. R. (1965). "Internal and External Deviation in Poetry," *Word* (21:225–237).

Levin, S. R. (1969). *Linguistic Structures in Poetry.* The Hague: Mouton & Company.

Lindholm, J. M. (1969). "Negative-raising and Sentence Pronominalization," in Papers from the 5th Regional Meeting of the Chicago Linguistics Society, Chicago, Illinois.

‡Lyons, J. (1969). *Introduction to Theoretical Linguistics.* Cambridge, England: Cambridge University Press.

Mandelbaum, D. (1963). *The Selected Writings of Edward Sapir.* Berkeley: University of California Press.

McCawley, J. (1968a). "Lexical Insertion in a Transformational Grammar," in Papers from the 4th Regional Meeting of the Chicago Linguistics Society, Chicago, Ill.

McCawley, J. (1968b). "The Role of Semantics in a Grammar," in E. Bach and R. Harms (eds.), *Universals in Linguistics Theory.* New York: Holt, Rinehart and Winston, Inc.

McCawley, J. (1968c). "Where Do Noun Phrases Come From?" Chicago: University of Chicago. Mimeographed.

McCawley, J. (1968d). "Concerning the Base Component of a Transformational Grammar," *Foundations of Language* (4;3:243–269).

McCawley, J., (1970a). "English as a VSO Language," *Language* (46;2:286–299).

McCawley, J. (1970b). "A Programme for Logic." Chicago: University of Chicago. Mimeographed.

McCawley, J. (1970c). "Syntactic and Logical Arguments for Semantic Structures." Chicago: University of Chicago. Mimeographed.

Mehler, J. (1963). "Some Effects of Grammatical Transformations on the Recall of English Sentences," *Journal of Verbal Learning and Verbal Behavior* (2:346–351).

Miller, G. A. (1962). "Some Psychological Studies of Grammar," *American Psychologist* (17:748–762).

Miller, G. A., E. Galanter, and K. H. Pribram (1960). *Plans and Structures of Behavior.* New York: Holt, Rinehart and Winston, Inc.

Minsky, M. (1967). *Computation: Finite and Infinite Machines.* Englewood Cliffs, N.J.: Prentice-Hall, Inc.

Morgan, J. (1969). "On the Treatment of Presuppositions in Transformational Grammar," in Papers from the 5th Regional Meeting of the Chicago Linguistics Society, Chicago, Ill.

Perlmutter, D. (1968a). "On the Article in English." Waltham, Mass.: Brandeis University. Mimeographed.

Perlmutter, D. (1968b). "The Two Verbs 'Begin.'" Waltham, Mass.: Brandeis University. Mimeographed.

Perlmutter, D. (1971). *Deep and Surface Structure Constraints in Syntax.* New York: Holt, Rinehart and Winston, Inc.

Peters, S., and R. Richie (1969). "On Restricting the Base Component of Transformational Grammar." Austin: University of Texas. Mimeographed.

Pike, K. (1947). "Grammatical Prerequisites to Phonemic Analysis," *Word* (3:155–172).

Popper, Karl R. (1968). *The Logic of Scientific Discovery.* 3d ed. rev. London: Hutchinson.

Postal, P. M. (1964). "Limitations of Phrase Structure Grammars," in J. J. Katz and J. A. Fodor (eds.), *The Structure of Language.* Englewood Cliffs, N.J.: Prentice-Hall, Inc.

Postal, P. M. (1968). *Aspects of Phonological Theory.* New York: Harper & Row.

Postal, P. M. (1970a). "On the Surface Verb Remind," *Linguistic Inquiry* (1;1:37–120).

Postal, P. M. (1970b). "On Coreferential Subject Complement Deletion," *Linguistic Inquiry* (1:439–500).

Postal, P. M. (1970c). "On the Derivation of Pseudo-Adjectives." Paper delivered to 44th Annual meeting of LSA, December 1969.

‡Postal, P. M. (1971a). *Cross-Over Phenomena.* New York: Holt, Rinehart and Winston, Inc.

Postal, P. M. (1971b). "Some Arguments for Raising in Random Order." Yorktown Heights, N.Y.: Thomas J. Watson Research Center, I.B.M. Mimeographed.

Postal, P. M. (1971c). "More on Raising." Yorktown Heights, N.Y.: Thomas J. Watson Research Center, I.B.M. Mimeographed.

Quine, W. (1960). *Word and Object.* Cambridge, Mass.: M.I.T. Press.

‡Reibel, D., and S. Schane (eds.) (1969). *Modern Studies in English.* Englewood Cliffs, N.J.: Prentice-Hall, Inc.

Riffaterre, M. (1959). "Criteria for Style Analysis," *Word* (15:154–174).

Robins, R. (1967). *A Short History of Linguistics.* Bloomington: Indiana University Press.

Rosenbaum, P. (1965–1967). *The Grammar of English Predicate Complement Constructions.* Cambridge, Mass.: M.I.T. Press.

Ross, J. R. (1966a). "Adjectives as Noun Phrases." Cambridge, Mass.: M.I.T. Mimeographed.

Ross, J. R. (1966b). "On the Cyclic Nature of English Pronominalization." Cambridge, Mass.: M.I.T. Mimeographed.

Ross, J. R. (1967a). "Auxiliaries as Main Verbs." Cambridge, Mass.: M.I.T. Mimeographed.

‡Ross, J. R. (1967b). "Constraints on Variables in Syntax." Unpublished doctoral dissertation. Cambridge, Mass.: M.I.T.

Ross, J. R. (1967c). "Gapping and the Order of Constituents." Cambridge, Mass.: M.I.T. Mimeographed.

Ross, J.R. (1968). "On Declarative Sentences." Cambridge, Mass.: M.I.T. Mimeographed.

Ross, J. R. (1969). "Guess Who," in Papers from the 5th Regional Meeting of the Chicago Linguistic Society, Chicago, Ill.

Schane, S. *Generative Phonology*. Englewood Cliffs, N.J.: Prentice-Hall, Inc. in press.

Searle, J. (1969). *Speech Acts: An Essay in the Philosophy of Language*. Cambridge, England.: Cambridge University Press.

Sebeok, Thomas A. (ed.) (1960). *Style in Language*. New York: John Wiley & Sons, Inc., and M.I.T. Press.

Shannon, C., and W. Weaver (1964). *The Mathematical Theory of Communications*. Urbana: University of Illinois Press.

Slobin, D. (1968). "Early Grammatical Development in Several Languages, with Special Attention to Soviet Research," Working Paper II. Berkeley: Language-Behavior Research Laboratory, University of California.

Smith, C. (1964). "Determiners and Relative Clauses in a Generative Grammar of English," *Language* (40:37–52).

Smith, F., and G. A. Miller (1966). *The Genesis of Language*. Cambridge, Mass.: M.I.T. Press.

Teeter, C. (1969). "Leonard Bloomfield's Linguistics," *Language Sciences*, No. 7. Bloomington: Indiana University.

Thorne, J. P. (1969). "Stylistics and Generative Grammars," *Journal of Linguistics* (1:49–59).

Trubetzkoy, N. (1969). *Principles of Phonology*. Berkeley: University of California.

Walker, D. (1970). "Diegueño Plural Formation," in *Linguistic Notes from La Jolla*, no. 4. San Diego: University of California.

Weinreich, U. (1966). "Exploration in Semantic Theory," in Thomas A. Sebeok (ed.), *Current Trends in Linguistics*, vol. III. The Hague: Mouton & Co.

Wells, R. S. (1947). "Immediate Constituents," *Language* (23:81–117).

Whorf, B. (1956). "Grammatical Categories," in John E. Carroll (ed.), *Language, Thought, and Reality*. New York: John Wiley & Sons.

Index